James Buchanan and the Political Crisis of the 1850s

President James Buchanan, by George P. A. Healey. Courtesy of Dickinson College.

James Buchanan
and the Political Crisis
of the 1850s

Edited by
Michael J. Birkner

SUP

Selinsgrove: Susquehanna University Press
London: Associated University Presses

Associated University Presses
440 Forsgate Drive
Cranbury, NJ 08512

Associated University Presses
16 Barter Street
London WC1A 2AH, England

Associated University Presses
P.O. Box 338, Port Credit
Mississauga, Ontario
Canada L5G 4L8

The paper used in this publication meets the requirements
of the American National Standard for Permanence of Paper
for Printed Library Materials Z39.48-1984.

Library of Congress Cataloging-in-Publication Data

James Buchanan and the political crisis of the 1850s / edited by Michael J. Birkner.
    p.   cm.
Includes bibliographical references (p.   ) and index.
ISBN 0-945636-89-X (alk. paper)
1. Buchanan, James, 1791–1868.   2. United States—Politics and government—1857–1861.   I. Birkner, Michael J., 1950–
E437.J36   1996
973.6'8'092—dc20   95-45041
                                                                          CIP

PRINTED IN THE UNITED STATES OF AMERICA

For Robin

Contents

Preface

Discussing one of his favorite subjects, James Buchanan, several years ago, the late Philip S. Klein mentioned some of the difficulties he faced writing a comprehensive account of the fifteenth president's public career. Among them was shaping an enormous mass of notes and documents he had collected over more than a decade into a readable narrative. His original typescript, Klein recalled, was a huge mass of paper, perhaps fifteen hundred pages in all. After the director of the Pennsylvania State University Press examined the draft Klein submitted in two big cardboard boxes, he sent it back with this injunction: "Cut it by half. No one will ever want to read this much about James Buchanan."

Philip Klein followed his editor's advice and produced an informed, highly sympathetic biography that remains the standard work on Buchanan, even though it has failed to change Buchanan's low standing in the presidential pantheon. Surprisingly, given its thrust, Klein's work never generated much dialogue about James Buchanan's conduct in the White House. Since the publication of Klein's biography, *President James Buchanan,* in 1962, shelves of new books have been written on the sectional conflict, the political crisis of the 1850s, partisan realignment, secession, and the coming of the Civil War. But aside from Elbert Smith's pithy contribution to the University of Kansas Press series on the presidency, little of this literature has focused on Buchanan's presidency. Consequently, when a friend of Franklin and Marshall College proposed convening a symposium to mark the two hundredth anniversary of the Sage of Wheatland's birth, the idea jelled. Some of the leading historians of the Civil War era convened in Lancaster for two days in September 1991 to discuss James Buchanan's life and times. A selection of these papers, together with one that was specifically commissioned for this volume and the transcript of a lively panel discussion featuring four distinguished historians of the 1850s, are published here on the premise that there really is more to say about James Buchanan and antebellum political culture.

* * *

9

Although the participants at the Lancaster symposium occasionally agreed to disagree about James Buchanan's presidential stewardship, most of them affirmed the consensus among current scholars that Buchanan belongs much closer to the bottom than the top of the list of American presidents. William E. Gienapp's "'No Bed of Roses': James Buchanan, Abraham Lincoln, and Presidential Leadership in the Civil War Era," makes one of the most straightforward arguments along these lines. Gienapp reminds us that long experience in government is no guarantee a new president will make the right moves—any more than limited experience assures failure. Gienapp faults Buchanan's management of his cabinet, his conduct of foreign affairs, his dealings with political allies and rivals, distribution of patronage, and major legislative initiatives, particularly in contrast with Abraham Lincoln's handling of these same matters. Whether the cause was political myopia, spitefulness, or simple miscalculation (and Gienapp suggests each of these factors was relevant at different times), Buchanan as president exacerbated rather than soothed sectional tensions.

Focusing on one aspect of a presidency—management of the press—Mark Summers offers a similarly harsh assessment of a president who was partly hapless, partly foolish, and almost always frustrated by his inability to control even Democratic newspapers in a turbulent time. It was not that Buchanan was inattentive to the need for a favorable press, Summers notes. But the president lacked the resources to support all claimants to printing contracts and patronage appointments, and needlessly alienated such long-time allies as Philadelphia's John Forney. Unfortunately for Buchanan, the 1850s witnessed the increasing independence of major metropolitan newspapers. Regardless of his ministrations, he was unlikely to enjoy the kind of loyalty that a predecessor like Andrew Jackson found so helpful in fighting his own battles in the 1830s. Moreover, Buchanan's major policy initiatives—notably his support for the notorious Lecompton Constitution in Kansas—were self-inflicted wounds so far as the press was concerned. Many otherwise loyal Northern Democratic newspapermen simply could not follow the administration's harsh line on Kansas, nor his bitter attacks on Illinois Senator Stephen A. Douglas. In the end, Summers concludes, Buchanan's attempts at news management boomeranged on him, showing him to be a "weak, treacherous, and ungrateful" party leader.

Robert E. May, by contrast, credits Buchanan with consistency and common sense in his conduct of foreign policy in the Caribbean—in particular, in his opposition to filibustering in Nicaragua. Based on a close examination of public documents, May demonstrates that Buchanan's rhetoric was matched by orders to civilian and military officials to restrain the filibustering efforts of William Walker and others. Buchanan's behavior, in this reading, was entirely principled, and it cost him some of his Southern support. May does not assert that Buchanan merits a higher ranking among presidents than he has generally received, but on the more limited question of whether the president's Caribbean policy exposed him as a lackey of the slave power, May argues forcefully that the president was not guilty.

Two final papers enrich the historiography of the political crisis of the 1850s. In "Another Look at the Election of 1856," Michael F. Holt provides a fresh look at the dynamics of a three-way campaign, with particular focus on the American Party. Holt observes that it is too easy in hindsight to dismiss Millard Fillmore's candidacy as hopeless as soon as the Northern wing of the "Know-Nothings" bolted from the party's February 1856 national convention. Fillmore and many of his supporters believed he could still win the election, and they were not foolish to believe so. But a variety of events and circumstances, Holt shows, ranging from the resilience of older party loyalties to the lack of an energizing American Party issue in 1856, to spectacularly polarizing events like Bleeding Kansas and Bleeding Sumner, all undercut the potential for a Unionist Party's success. Holt's essay sheds light on the Americans' delicate courtship of the nativist Know-Nothings, on the basis for Robert Toombs's surprisingly moderate Kansas bill in 1856, and on the failure of the Americans to energize a grassroots constituency as the Republicans were so effectively doing in the North.

In his reassessment of the election of 1860, Peter Knupfer places noncandidate James Buchanan at the center rather than the periphery of the action. Buchanan's policies, Knupfer argues, presaged an electoral revolution in 1860, manifest in the end of Jacksonian politics and the emergence of a new political order dominated by a sectionally based party, the Republicans. They provided the "spark" for Republican activism and increasing Republican appeal in the North, culminating in the election of a president who represented a dramatic shift in leadership style and political values from the old-war horse then inhabiting the White House. For Knupfer, a student of generational politics, Buchanan was a symbol of the "declining Jacksonian generation." His feckless policies, heavy-handed disposition of the patronage, and insensitivity to corruption that was rampant in his own administration contributed to the public's disenchantment with politics as usual and its willingness to sweep away the old regime. "Few presidents," Knupfer concludes, "have equaled Buchanan's record for misjudging public opinion and rigidly insulating the White House from the trend of national events."

Such a harsh assessment would face challenge by Philip S. Klein, but it is reinforced in the comments of Kenneth Stampp, Elbert Smith, and Don Fehrenbacher in the panel discussion that concludes this volume. None of these scholars credits Buchanan with the vision, flexibility, or generosity of spirit that was essential were any president to hold a divided republic together. Not only did President Buchanan fail to conciliate a critical constituency in his own party—the Douglas Democrats—he demanded it accede to his approach to the sectional issue and punished otherwise faithful Democrats who on this issue of principle refused to go along. At the same time, Stampp and Fehrenbacher suggest that Buchanan's leadership during the secession crisis was probably as good as it could have been under the circumstances. He conceded no essential point about the rights and responsibilities of the federal government, and he was able to hand over power to Abraham Lincoln with the Union still intact and Fort Sumter still flying the American flag. Another participant in the panel discussion, Robert Johannsen, joined the defense of Buchanan's management of the secession crisis as part of a broader-based argument that Buchanan's presidency merits a more sympathetic assessment than the other panelists were prepared to offer.

No short book could do justice to all the issues relevant to the Buchanan presidency, and this one makes no claim to comprehensiveness. The contributors to this volume have, however, provided a thoughtful and often provocative contribution to the ongoing dialogue about a critically important period in the nation's history.

* * *

The Buchanan Conference and this book were made possible by the inspiration of William MacKinnon of Bloomfield Hills, Michigan (himself a student of the Buchanan presidency) and by the hard work of many people. Of those individuals, Dr. David Stameshkin, then executive assistant to the President at Franklin and Marshall College, merits special appreciation. Stameshkin was the indispensable figure in assuring the success of the conference and in supporting publication of a selection of its proceedings. John C. C. Loose, former president of the Lancaster County Historical Society, provided thoughtful counsel in the planning stages and, during our conference, exemplary hospitality at the society. Wheatland's executive director, Sally Cahalan, was similarly helpful during the planning process and graciously opened Buchanan's magnificent home to conference participants. Dr. Richard Kneedler, president of Franklin and Marshall College, provided support in kind and cash for the project. A generous grant from the Pennsylvania Humanities Council helped underwrite the Buchanan conference and publication of this book. The Pennsylvania Historical Association granted permission to reprint a version of the panel discussion that was originally published in the July 1993 number of *Pennsylvania History.* My thanks go to editor William Pencak of Penn State University for his encouragement and support. The Special Collections Department of Spahr Library, Dickinson College, Carlisle, Pennsylvania, has graciously supplied many of the illustrations in the book.

Finally, I want to acknowledge my former student, Scott Webster, for research assistance early in the gestation of this project; my department secretary, Joy Sunderland McDannell, who provided essential technical assistance in the latter stages of production; and my student research assistant, Adam Fernandez, who helped track down illustrations, assisted with the bibliography, and cheerfully performed many other chores as we moved this work toward publication. My wife, Robin Wagner-Birkner, has, as always, been an invaluable accomplice.

James Buchanan
and the Political Crisis
of the 1850s

Introduction: Getting to Know James Buchanan, Again

Michael J. Birkner

Pennsylvania's only president is today not considered much of an advertisement for Pennsylvania, Pennsylvania politicians, or the presidency. Even in places like Carlisle (where he attended college) and Lancaster (where he spent most of his life), it is difficult to ignore the stigma attached to his name.

Buchanan is perhaps best remembered, or misremembered, as the weak-kneed, dough-faced president who allowed the South to break up the Union. "Poor, foolish, Buchanan!" wrote Samuel Eliot Morison in *The Oxford History of the American People.* He "prayed and twittered and did nothing" while the states of the Deep South seceded in 1860–61, thereby setting the stage for a terrible Civil war. Buchanan, Henry Steele Commager wrote two decades ago, was "by universal consent the worst president in the history of the country."[1]

Even historians who question the validity of Commager's statement tend not to argue the point too vigorously. The consensus in the profession holds that Buchanan was, as president, a failure. In the latest polls of historians on American presidents, Buchanan is ranked at the bottom, along with Warren Harding, Andrew Johnson, and Ulysses S. Grant.[2] The most influential recent scholarly accounts of Buchanan's administration, among them Michael Holt's *The Political Crisis of the 1850s,* Mark Summers's *The Plundering Generation,* and Kenneth M. Stampp's *America in 1857,* are highly unflattering to Buchanan. Holt and Summers, for example, portray Buchanan's single term in the White House as politically disastrous and extraordinarily corrupt. While neither historian charges Buchanan with taking bribes or knowingly engaging in corrupt acts, both say that Buchanan set a low moral standard in office. Both suggest that widespread revulsion among reform-minded Americans toward the Buchanan administration contributed significantly to the Republicans' victory in the election of

17

1860. For his part, Stampp argues that Buchanan's bumbling was the Republican Party's best political weapon.[3] Textbook interpretations of the 1850s—for example, David Herbert Donald's *Liberty and Union*—follow a similar track.[4]

There are two notable exceptions to this consensus on Buchanan's failings as chief executive. One is the impressive Buchanan biography published in 1962 by Philip S. Klein. The other is John Updike's meditation on Pennsylvania's only president, first in the play *Buchanan Dying* and more recently the novel, *Memories of the Ford Administration.*[5]

Both authors defend Buchanan from the derision of Morison and Commager and their contemporary, Allan Nevins.[6] Klein and Updike, in their respective works, suggest that Buchanan's presidency has been underestimated, and that he has been unfairly stigmatized by a crisis he neither created nor exacerbated. During the secession crisis of 1860–61, each argues, Buchanan performed about as well as possible under extraordinary trying circumstances—indeed, performed as well as Abraham Lincoln could have done or did. As Klein portrays it, Buchanan's policy in 1861 was Lincoln's policy, and Lincoln's policy was Buchanan's.[7]

* * *

In their sympathetic reading of Buchanan's behavior in the final months of his presidency and, for that matter, throughout a long and active political career, Klein and Updike populate a small fraternity. To appreciate the context for Buchanan's historical reputation, consider some of the adjectives historians have used in describing or characterizing him during his long political career. On the positive side, Buchanan is considered "able," "prudent," "shrewd," "judicious," "urbane," "canny," and "engaging." Words like "courageous," "principled," "visionary," or "honest" are absent from published works about Buchanan, but he does enjoy respect for his evident ability and, virtually all scholars agree, was well credentialed for the presidency.[8]

At the same time, a host of other adjectives—one might even say epithets—are used to depict a less than admirable figure. Buchanan, several historians suggest, was a "supple" politician. The suggestion here is that his known pragmatism sometimes slid into sheer expedience, and that his "cautious" nature was really an "ever cautious" or even "timid" character. Buchanan was not simply "proud," but "self important" and "pompous"; not simply solicitous of colleagues or acquaintances, but "obsequious"; not merely "careful," but "shifty," "wily," or "untrustworthy"; not simply interested in a good appearance, but "fussy, "old-maidish," and "vain." One historian, the Jacksonian scholar Robert V. Remini, dismisses Buchanan as "a born busybody."[9]

Contemporaries were often even harsher. And even if one discounts some of this commentary because it was offered by men not sympathetic to Buchanan's politics, the fact remains that even Buchanan's allies knew him through a faintly contemptuous nickname. Andrew Jackson was "The Old Hero" to his supporters; Abraham Lincoln was "the railsplitter"; Stephen A. Douglas was "The Little Giant." Even Martin Van Buren, the consummate wire-puller, was respected. "The Sly Fox," he was called. Buchanan, by contrast, was best known as "The Old Public Functionary."[10]

Not even so portentous an event as the bicentennial of Buchanan's birth affected his tarnished reputation. Still, to acknowledge a stigma is not to say that something fresh cannot be unearthed or argued about any notable historical figure, including James Buchanan. Even for historians who cannot embrace the sympathetic spin on Buchanan's career offered by Philip S. Klein, there *is* something in Buchanan that commands attention. That something is success. Like him or not, Buchanan was a formidable figure. He was a capable lawyer, a shrewd diplomat, and one of only forty-one Americans who have ever held the first office in the land, the presidency of the United States.[11]

* * *

James Buchanan was born on 23 April 1791, near Mercersburg, Pennsylvania, of Scots Irish immigrant parents. His father, James, Sr., prospered, first as a farmer, then a businessman, and encouraged his eldest son to attend college in Carlisle in order to prepare for a career as a lawyer. Although all evidence suggests that James felt emotionally much closer to his mother, James Buchanan, Sr., nonetheless taught his son the importance of hard work.[12]

James Buchanan entered Dickinson College in September 1807 and graduated two years later. Buchanan's Dickinson experience is not well documented. According to Philip Klein, Buchanan was a good, even brilliant student, but annoyingly conceited and sometimes simply obnoxious. Apparently some of these latter qualities grated on college faculty and administration, because in 1808 Buchanan was briefly suspended from Dickinson for "disorderly conduct," and permitted to return only after the intercession of a friend of the family, the Reverend John King, who served as a Dickinson trustee.[13]

Even then the young man did not fully learn his lesson. Approaching graduation from Dickinson in 1809, Buchanan pressed college authorities to give him and his friends certain honors, but he was rebuffed and even denied the honors he had in fact earned. It is not surprising, in this context, to learn that Buchanan had little to do with his alma mater in subsequent years, though he did continue to associate with Dickinsonians in politics, and a number of Dickinson alumni, including two future United States Supreme Court justices, were in his circle of friends.[14]

Although the Dickinson years were not necessarily happy ones for James Buchanan, they did leave an impress on him. According to Philip S. Klein, Buchanan at Dickinson learned a respect for law and property, qualities that would complement his essentially conservative philosophy of life and politics. At Dickinson, too, Buchanan "developed a respectful attitude toward religion" and a deep-seated, if semiconscious, commitment to playing peacemaker. Philip S. Klein says that while Buchanan as a student freely made fun of President Robert Davidson because of the latter's solemnity, formality, and vanity, as a mature adult Buchanan increasingly resembled Davidson, especially in his desire to "settle disputes without force" and to "solve problems by a friendly meeting of the minds."[15]

Buchanan's true vocation, however, was not law as a force for conflict resolution but, rather, politics. Politics in early nineteenth-century America was not at all pacific; it was, rather, a rough-and-tumble game. Politicians had to be able to hold their own in a rowdy arena. They had to take hard verbal shots and, on occasion, be prepared for roughhousing.[16] Examples of politicians wrestling with one another, pushing one another, even stabbing and shooting one another are commonplace in the early republic. According to legend, Andrew Jackson made friends with Thomas Hart Benton only after nearly being killed by Benton and his cronies in a barroom brawl. There are many readily verifiable examples of mayhem in the halls of Congress and on the political stump.[17] Buchanan himself was unlikely to put anyone in a bear hug or bite another politician's ear. But his skin had to be tough enough to weather frequent sharp assaults on his character and his politics, and by all evidence, it was.

As an ambitious young lawyer and politician in Lancaster, Buchanan revealed himself less for vision or brilliance than for tireless and painstaking preparation, shrewd parry and thrust, and sheer competence. Combined with his affability and easy repartee with a cigar in his mouth and a drink in his hand, these qualities propelled Buchanan upward in Pennsylvania politics.[18]

Buchanan's appearance is always raised when his politics is discussed. The best-known portraits of Buchanan that survive represent an older and less vigorous man than Buchanan was, and tend to emphasize his foppishness rather than his vitality.[19] Young or old, Buchanan had a distinctive and perhaps a peculiar appearance—highlighted by his set of mismatched eyes, one blue, the other hazel. Myopia in one eye, moreover, necessitated that he tilt his head and neck forward and sideways to compensate for his visual impairment. This posture was not necessarily a handicap, because it conveyed the impression that Buchanan was particularly solicitous of whomever he was talking with at the time.[20]

Buchanan's personal charm was real and it was not irrelevant to his political advancement. He could not have so readily risen from the ashes of the Federalist Party to which he gave his youthful allegiance had he not been pleasant and quick-witted. During the so-called Era of Good Feelings, in which Federalism died a slow death, Buchanan spent most of his time making his way as a lawyer and building a network of contacts that would serve him well later. During these years, too, he courted and then mourned his one true love, Anne Coleman, who died mysteriously in 1820 following an apparently trivial quarrel.[21]

Buchanan's love life is inevitably the subject of speculation. What we know would not give even the most adventurous psychobiographer much to go on. It would seem that Buchanan genuinely loved Anne Coleman and deeply grieved her untimely death. But it could well be that Coleman's demise was also a relief for a man who had great difficulty making emotional connections with anybody, male or female.

Buchanan was renowned as a dinner table conversationalist, and there's no question that among his most fervent admirers in this respect were women. He seems to have enjoyed female companionship—so long as it was in safe company. Serious relationships were rare. He may have feared sexuality, or simply lacked a capacity for emotional intimacy. Buchanan's failure to connect closely with anyone, save possibly his long-time roommate in Washington, Senator William R. King, contributes to the air of mystery about him that existed in his lifetime and exists today. It is also doubtless one reason why his motives were always subject to question. No one save Buchanan really knew what he was up to.[22]

Even as a rising young politician, Buchanan gained a reputation for intelligence and sagacity. He knew when to jump on, and when

James Buchanan as an aspiring lawyer and politician. Courtesy of Dickinson College.

to jump off bandwagons. He was most adept at denying his own ambitions while, behind the scenes, he maneuvered vigorously for the very office he said he did not seek.[23] The small-town lawyer in fact had large ambitions that transcended the Pennsylvania state line. He wanted to be a person of influence in Washington, perhaps in the U.S. Senate, perhaps in the president's cabinet, perhaps ultimately as president. Unlike most bright and ambitious young politicians, Buchanan achieved every one of his ambitions.

In 1820, following a brief political retirement, Buchanan won election to Congress from Lancaster. By 1824 he was playing presidential politics at the highest level. Indeed, he was out of his league and got burned when he made a baseless charge about Henry Clay's motives in the race between John Quincy Adams and Andrew Jackson for a majority in the House of Representatives in that election. From this experience, Buchanan learned to play his cards much more closely to his chest.[24]

Buchanan's candidate that year, General Jackson, came up short; but he was back four years later and decisively defeated his old nemesis Adams, in part because of Buchanan's support in Pennsylvania. When Buchanan made noises about rewards, Jackson doubtless recalled the younger man's unreliability four years earlier. He offered Buchanan the ambassadorship to Russia. This was as close to exile as any American politician can be sentenced. Jackson, moreover, channeled most Pennsylvania patronage to Buchanan's political rivals.[25]

If Buchanan had gained an unwanted reputation in 1824 and 1825 as untrustworthy, he did learn from his blunder. He was much more careful thereafter, both with characterizations and with promises. He developed tact. He deepened his preternatural tendency to pragmatic behavior. Buchanan was no excitable crusader, like his ostensible hero, Jackson. Rather, he exemplified the new generation of professional politicians, who believed that an ounce of compromise is worth a pound of principle.[26]

Although Buchanan espoused certain principles like strict construction and limited government, he was extraordinarily flexible on details. Over the years he became known for talking so circumspectly that it was often difficult to grasp his point. Consequently, his words were subject to the listener's interpretation. Sometimes this enabled Buchanan to smooth over potential disagreements; sometimes it simply caused confusion. In general it created the impression that James Buchanan was a trimmer.[27] When Buchanan nodded in one direction, friends and foes alike looked the other way, just in case.[28]

Because he was politically astute and because he knew as well as any man how to forge an alliance or cut a deal, Buchanan could never be ignored or dismissed, even among politicians on the Whig side of the aisle. Peers may not have trusted him, but they respected him and generally liked him, too. Like most good politicians, Buchanan recognized the importance of not holding grudges and not carrying disagreements outside the political cloakroom. He would drink with practically anyone, and he was known for his generosity and hospitality. Buchanan's social skills were among his most winsome qualities, and they served him well in his long climb to the White House.

Buchanan overcame tremendous odds in his quest for the presidency. Although he was Pennsylvania's leading politician from 1830 on into the 1850s, Buchanan never controlled his state Democratic Party. George Mifflin Dallas, a formidable infighter in his own right, battled with Buchanan for nearly three decades.[29] Aside from the rigors of factional and partisan politicking in antebellum Pennsylvania, Buchanan had to build a cross-sectional alliance with an extraordinary complex and increasingly volatile Democratic coalition. Not surprisingly, he cloaked himself as a centrist, took refuge in controversies by embracing "constitutionalism," and tended to come up with safe schemes, like the extension of the Missouri Compromise line to the Pacific, when pressed for his views on thorny sectional issues. Buchanan preferred generalities and ambiguity in any case. When really pushed, he did not mind leaving the country, as he did from 1853 through 1856, at a time when the nation was bitterly divided over slavery expansion. Residence abroad gave Buchanan room to maneuver and time to assemble support as rivals one by one made too many enemies to sustain their respective presidential bids.[30]

Assessments of Buchanan as politician vary. His sympathetic biographer, Philip S. Klein, highlights Buchanan's pragmatism within the context of consistent commitment to basic Democratic values, such as strict construction of the Constitution and recognition of the rights of the slaveholding South. By contrast, scholars like Elbert B. Smith (and others) have detected a pro-Southern orientation to his politics. In a variation on this theme, Don Fehrenbacher portrays the Pennsylvanian less as pro-Southern than anti-antislavery in his political slant. Buchanan's severest critics, including such prominent historians as David Donald and Roy F. Nichols, would probably accept that assessment, but they depict him preeminently as a wire-puller and self-promoter.[31]

In a speech delivered at Dickinson College four decades ago,

Engraving of Buchanan during his tenure as Minister to England under President Franklin Pierce (1853–56). Courtesy of Dickinson College.

Nichols argued that Buchanan was essentially a "scribe"—a person who could cultivate people effectively, write a deft letter, or deliver a successful speech, but someone who never could or would take a constructive stand on a controversial question.[32] Philip Klein passionately rejected this assessment and the disagreement is, at bottom, not resolvable. Nor is it critical to resolve it. Buchanan was what he was, a canny wheeler-dealer with a certain demagogic appeal on foreign policy issues.[33] Until the end of his career, it worked for him.

By 1843 Buchanan was being touted for the presidency.[34] He

An idealized view of Buchanan's Lancaster estate, "Wheatland." From *Leslie's Illustrated Magazine.* Courtesy of Dickinson College.

knew that 1844 was too soon for him to make a serious bid, but Buchanan parlayed his availability that year into a major post in the administration of fellow Democrat James K. Polk. Buchanan's years as secretary of state were tumultuous. He promoted, unsuccessfully, an intriguing scheme for a canal in Central America. He presided over a successful negotiation with Great Britain on Oregon and tense negotiations with Mexico on Texas. And he had a voice, albeit not a dominant voice, in wartime diplomacy during the Mexican conflict that yielded a vast new domain in the southwest United States.[35]

On this ground alone, Buchanan was a significant secretary. Perhaps more interesting is something that few beyond the ranks of professional historians know. Never in American history have a president of the United States and his secretary of state been less in harmony than were James Buchanan and James K. Polk. Their relationship was not merely expedient; it was painfully unpleasant for both of them—particularly so for Polk.[36] Put most simply, Buchanan did not like or trust Polk, and Polk did not like or trust Buchanan. Polk's diary from 1845 through 1849 is filled with references to Buchanan's working behind his back or even contradicting him. At one point, Polk wrote of Buchanan that the man who was supposedly his key adviser was in truth the enemy within. Buchanan "has been selfish, & all his acts and opinions seem to have been controlled with a view to his own advancement, so much so that I can have no confidence or reliance on any advice he may give upon public questions."[37]

On another occasion, taking note that Buchanan was prone to shift his position on key questions like the Oregon boundary, Polk observed, probably justly, that Buchanan "is governed by his own views of his chances for the Presidency."[38] For his part, though he was never so candid about his frustrations with Polk, Buchanan was embittered when he asked Polk for a nomination to the Supreme Court, and when one came available, Polk proved unwilling to give it to him, despite the fact that the president wanted Buchanan out of his cabinet.[39]

Why did this uncomfortable duo not separate? Aside from the answer a psychohistorian might give—that Buchanan was a constant pain the masochistic Polk needed to be truly happy—there is a more practical explanation. Despite his contentiousness and his double dealing, Buchanan was so effective as secretary of state that Polk could not discharge him. This is the conclusion drawn by Polk's biographer, Charles G. Sellers. Paul H. Bergeron, author of an authoritative study of the Polk presidency, offered a similar judgment.[40]

Buchanan hoped to succeed Polk as president. In this he was thwarted by factors he could not control, among them the voters' taste for war heroes. Buchanan played the good soldier in 1848, and contented himself with a brief retirement back in Lancaster, during which he plotted yet another presidential bid in 1852. This time, too, the prize eluded Buchanan, as the Democrats turned to Franklin Pierce of New Hampshire—in many respects Buchanan's inferior, save in having a helpful war record that Buchanan lacked. Buchanan gained the London mission as his consolation prize.

Conveniently distanced from the storm over Stephen Douglas's efforts to repeal the Missouri Compromise, Buchanan's stock rose as Douglas's and President Pierce's fell. In 1856 Buchanan was the available man for the democracy. John Updike, in *Buchanan Dying,* captured the dynamic of Buchanan's shrewd and cynical strategy for the nomination, by putting these cutting words in the mouth of Buchanan backer, Louisiana Congressman John Slidell: "Hide yourself, Buchanan, and trust to the South. Hide yourself in London while Bleeding Kansas stains Pierce and Douglas beyond redemption; hide yourself in Lancaster while Southerners hawk Union soothing spirit all over the North."[41]

Updike's fiction cuts very close to the historical realities. Bu-

Buchanan greeting friends in the Governor's Room, New York City Hall, 1856. From *Leslie's Illustrated Magazine*. Courtesy of Dickinson College.

chanan won the Democratic presidential nomination in 1856 because he was not tarred or pinned down by a position on Kansas; because he was a Northern man from an important state; because, above all, he was acceptable to the South.[42] Running in 1856 primarily as the safe alternative to Republican radicalism and a possible dissolution of the Union, Buchanan swept the South, carried Pennsylvania and Indiana, and reached the objective he had dreamed of for years.

The presidency was, alas, a hugely disappointing and dispiriting experience. Possibly under different circumstances—for example, during the mid-1840s—Buchanan could have been a successful president. He had the skills, if not the vision, to be a very good president. But he was too old, too ill, too poorly leveraged in the late 1850s to serve effectively. He was representative of an increasingly unstable and unpopular Jacksonian political order, working with tools unequal to the task he faced. Time had passed his like by. This, combined with the mismanagement and blundering that historians continue to attribute to his presidency, doomed Buchanan to a miserable experience in the White House.[43]

Although it is extreme to call Buchanan, as Henry Steele Commager does, America's worst president, it is true that little went right and much went wrong for President Buchanan, and that many of his troubles he brought on himself. Buchanan's cabinet, which he took months to construct, was ill-designed to strengthen the national Democratic Party or conduct the nation's business effectively. Buchanan's mean-spirited treatment of Stephen Douglas and Douglas's political friends divided the Northern wing of his party and demoralized many faithful functionaries. His meddling in the Dred Scott case was unfortunate at best and obviously unethical. And his decision to stake most of his political capital on the Lecompton Constitution in Kansas was a blunder of the first magnitude. Politically speaking, Buchanan's presidency was a disaster.[44]

Whatever his responsibility for exacerbating sectional tensions, James Buchanan did not cause civil war, and a case can be made that he managed the secession crisis that was its preliminary as effectively as anyone could have.[45] Had Buchanan acted more forcefully in 1860–61, he probably would have hastened the secession of the Upper South and put the federal government in the position of having provoked the conflict. Even Abraham Lincoln recognized that the federal government could not strike first or even appear as the aggressor. As Updike shrewdly puts it, Buchanan's frequently expressed desire not to fire the first shot re-

An artist's rendering of Buchanan parting for Washington from the Lancaster railroad station en route to his inauguration, February 1857. From *Leslie's Illustrated Magazine*. Courtesy of Dickinson College.

A NEW APPLICATION OF THE RAREY SYSTEM.

Mr. Rarey Buchanan doesn't see why he can't put the Federal straps on that spunky little colt Miss South Carolina. When he tries to pat her—she bites; when he tries to apply the strap—she kicks. He really doesn't see what is to be done with her—s'poses she'll have to have her own way. To which remark Miss Carolina doesn't say, neigh!

Contemporary cartoon depicts Buchanan's troubles with South Carolina during the secession winter. South Carolina is portrayed as a bucking bronco, and the caption reads: "Mr. Rarey Buchanan doesn't see why he can't put the Federal straps on that spunky little colt Miss South Carolina. When he tries to pat her—she bites; when he tries to apply the strap—she kicks. He really doesn't see what is to be done with her—s'poses she'll have to have her own way. To which remark Miss Carolina doesn't say, neigh!" From *Leslie's Illustrated Magazine.* Courtesy of Dickinson College.

flected not so much his timidity as a "wise instinct that in a democracy . . . the people can only be rallied . . . to a cause that is made to appear righteous."[46] Many historians, among them Arthur Schlesinger, Jr., without directly refuting this point, see Buchanan's assertion that the federal government had no power to put down secession as only encouraging the South to try it.[47]

James Buchanan left office in March 1861 with the nation precariously poised between war and peace. He was relieved to go, and he left without regrets. As he put it in a letter to newspaper publisher James Gordon Bennett a week after departing Washington, "under heaven's blessing the administration has been eminently successful in its foreign & domestic policy unless we may except the sad events which have recently occurred. These no human wisdom could have prevented. Whether I have done all I could consistently with my duty to give them a wise & peaceful direction towards the preservation or reconstruction of the Union, will be for the public & posterity to judge. I feel conscious that I have done my duty in this respect & that I shall at last receive justice."[48] He spent his last years in Lancaster, tending to his estate at Wheatland, corresponding with friends, friendly acquaintances, and autograph seekers across the nation. He wrote a dense, self-justificatory memoir and he charmed a succession of visitors as he had been doing for more than half a century.[49] James Buchanan died at Wheatland, a "Christian Statesman" at peace with himself, on 1 June 1868.[50]

Notes

1. Samuel Eliot Morison, *The Oxford History of the American People* (New York: Oxford University Press, 1965), 593, 608; Henry Steele Commager's assessment, cited by John Updike in *Buchanan Dying: A Play* (New York: Knopf, 1974), 202, derives from a garbled passage in the *New Republic* (6 July 1968): 18. It is repeated by Arthur Schlesinger, Jr., in an essay review of *Buchanan Dying* for the *Atlantic Monthly* 233 (June 1974): 54. For a more recent assertion that Buchanan "dithered" as the Deep South seceded, see Harold M. Hyman, "Lincoln and Other Antislavery Lawyers: The Thirteenth and Fourteenth Amendments and Republican Political Agendas," in Lloyd E. Ambrosius, ed., *A Crisis of Republicanism: American Politics in the Civil War Era* (Lincoln: University of Nebraska Press, 1990), 101.

2. See, for example, Robert K. Murray and Tim H. Blessing, *Greatness in the White House: Rating the Presidents, Washington through Carter* (University Park: Pennsylvania State University Press, 1988). Another poll conducted by the Chicago *Tribune* in 1982 placed Buchanan third from the bottom of the nation's "worst presidents," ahead only of Richard M. Nixon and Warren G. Harding. *ibid.*, p. 16. And a 1990 survey conducted by Siena College historians also ranked Buchanan third from the bottom—in this instance just ahead of Andrew Johnson and Warren G. Harding.

3. Michael F. Holt, *The Political Crisis of the 1850s* (New York: Wiley, 1978), especially 255; Mark W. Summers, *The Plundering Generation: Corruption and the Crisis of the Union, 1849–1861* (New York: Oxford University Press, 1987), especially chap. 15, "The Buchaneers"; Kenneth M. Stampp, *America in 1857: A Nation on the Brink* (New York: Oxford University Press, 1990). On p. 14 Stampp observes that Buchanan's handling of the Kansas issue in 1857 could not have served the Republicans better had they "themselves written the script."

4. David Herbert Donald, *Liberty and Union* (Boston: Little, Brown, 1978), esp. 58, 78. See also Elbert Smith, *The Death of Slavery, 1837–1865* (Chicago: University of Chicago Press, 1967), 154, 156.

5. Philip S. Klein, *President James Buchanan: A Biography* (University Park: Pennsylvania State University Press, 1962); Updike, *Buchanan Dying*.

6. See, for example, Allan Nevins, *The Emergence of Lincoln*, 2 vols. (New York: Charles Scribner's Sons, 1950); and "The Needless Conflict: If Buchanan Had Met the Kansas Problem Firmly He Might Have Avoided Civil War," *American Heritage* 7 (August 1955): 4–9, 88–90.

7. See Klein, *President James Buchanan,* chaps. 27–29, and "Patriotic Myths and Political Realities: Buchanan and the Origins of the Civil War," *Lock Haven Review* 15 (1974): 65–77; also Michael J. Birkner, "A Conversation with Philip S. Klein," *Pennsylvania History* 56 (October 1989): 267–70; and Updike, *Buchanan Dying,* especially 204–5, 210. For a different view, see William Gienapp's essay in this volume.

8. On Buchanan as "canny," Roy F. Nichols, *The Disruption of American Democracy* (New York: Macmillan, 1948), 26; as "urbane" and "engaging," John M. Belohlavek, *Let the Eagle Soar: The Foreign Policy of Andrew Jackson* (Lincoln: University of Nebraska Press, 1985), 84–85; as "judicious," Andrew C. McLaughlin, *Lewis Cass* (Boston: Houghton, Mifflin, 1891), 205; as "shrewd," John Niven, *Martin Van Buren: The Romantic Age of American Politics* (New York: Oxford University Press, 1987), 535.

9. For characterization of Buchanan as "supple" and "shifty," see John Niven, *John C. Calhoun and the Price of Union: A Biography* (Baton Rouge: Louisiana State University Press, 1988), 248, 291; as "timid," Nevins, *Emergence of Lincoln,* 1:72; as "old maidish," William Nisbet Chambers, *Old Bullion Benton: Senator from the New West* (Boston: Little, Brown, 1956), 251; as "ever-cautious," John M. Belohlavek, *George Mifflin Dallas: Jacksonian Politician* (University Park: Pennsylvania State University Press, 1977), 104; as "fussy" and "vain," see, for example, Charles G. Sellers, *James K. Polk: Continentalist, 1843–1846* (Princeton: Princeton University Press, 1966), 304; John A. Garraty, *Silas Wright* (New York: Columbia University Press, 1949), 256, 371; Belohlavek, *Let the Eagle Soar,* 86; as "shifty" and "selfish," Theodore Roosevelt, *Thomas H. Benton* (Boston: Houghton Mifflin, 1914), 254. Robert Remini's quotation is from *The Election of Andrew Jackson* (Philadelphia: J. B. Lippincott, 1963), 22.

10. There are many examples from which to draw. Particularly pungent are the comments of the journalist Murat Halstead, as recorded in William B. Hesseltine and Rex G. Fisher, eds., *Trimmers, Trucklers, and Temporizers: Notes of Murat Halstead from the Political Conventions of 1856* (Madison: State Historical Society of Wisconsin, 1961), xi, 17, 234, 264. See also Charles Francis Adams, ed., *Memoirs of John Quincy Adams,* 12 vols. (Philadelphia: J. B. Lippincott, 1874–77), 10:402; Allan Nevins and Milton Halsey Thomas, eds., *The Diary of George Templeton Strong: The Civil War, 1860–1865* (New York: Macmillan, 1952).

11. For a balanced assessment of Buchanan's diplomatic career, see Frederick Moore Binder, *James Buchanan and the American Empire* (Selinsgrove, Pa.: Susquehanna University Press, 1994).

12. Klein, *President James Buchanan,* 4–7.

13. Ibid., pp. 7–12, which is drawn largely from Philip S. Klein, "James Buchanan at Dickinson," in *John and Mary's College: The Boyd Lee Spahr Lectures* (Carlisle, Pa.: Dickinson College, 1956), 157–80. See also Charles Coleman Sellers, *Dickinson College: A History* (Middletown, Conn.: Wesleyan University Press, 1973), 133; and Christine Deardorff, "The Original Dickinson Devil," *Dickinson Magazine* 1 (Spring 1991): 29–32.

14. The justices were Roger B. Taney (Dickinson class of 1795) and Robert C. Grier (Dickinson class of 1812). On Buchanan's "bitter frame of mind" toward his alma mater for many years following his graduation, see Nichols, *Disruption,* 77. As time passed, Buchanan seems to have softened toward his alma mater. In the 1830s he corresponded periodically with Dickinson President James Price Durbin, regarding a ward of his who was then a student at the college, and he made a financial contribution to the Union Philosophical Society's library. In 1842 Dickin-

son awarded Buchanan, then a U.S. senator, a Doctor of Law degree. And in 1851 Buchanan agreed to mediate a dispute between college students and the Dickinson's administration after an incident provoked a mass dismissal of the junior class. On this, see Klein, "James Buchanan at Dickinson," and Sellers, *Dickinson,* 233.

15. Klein, *President James Buchanan,* p. 12.

16. On the rough and tumble nature of politics in the early republic, see Michael J. Birkner, "Was There a Second Great Generation?" *Virginia Cavalcade* 40 (Autumn 1990): 52–64, and Donald B. Cole and John J. McDonough, eds., *Witness to the Young Republic: A Yankee's Journal, 1828–1870* (Hanover, N.H.: University Press of New England, 1989).

17. Cole and McDonough, *Witness to the Young Republic,* especially pp. 45–46, 64, 75, 78–79, 86, 124.

18. Klein, *President James Buchanan,* chaps. 2–5, has the most detailed account of Buchanan's rise in politics; for a brief overview, see Kent D. Zwikl, "The Political Ascent of James Buchanan," *Pennsylvania Heritage* 17 (Spring 1991): especially 16–18.

19. For a portrait of Buchanan as a young man, see the illustration in *President James Buchanan,* immediately following p. 12. The original is in the Smithsonian Institution. Compare with a presidential portrait, for example, Buchanan posing with his cabinet in mid-1859, in the next to last illustration in this sequence (original in Library of Congress).

20. Nichols, *Disruption,* 76. Buchanan's niece Anna told George Ticknor Curtis that Buchanan was nearsighted in one eye and farsighted in the other. This physiological oddity provided an angle for John Updike's account of Buchanan's politics in *Buchanan Dying.* For a less sympathetic reading, using the same motif, see Schlesinger, "Historical Mind and the Literary Imagination," 55–59.

21. Klein, *President James Buchanan,* 27–33. For a psychologically plausible reconstruction of the Buchanan-Coleman relationship and its tragic denouement, see John Updike, *Memories of the Ford Administration* (New York: Knopf, 1992).

22. On the relationship with King, Updike's account in *Memories of the Ford Administration* is most suggestive.

23. See Roy F. Nichols, "James Buchanan: Lessons in Leadership in Trying Times," in *Boyd Lee Spahr Lectures in Americana* (Carlisle, Pa.: Library of Dickinson College, 1950), 165–74.

24. Remini, *Election of Andrew Jackson,* 22, 66.

25. According to one account, when Andrew Jackson was asked in 1845 why he had appointed Buchanan minister to Russia if he didn't think much of the Pennsylvanian, Jackson is supposed to have replied: "It was as far as I could send him out of my sight; and where he could do the least harm. I would have sent him to the North Pole if we had kept a minister there!" Quoted in Paul F. Boller, *Presidential Anecdotes* (New York: Oxford University Press, 1981), 118. On Jackson's channeling of patronage, see Belohlavek, *George Mifflin Dallas,* 282.

26. Birkner, "Second Great Generation," is relevant, as is the commentary of J. Mills Thornton at a session, "The South and Nineteenth Century American Politics," Organization of American Historians Annual Convention, Washington, D.C., 23 March 1990. For a different view, see Klein, *President James Buchanan.*

27. Henry S. Foote observed that "even among close friends, he very rarely expressed his opinions at all on disputed questions, except in a language especially marked with a cautious circumspection almost amounting to timidity." Quoted in Nevins, *Emergence,* 63. Another contemporary, Murat Halstead, called

Buchanan "the personification of evasion, the embodiment of an inducement to dodge." Quoted in *Trimmers, Trucklers, and Temporizers,* 17, 24. See also Simon Cameron to Samuel Ingham, 9 January 1858, Buchanan Papers, Dickinson College Archives.

28. For an excellent example of Buchanan's capacity to express himself ambiguously when exigency demanded, see Buchanan to James X. McLanahan, 22 June 1842, regarding the removal, by President John Tyler, of the postmaster at Chambersburg. Buchanan Papers. See also Nichols, *Disruption,* 76–77.

29. Belohlavek, *George Mifflin Dallas,* especially 3–21. As president, Buchanan also faced division within the Pennsylvania democracy, on patronage and substantive issues. On this, see John F. Coleman, *The Disruption of the Pennsylvania Democracy, 1848–1860* (Harrisburg: Pennsylvania Historical and Museum Commission, 1975), especially chaps. 8–9.

30. See, for example, Don E. Fehrenbacher, *Slavery, Law and Politics: The Dred Scott Case in Historical Perspective* (New York: Oxford University Press, 1981), 64. In a letter to Robert Tyler, 11 June 1857, Buchanan observed that "my constant adhesion to the Missouri Compromise has been the cause of many attacks against me from the fishy Democrats of our state" (Buchanan Collection, Dickinson College Archives).

31. Nichols, "James Buchanan: Lessons in Leadership in Trying Times."

32. Ibid., 172–73.

33. On Buchanan's foreign policy jingoism, see, for example, Paul A. Varg, *United States Foreign Relations, 1820–1860* (East Lansing: Michigan State University Press, 1979), 217, 226, 247, 251, 252, 254, and C. Thomas Burns, "James Buchanan's Diplomatic Mission to England, 1853–1856" (M.A. thesis, University of Delaware, 1967). Frederick Moore Binder emphasizes Buchanan's commitment to Manifest Destiny in "James Buchanan: Jacksonian Expansionist," *Historian* 55 (Autumn 1992): 69–84.

34. See Charles M. Wiltse, *John C. Calhoun: Sectionalist, 1840–1850* (Indianapolis: Bobbs Merrill, 1951), 92; Klein, *President James Buchanan,* chap. 12.

35. See, for example, Sellers, *Polk,* and Paul K. Bergeron, *The Presidency of James K. Polk* (Lawrence: University Press of Kansas, 1987), especially 34, 42, 165.

36. Bergeron, *Presidency of Polk* 35, 37, 38, 39; Klein, *President James Buchanan,* chaps. 13, 14; and Binder, *Buchanan and the American Empire,* chap. 4.

37. Milo Milton Quaife, ed., *The Diary of James K. Polk, During His Presidency, 1845 to 1849* 4 vols. (Chicago: A. C. McClurg & Co., 1910), 3:403.

38. Ibid., 1:297.

39. See Bergeron, *Presidency of Polk,* 163–66. The nomination went to another Dickinsonian from Pennsylvania: Robert C. Grier.

40. Ibid., 391.

41. Updike, *Buchanan Dying,* 19.

42. Nichols, *Disruption,* 26–27; Summers, *Plundering Generation,* 239–40; and Roy F. Nichols and Philip S. Klein, "The Election of 1856," in Arthur M. Schlesinger, Jr. and Fred L. Israel, eds., *History of American Presidential Elections, 1789–1968,* 4 vols. (New York: Chelsea House, 1971), 2:1025.

43. Richard Cobden, a British reformer who had known Buchanan during the latter's service in London in the early 1850s, visited the president in 1859. He "found him looking much older, and apparently out of spirits, and not so happy as when I knew him in London. Having attained the highest object of his worldly ambition, he is disappointed with the result." Quoted in *Emergence of Lincoln,*

1:432. For a similar analysis, see the letter of Justice Robert Grier to W. H. Smith, 29 December 1860, as quoted in Nevins, *Emergence of Lincoln,* 2:360. Relevant here are the tart comments by Kenneth M. Stampp in the panel discussion in this volume, "The Presidency of James Buchanan: A Reassessment."

44. Fehrenbacher, *Slavery, Law, and Politics,* pp. 164–69; David Potter, *The Impending Crisis, 1848–1861* (New York: Harper and Row, 1976), especially chaps. 11–12; and Michael F. Holt, *Political Parties and American Political Development from the Age of Jackson to the Age of Lincoln* (Baton Rouge: Louisiana State University Press, 1992), 80–83. See also the essays by William Gienapp, Mark Summers, and Peter Knupfer, and comments by Kenneth Stampp, Don Fehrenbacher, and Elbert Smith in this volume.

45. See, Klein's Fortenbaugh Lecture at Gettysburg College, 1978, as recounted in *Gettysburg Times,* 20 November 1978, pp. 1, 8; Klein, *President James Buchanan,* 353–402; and Birkner, "A Conversation with Philip S. Klein," 67–70. For an early formulation of the argument that Buchanan's policy during the secession crisis was at least as firm as Lincoln's, consult W. U. Hensel, *Buchanan's Administration on the Eve of the Rebellion: A Paper Read before the Cliosophic Society, Lancaster, Pa., January 24, 1908* (Lancaster, Pa.: n.p., 1908), esp. 10–12.

46. Updike, *Buchanan Dying,* 204–5.

47. Schlesinger, "The Historical Mind and the Literary Imagination," 57–59.

48. Buchanan to Bennett, 11 March 1861, Buchanan Papers. Dickinson College Archives. Buchanan took a similar tack in a letter to Henry Slicer, 16 May 1863, Buchanan Papers, Dickinson College Archives. Relevant is Stephen Skowronek's observation that "successful political leaders do not necessarily do more than other leaders; successful leaders control the political definition of their actions, the terms in which their places in history are understood. The failures are those who, upon leaving office, look to some time in the distant future when people might begin to appreciate the wisdom of what they did." *The Politics Presidents Make* (Cambridge, Mass.: Harvard University Press, 1993), 17–18.

49. James Buchanan, *Mr. Buchanan's Administration on the Eve of the Rebellion* (New York: Appleton, 1866). For Buchanan's reference to a steady stream of autograph seekers, see his letter to Thomas A. Goodman, 8 May 1862, Buchanan Papers, Dickinson College Archives.

50. The "Christian Statesman" motif is from W. U. Hensel, *A Pennsylvania Presbyterian President: An Inquiry into the Religious Sentiments and Character of James Buchanan . . .* (Philadelphia: n.p., 1907), 14.

Another Look at the Election of 1856

Michael F. Holt

Spanning almost fifty years, James Buchanan's political career included service as state legislator, United States representative and senator, secretary of state, and minister to England. Without question, however, Buchanan's historical significance and reputation rest primarily on his controversial presidency between 1857 and 1861. The long-time Democrat won that office after an unusual three-way contest in 1856 when he bested John C. Frémont, the candidate of the fledgling Republican Party, and ex-president Millard Fillmore, the nominee of both the new American or Know-Nothing Party and the expiring Whig Party. Because the Democratic triumph put Buchanan in the White House for four crucial years that led to Civil War, because the election also played a pivotal role in the rise and impending success of the Republican Party, and because those organizations have endured as our two major parties until the present day, historians' accounts of the 1856 election have usually been told from their perspective.[1]

Conversely, because Fillmore ran third in the popular vote and far behind in the electoral count and because the American and Whig parties utterly collapsed after the election, the Fillmore campaign has received far less attention from historians.[2] This essay seeks to right that imbalance by briefly reexamining the election from the perspective of Fillmore and the groups that backed him. No claim is made that such a vantage point casts new light on Buchanan, on his presidency, or on the coming of the Civil War. Nonetheless, it allows one to correct careless errors in some of the leading accounts of the dynamics of the 1856 campaign, if not about its short- and long-term results.

The Fillmore campaign merits examination for another reason. The presidential election of 1856 was indeed a crucial turning point on the road to the Civil War and an absolutely critical episode in the rise of the Republican Party as William E. Gienapp, among other historians, has recently reminded us.[3] But that election also constituted the final chapter in the life of an earlier framework of political competition between the Whig and Democratic parties that lasted from 1834 to 1856. It was a conclusion as well as a beginning, and viewing the campaign from the perspective of Fillmore helps us better understand that conclusion.

The election of 1856 occurred in the midst of a dramatic voter realignment and partisan reorganization that were fueled by exceptional sectional, social, and political turmoil. The passage of the Kansas-Nebraska Act in May 1854 had reaggravated sectional conflict over slavery expansion, contributed to massive Democratic defeats in off-year Northern elections during 1854 and 1855, and spurred the creation of the new, exclusively Northern Republican Party. Simultaneously, widespread and intense hostility toward existing parties, immigrants, and Catholics had spawned the powerful Know-Nothing movement in both the North and South which by the end of 1855 appeared to be the most rapidly growing political force in the country. Although the incumbent Democratic Party was the chief target of both new parties and of the voters' wrath that spawned them, ironically the Whig Party would be their chief victim. What occurred between 1852 and 1856, in short, was not simply a weakening of the Democratic Party but the displacement of its major opponent by differently constituted anti-Democratic organizations. The undeniable appeal of the two new parties vitally contributed to that reorganization, but it was also a product of the unraveling of the Whig Party. Its final death throes are illuminated by the Fillmore campaign.[4]

Developments during 1856 itself are familiar and can be sketched rapidly. Both sectional antagonism and partisan volatility intensified. Though many predicted at the beginning of the year that the rapidly rising Know-Nothings would win the presidential sweepstakes, by the end of the year the party had been reduced to an also-ran. When the American national convention in February refused to demand repeal of the Kansas-Nebraska Act, Northern members of the organization were infuriated. The nomination of Fillmore, who as Whig president between 1850 and 1852 had vigorously enforced the odious Fugitive Slave Act, further incensed them. Consequently, many Northern Know-Nothings bolted the party and called for a meeting of a North American convention to nominate another candidate in New York City on 12 June, five days before the Republican national convention was to choose a candidate in Philadelphia.

Unlike the sectionally riven Know-Nothings, the Democrats preserved a tenuous sectional unity at their convention in early June

Campaign portrait of the 1856 Democratic ticket: James Buchanan of Pennsylvania and John C. Breckinridge of Kentucky. From *Leslie's Illustrated Magazine*. Courtesy of Dickinson College.

behind Buchanan's candidacy. Their platform endorsed the ambiguous popular sovereignty provisions of the Kansas-Nebraska Act. That success, however, drove even more anti-Nebraska Democrats into the enemy camp. Additional Democratic defections were also attributable to events that occurred only weeks before the Democrats met. Those events transformed the election.

During May violence on the plains of Kansas and the caning of Massachusetts's Republican Senator Charles Sumner by a South Carolinian caused Northern anger to soar. North Americans and Republicans then united behind the candidacy of Frémont in June. The ensuing campaign focused primarily on the issues of slavery extension, purported sectional aggressions, and the threat that sectional agitation posed to the Union. As a result, Republicans and Democrats eventually emerged from the fray as the race's major contestants.

Ultimately Buchanan won with 45 percent of the popular vote by carrying every slave state but Maryland and five key Northern states. Frémont swept the rest of the North and the plurality of that region's popular vote. Because Frémont won virtually no Southern

Campaign portrait of the Republican nominee for President in 1856, John Charles Frémont. From *Leslie's Illustrated Magazine.* **Courtesy of Dickinson College.**

votes, however, he garnered only 33 percent of the nationwide popular poll. Fillmore took the remaining 21.6 percent of the popular vote, 13.4 percent of the North's, and 43.9 percent of the South's. Maryland was his sole trophy in the electoral vote column.

Even though Fillmore amassed a larger percentage of the popular vote than any other third-party presidential candidate in our history with the exception of Theodore Roosevelt in 1912, his poor showing, especially in the crucial Northern states, has caused most historians to give his campaign short shrift. Fillmore is dismissed as at best a regional candidate and spoiler but more customarily as a certain loser and nonfactor in the race. Specifically, the conventional wisdom about the election maintains that from the moment Northern Know-Nothings bolted from the American national convention in February 1856, the American Party was irreparably split along sectional lines and ceased to be a competitive factor in the North. Consequently, the election featured two entirely separate campaigns with Buchanan pitted against Republicans in the North and against Americans in the South. In these circumstances Buchanan was the only candidate who had to worry about winning votes in both sections, and he won because he was properly perceived as the only credible nationalist or pro-Union candidate in the race.[5]

Allan Nevins writes in *Ordeal of the Union,* for example, "The moment the American convention broke into two parts [in February], it had become clear the real contest in 1856 would lie between the Democrats and Republicans." Fillmore "was a respectable mediocrity" who "had never counted for anything in American politics except the [obsolescent] idea of sectional compromise" and whose "sole importance would lie in attracting enough conservative Whig votes in the North to weaken the Republicans." Hence, "in practical terms, the battle lay essentially between Buchanan and Frémont—for while Fillmore might get a large minority of the vote, he could not win."[6]

According to Roy Nichols in his prize-winning *Disruption of American Democracy,* when "most of the northern wing of the Know Nothings went over to the Republicans," after the American convention split in February, "the Americans became almost wholly a Southern party with no Northern contingent to conciliate. The result was that this new party could go all out for Southern power and interests to an extent which the Democracy, with its Northern wing could not match. Likewise the Republican party with no Southern support at all could concentrate on promoting Northern interests. The Democracy therefore must fight two campaigns against two enemies."[7]

David Potter echoes Nichols in *The Impending Crisis, 1848–1861:*

From this time [February, 1856] forward, northern and southern Know Nothings were completely divided . . . The basic peculiarity of this election lay in the fact that although it appeared superficially to present

a triangular rivalry, there were actually two separate contests in progress at the same time—one between Buchanan and Frémont in the free
states, the other between Buchanan and Fillmore in the slave
states. . . . In one sense the nature of the contest placed Buchanan at
a disadvantage, for it forced him to take a position that would win favor
in both the North and the South, while Frémont could court northern
voters exclusively, and Fillmore could concentrate on winning southern support. But in the long run, this situation helped Buchanan, for
it identified him as the only truly national candidate in the race—the
only one whose victory would not be a clear-cut sectional victory.[8]

Even a cursory examination of the Fillmore campaign exposes
these separate-but-related contentions about the 1856 election as
caricatures. Here is a classic case where hindsight knowledge of
the results distorts understanding of the campaign that preceded
them. Not only does such a focus lead to mischaracterizations of
the campaign itself by telescoping developments. It also deflects
attention from interesting questions such as why Fillmore and his
supporters believed he could win, as they did until the last month of
the campaign, and what strategies they pursued to secure victory.
Palpably those expectations were frustrated, but contending that
they were doomed from the outset is no substitute for an analysis
of what their basis was and why they aborted.

Nothing could be further from the truth than the assertion that
Fillmore focused on only one section, whether it was the North as
Nevins maintains or the South as Nichols and Potter contend. Nor
is it true that only the Democrats had to fashion an appeal for both
sections or that only Buchanan was a national candidate whose
triumph would not be a clear-cut sectional victory. The central
theme of the Fillmore campaign was that he was the only candidate
whose victory would preserve the Union, and it is an egregious
distortion to suggest that he was somehow in a position to outflank
Buchanan in the South by posing as a more devoted champion of
Southern rights and interests. For tactical reasons alone, the Fillmore campaign had to run hard in the North. His Southern supporters repeatedly told him that they could hold votes in Fillmore's
column only if they had hard evidence that he could carry New
York and other Northern states like New Jersey, Pennsylvania,
and California. Simultaneously, Northern Fillmore men constantly
warned that his hope of carrying Northern states depended heavily
on American prospects in the South, prospects that would be
gauged by the Know-Nothing performance in August elections in
Kentucky, North Carolina, and Missouri. Thus the Fillmore campaign in the North was inextricably tied to its efforts in the South.[9]

Fillmore, who played a leading managerial role in the American campaign, was in fact unwilling to write off any part of the North. Even after he received discouraging reports from New England in the summer that "the late outrageous proceedings in Kansas & the assault on Mr. Sumner" had laid "Conservatism, in all its forms, . . . prostrate," he and his supporters insisted that Americans battle for every New England state and not concentrate all their energies on the lower North where Fillmore had greater strength.[10]

To be sure, fashioning an appeal that could sell equally well in the North and South confronted the Fillmore campaign with severe difficulties, and given his small share of the vote, especially in the more populous North, he does appear, at least in hindsight, to be the certain loser various historians have labeled him. Given his forlorn performance, indeed, we might ask why Fillmore and his supporters remained sanguine until mid-October. The answer to this question is complicated if only because the calculations and strategies of the Fillmore team changed rapidly over time. Whereas they expected for most of the Spring to win a clear electoral majority, for example, by late summer they pinned their hopes on throwing the election into the House where all opponents of Buchanan might unite on Fillmore. Throughout the campaign, moreover, there *was* an air of unreality about their assumptions that may explain the contemptuous dismissal of it by various historians. Their belief that the stronger Republicans appeared in the North the better Fillmore's chances because conservatives would desert Buchanan seems, in retrospect, especially surreal.[11] Nonetheless, their tactics were not totally farfetched, and they merit investigation.

Initially, when Fillmore was nominated in February, his supporters' hopes rested on three considerations. First, as William Gienapp makes amply clear in his book on the origins of the Republican Party, by February 1856 the Republicans had not yet formed a national organization or even emerged yet in several Northern states while the Know-Nothings appeared to be soaring on an upward trajectory.[12] Thus they hoped to attract the great majority of the anti-Democratic vote in both sections. But how could they believe this in light of the sectional split in the Know-Nothing convention, Northerners' dissatisfaction with the candidate and the slavery plank of the platform, and the bolt of the North Americans?

The answer is the second reason for Fillmore's hopes. His closest advisors did not believe that the sectional split in the party was irreparable. They dismissed the delegates who bolted the February

FANCIED SECURITY, OR THE RATS ON A BENDER.

A pro-Fillmore campaign cartoon in 1856 depicts major party politicians as rats and suggests that an agrarian-minded Fillmore will keep rodents out of the government corncrib for the next four years. Courtesy of Dickinson College.

convention as Republican saboteurs whose departure marked a good riddance. Nor did all Northern Know-Nothings join the North American movement. Probably the majority remained loyal to Fillmore in Pennsylvania, New York, and New Jersey as did significant minorities elsewhere.[13] In February and indeed until November, moreover, many campaign insiders believed they could woo back the bolting North Americans and prevent them from merging with the Republicans. Of course they did not foresee the dramatic impact that Bleeding Kansas and Bleeding Sumner would have in driving Northerners toward the Republican Party, but even after those events and the joint North American/Republican nomination of Frémont they continued to court the bolters.[14]

The tactics Fillmore's campaign adopted to bring these strays back into the fold varied over time. First, they tried to have another meeting of the national council in New York prior to the North American convention on 12 June to persuade the delegates to endorse Fillmore.[15] When that effort failed, they tried to exploit the resentment among North Americans caused by the Republicans' refusal to accept their vice-presidential candidate, William F. Johnston.[16] More important, they appealed to the genuine nativist and anti-Catholic biases of North Americans by enhancing Fillmore's nativist credentials and tarnishing those of Frémont.

Fillmore had been out of the country when he was nominated, and many people had no idea that he had secretly joined the Know-Nothing order.[17] Certainly he had no public reputation as a nativist. His closest lieutenants who secured his nomination in his absence, like Solomon G. Haven and John Pendleton Kennedy, tried to reassure nativists by releasing letters Fillmore had written sympathizing with Know-Nothing principles and revealing his membership. They also urged him to endorse Americanism and Protestantism in his letter accepting the nomination, but that letter was not mailed from Europe until late May and not published widely after its reception.[18]

Once Fillmore returned to the United States in late June, however, he quickly took steps to make up for lost time. Fillmore made several speeches as he proceeded from New York City to Buffalo, which the campaign later published in pamphlet form as *Fillmore at Home* and circulated as its main campaign document. Most of those speeches dwelled on the central theme of the Americans' campaign, his devotion to the Union, and his availability to conservatives who disliked the sectional extremists who seemed to dominate the Republican and Democratic parties. Yet to the absolute delight of his managers, Fillmore's brief speech at the Hudson River town of Newburgh embraced almost all of the nativist creed. Whatever Frémont may have told Know-Nothings in private, Fillmore publicly endorsed the cry that Americans must rule America, that foreign paupers and criminals must be banned, and that "if any sect or denomination, ostensibly organized for religious purposes, should use that organization or suffer it to be used for political objects, I would meet it by political opposition." Through these code words, Fillmore thus aligned himself on the side of anti-Catholics.[19]

Refurbishing Fillmore's nativist reputation with one hand, his supporters tried to destroy Frémont's appeal to nativists with the other by circulating the rumor that Frémont was Catholic, a charge that Gienapp and I have argued probably did more than any other to cost the Republicans the election.[20] Finally, they apparently tried to sabotage the Republican–North American coalition from within. The key saboteur here was a wealthy rubber manufacturer from New York City named Horace Day, who had previously been involved in the campaign to get Nathaniel Banks the North Americans' nomination in June and who was a member of the North

American National Council. Day may have simply been blowing smoke, but during the last three months of the campaign he repeatedly wrote Fillmore that he had made unspecified arrangements in a number of Northern states to make sure that North American tickets were not cast for Frémont.[21]

Exploiting nativist and anti-Catholic sentiment to woo back North Americans to the Fillmore camp was a plausible strategy, but it did nothing to obviate the chief cause of their bolt, their contempt for Fillmore as a doughface and their anger that the American platform refused to call for repeal of the Kansas-Nebraska Act. Just like Buchanan, Fillmore tried to fashion a stance on the slavery issue that was palatable to both Northerners and Southerners. Buchanan did so by embracing the Democratic platform, which praised the Kansas-Nebraska Act and the doctrine of popular sovereignty. Buchanan's stance, in fact, seemed like a grave blunder to Fillmore's Southern supporters because it appeared to endorse the doctrine of squatter sovereignty or a decision on slavery during the territorial stage. Hence Southerners urged Fillmore to exploit that mistake by insisting forthrightly that no decision on slavery would be made in a territory until it was ready to apply for statehood.[22] Had Fillmore been as free to concentrate on the South as Nichols and Potter contend, he could have done so, but he was unwilling to write off the North. Nor did he accede to demands from Southerners to retreat from the position he did take on the Kansas issue in order to win Northern support—that was to condemn the repeal of the Missouri Compromise as an outrageous and reckless act of the Democrats that reignited sectional strife and then to pose as the only candidate who could save the Union.[23]

Northerners considered this position inadequate and anachronistic because of the course of events since the spring of 1854, and they repeatedly called on Fillmore to come out for restoration of the 36° 30′ line. Southerners, in contrast, criticized it for implying that Fillmore wanted to restore the Missouri Compromise's ban, and they begged him explicitly to renounce such an intention. Privately, Fillmore believed that the best solution for Kansas was to admit it immediately as a free state, but publicly he refused to move beyond his criticism of the passage of the Kansas-Nebraska Act despite the outpouring of criticism from both sections. "I cannot be one thing to the North and another to the South," he wrote to Virginia's William C. Rives in exasperation.[24]

Fillmore's refusal to change his stance and to tilt one way or the other may strike some as an example of the seemingly congenital indecisiveness that characterized his career. Why alienate both Northerners and Southerners when he could easily have appeased one of the groups? But to fault Fillmore in this regard is to ignore the central strategy of his campaign. Fillmore and his managers saw the American Party as the party of the center, not of either section. The center of the sectional spectrum was where they believed most votes resided, and to mobilize those voters they presented the American Party as the only authentic Union Party in the race.[25] It is easy to view the American Party's well-known stress on unionism as simply a response to the context of the election or as an attempt to provide a refuge for conservatives frightened by extremists in both sections. But it in fact represented something far more than that, and it was the utter conviction of Fillmore and the men who secured his nomination about the appeal of a Union Party that was the third, and most important, reason they believed Fillmore could win the election.

The idea of creating a new Union Party had a lineage that dates back to Fillmore's own service as president between 1850 and 1853. The story of what I shall call the Union Party movement is intimately involved in the final collapse of the Whig Party between 1852 and 1856. That disintegration is usually told in terms of the party's sectional rupture over slavery and the defection of different elements in it to the new parties that appeared in 1854 and 1855— the Republicans on one hand and the Know-Nothings on the other. But there was a third group of self-defined conservative Whigs who wanted no part of those new parties. Some clung stubbornly to the Whig banner, and those diehards would be in part responsible for the separate nomination of Fillmore by a poorly attended Whig national convention in September 1856. Others in disgust withdrew from active political participation altogether. Still others would ultimately endorse Buchanan's candidacy in 1856. Yet the most interesting and active group of these conservative Whigs had from the early 1850s on persistently promoted the idea of replacing the old party with a new national conservative Union party that could combine pro-Union Whigs and Democrats from both sections. By a process of iteration and reiteration over five years, the proponents of this new party absolutely convinced themselves that it could mobilize a huge majority of voters in both sections and put Fillmore in the White House.

The idea of forming a new Union Party first emerged in the summer of 1850 after Fillmore became president when Democrats and Whigs in Congress were cooperating to pass the Compromise of 1850 over the opposition of anti-Compromise men from both parties.[26] It grew more powerful in the fall of 1850 and winter and spring of 1851 when bipartisan Union parties were formed in Deep South states and bipartisan Union meetings were held in numerous Northern cities to support the compromise. As early as October 1850, for example, the Baltimore Whig John Pendleton Kennedy reported that a Union meeting in New York marked "the beginning of a great conservative National party which will overwhelm the old divisions of Whig and democrat and make a new order of politics."[27] Originally, proponents of this new party expected it to form behind the presidential candidacy of Daniel Webster in 1852, and in the fall of 1851 one of Webster's supporters from Newburyport, Massachusetts, named Benjamin Balch issued a circular calling for the organization of a National Union Party that would nominate Webster.[28]

After Webster's death in 1852, the hopes of these men turned to Fillmore, and from the moment of Winfield Scott's defeat in November 1852 a small group of Whigs with intimate ties to Fillmore became the leading proponents of replacing the Whigs with a new Union Party that would elect Fillmore president in 1856.[29] This group included William L. Hodge, a Louisiana newspaper editor who worked in the Treasury Department under Fillmore and remained in Washington after the close of his administration; Daniel Lee, a Georgian who served in the Interior Department and who, after Fillmore left office, was brought to Rochester, New York, to help edit a pro-Fillmore newspaper; Isaac Newton of Pennsylvania, who also served in the Interior Department and to whom Fillmore would send a letter in January 1855 for private circulation among Know-Nothings that made clear Fillmore sympathized with their principles; Alexander H. H. Stuart of Virginia, the secretary of the interior in Fillmore's administration; Nathan K. Hall, Fillmore's law partner from Buffalo and his postmaster general; Solomon G. Haven, another of Fillmore's Buffalo law partners who represented that city in Congress from December 1851 through the 1856 election; and, above all, John P. Kennedy of Baltimore, who served as Fillmore's navy secretary during the last nine months of his administration and who, in the Spring of 1854, accompanied Fillmore on a tour of Southern states that was clearly meant to whip up enthusiasm for his presidential prospects.[30] Despite Fillmore's repeated public professions of disinterest in political affairs, it is absolutely clear that Millard Fillmore himself was committed by the fall of 1853 to this scheme to replace the Whigs with a new Union Party that could elect him president in 1856.[31]

From 1850 until 1856 the calculations of this group about which elements would compose this new Union Party remained the same. Its nucleus would be a merger of Silver Gray or Fillmorite Whigs from New York with Hunker or Hardshell Democrats there that could dominate the Empire State. To this core would be grafted other pro-Compromise Whigs in the North and the equivalent of Hunker Democrats from other Northern states, that is, Democrats who supported the Compromise of 1850, who insisted that sectional agitation be stopped, and who opposed any coalition between Democrats and Free Soilers. Proponents of the new party also counted on the support of all unionist or pro-Compromise men in the South, that is, virtually all Southern Whigs and what they called National or Union Democrats in the South—the Democrats who supported formal Union parties in Georgia, Alabama, and Mississippi and who, in other slave states, applauded the Compromise. Kennedy, for one, was absolutely convinced these Southern Democrats would support Fillmore in 1856.[32]

If the calculations about the potential constituency for a new Union Party remained constant from the start, it is also true that the Union Party movement met constant frustration and never jelled. It is important to understand what proponents of the idea identified as the major obstacles to it, for such an understanding explains why they eventually turned to the Know-Nothing Party as a substitute for the new organization they had long contemplated and why they were so confident Fillmore could win in 1856.

From the start, one problem was the lack of a distinctive issue or need for a Union Party when a national consensus in support of the Compromise of 1850 seemed quickly to emerge in 1851 and 1852. As the very conservative Boston Whig Samuel Eliot wrote in the fall of 1851, no Union Party could ever be formed because no one would oppose a platform calling for preservation of the Union. "How," he asked, "can a party exist without an opposition?" Creating a Union Party was thus a "no go." "It cannot live alone, & it cannot find a vis-à-vis." Or, as Kennedy wistfully wrote a year earlier in reference to the impending second session of the 31st Congress, "An attempt to repeal the fugitive slave law this winter, will inevitably draw the dividing line between the 'great [national conservative] party' and the small one five to one in any combat hereafter." To Kennedy's dismay, however, no such clarifying attempt at repeal was made. Again, in December 1851, Howell Cobb, who had been elected governor of Georgia on the Union Party ticket, warned Alexander Stephens, another member of Georgia's Union Party, that the party was disintegrating because it no longer had anything to fight about with its foes. Thus he urged

Stephens to push for some kind of vote in Congress as he would in the Georgia state legislature that clearly defined the differences between the Union Party and its foes. Other proponents of a new National Union party in 1851 and 1852 urged that it be built around distinctive economic programs such as aid to a Pacific railroad and the establishment of a national free banking system, but those efforts to generate a distinctive platform also aborted.[33]

A second obstacle that proponents of a Union Party identified in the early 1850s was that outside of the Deep South pro-Union Whigs and pro-Union Democrats refused to abandon their old parties to combine together in a new organization. Five factors were cited for that reluctance. First, conservative elements in both major parties still believed they could win control of their national and state organizations over rival factions. Conservative Whigs, after all, had the backing of Fillmore's administration; Hunker Democrats had the prestige of backing the Compromise.[34] Second, after twenty years of combat Whigs and Democrats still distrusted each other, and both regarded the Union Party movement as a trick of the other, not a mutual alliance. "No *coalition* with *Locofocos* even under the plausible title of *Union party* can succeed," thundered one Ohio Whig. It was simply an effort to put Democrats like Daniel S. Dickinson in the Senate.[35] Third, despite their common support for the Compromise, conservative Whigs and Democrats still disagreed sharply over a host of state issues they were unwilling to ignore. Even though both parties in his state were equally attached to the Union, carped a Tennessee Whig, "on most other important questions, on which there can be a difference of opinion, they differ now as they have always done."[36] Fourth, the very divisions within both major parties, especially in New York, which was considered the linchpin of the movement, rather than spawning realignment, instead encouraged hopes of an easy victory over their divided foe among both Whigs and Democrats, which were irresistible since victory in New York meant control of lucrative canal contracts.[37] Fifth, and most important, the pressure of the impending presidential election of 1852 kept Whigs and Democrats in their parties and drew back to them previous defectors to bipartisan Union parties in the South. With both parties' national platforms acquiescing in the Compromise of 1850 as a final settlement of the slavery issue, moreover, the rationale for a new party was undermined. Without a cause and a presidential candidate around whom conservatives could rally, the Union Party movement proved stillborn.[38]

After the 1852 election, hopes that a national Union Party could be created again rose. For one thing, the well-publicized rift between Hardshells in New York and the Pierce administration and the discontent of Union Democrats in the South with Pierce's patronage allocation made them seem once again a likely partner for merger. "The whole Union Democratic party at the South are ready to cut loose from the Pierce administration," Hodge wrote Fillmore in September 1853, and in December of that year, when dissident conservative Democrats in the Senate joined with Whigs to elect the printer, Fillmore himself exulted that it "looks very much as though a *nucleus* had been formed around which the *Union men* of all parties may rally and form a Union party." As late as December 1855 Kennedy was certain that "the National Hard Democrats North and South are too much offended with the administration and the Softs" ever to support the Democratic presidential nominee in 1856.[39]

Democratic divisions, however, did not solve the conservatives' need for a defining issue that divided pro-Union men from their opponents in the North and South. Fillmore astutely wrote Kennedy in the fall of 1853 that while the old Whig and Democratic parties could be "broken up by local causes and that centrifugal forces which throws individuals and masses beyond the attraction of the central power," new national parties could only be forged in reaction to events in Washington. "Will any question present such a magnet at the ensuing session of Congress?" he asked. "If so, then may we hope to see a national Union party which will cast off the secessionists of the South and the abolition free soilers of the North and rally around the constitution."[40]

What the ensuing session of Congress produced, of course, was the Kansas-Nebraska Act, which once again frustrated efforts to start a new conservative party where it was always thought it had to be started—in New York. That was because the Kansas-Nebraska Act was enthusiastically supported by Hardshell Democrats while it simultaneously drove conservative Whigs into the arms of the Sewardite antislavery wing of the party to fight it. "The Nebraska Swindle has driven National & Sectional Whigs into the same camp where they must mess together," groaned one Silver Gray. "The Whigs will be united . . . and will swallow anything, on account of Nebraska."[41]

Even worse, since most Southern Whigs in Congress supported the Nebraska bill, opposition to it by conservative Northern Whigs would hinder the creation of a new national coalition. That Southern support, sputtered Haven from the House, "cuts off all communion between us & the Whigs of the South and gives decided preponderance to the woolly head [Sewardite] influence of the north. Nothing can be worse, & yet nothing is more likely to happen." But that was not all, he moaned. "The Hards of the North (together with some Softs) will vote for it. So we are isolated from the hards, and made particularly subordinate & secondary amongst the Whigs of the North." Warned by Haven, Daniel Lee, and others that Silver Gray opposition to Nebraska could destroy Southern support for Fillmore's candidacy in 1856, Fillmore, who was genuinely appalled by the repeal of the Missouri Compromise line, could only urge his Northern friends not to publicize his anti-Nebraska views in 1854 lest they abort his incipient candidacy. Yet as early as January and February 1854, the Boston patrician Robert C. Winthrop, a natural recruit for a new conservative party, was warning that the Nebraska Act had doomed the chances of such a party and that Fillmore to have any chance for Northern support must openly condemn the bill. So damaging did the sectional rupture over Nebraska appear, indeed, that some correspondents urged Fillmore to cancel his impending trip to the South to avoid being forced by questioners there to reveal his hostility to the bill.[42]

The second important political development of 1854—the mushrooming of the Know-Nothing Party—also seemed at first to block the formation of the kind of Union Party Fillmore and his advisors sought. Not only were its nativism and anti-Catholicism irrelevant to their needs and repugnant to many conservative Whigs, but it had preempted the middle ground between proslavery Democrats and the new, rapidly growing antislavery coalitions in the North, the middle ground that proponents of a Union Party had long sought to occupy.

It is a great mistake to think that Fillmore's supporters and other conservative Whigs rushed pell-mell into the Know-Nothing order as an alternative to the emerging Republican Party. For most of 1854 they held back to see what would happen. As late as October 1854, indeed, Fillmore's conservative Whig allies in New York circulated a call throughout the country for a convention of conservative Whigs to meet the following January to reorganize the national *Whig* Party.[43] Only after the results of the 1854 elections were in and the strength of Know-Nothings was clear did they drop plans to resuscitate the Whig organization. Instead they now decided to try to take over the Know-Nothing organization and make it a unionist rather than a nativist party.[44] Kennedy and Haven concluded that Know-Nothings could form a nucleus around which Union Whigs and Democrats in the North and South could cohere,

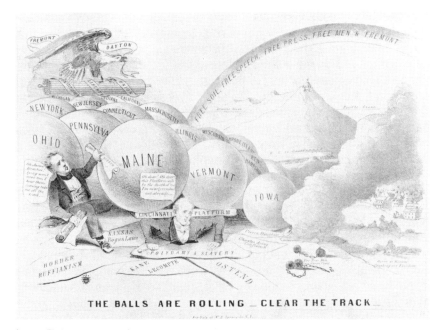

THE BALLS ARE ROLLING _ CLEAR THE TRACK

A pro-Frémont campaign cartoon in 1856 titled "The Balls are Rolling—Clear the Track," suggests that Millard Fillmore's support for the Fugitive Slave Bill of 1850 and Buchanan's identification with the Democratic platform doom both of these candidates with the northern electorate. Courtesy of Dickinson College.

and Fillmore himself exalted that *"Know Nothingism or Americanism* is fast purging a political party from sectionalism and slavery agitation, and may lay the foundation for a party useful to the country and entirely national in its character."[45] Confiding to the Virginian Stuart in January 1855 that "my mind inclines to the K.N.s as the best remedy for existing evils," Fillmore urged his friends to join the order, and Haven, Stuart, and eventually Fillmore himself did so. Kennedy remained outside the order, but he worked closely with insiders to secure Fillmore's nomination.[46]

By the end of 1855 all the elements seemed in place to convert the American Party into the long-sought Union Party that would elect Fillmore. The sectional split over the Kansas-Nebraska Act and the emergence of the Know-Nothings had seemingly wrecked both the Whigs and the Democrats. Thus the reluctance to leave old parties that had frustrated the Union Party movement earlier no longer seemed operative. Unlike 1852 as well, the conservatives would have a candidate of their own in the 1856 presidential election, although Fillmore's friends originally hoped he could be nominated by newspapers and local meetings rather than a national convention. Finally, proponents of a Union Party had an issue that could justify its existence and differentiate it from its foes. This was not so much the Kansas-Nebraska Act itself as the sectional turmoil that ensued after its passage. Fillmore and his supporters could and did denounce the Democrats for recklessly endangering the Union by pushing that act through Congress. Clearly such a party, they argued, no longer deserved the trust of Union-loving men. Simultaneously, they assailed Republicans as sectional extremists whose victory would provoke disunion.

This tack, they were sure, would not only attract conservative Whigs in both sections of the country, both inside and outside of the Know-Nothing order. It would also attract Hardshell or National Democrats in the North and South who had been shortchanged by Pierce on patronage and who blamed Pierce for needlessly reopening sectional agitation at no advantage to the South because, as they endlessly repeated, no one in his right mind believed slavery could ever expand to Kansas.[47] Simply by promising, as he explicitly did, that he would conduct the presidency just as he had between 1850 and 1853, Fillmore would mobilize an overwhelming majority of voters in the North and South.[48]

Such was the basis for the optimism of Fillmore's supporters in the spring of 1856, a confidence that of course proved badly misplaced. The most important reasons why these hopes were unrealized are well known. Bleeding Kansas and Bleeding Sumner helped the Republicans at the expense of the Americans in the North, and the growing strength of the Republicans in the North, which Fillmore and his men unrealistically believed would drive Democrats into Fillmore's column by showing Buchanan's inability to defeat Frémont, instead drove Southern Americans and Whigs into Buchanan's column. Those events could not have been predicted in the early spring, but three other developments also contributed to the dashing of Fillmore's hopes.

The first was the very nomination of Buchanan itself. The conviction that conservative Democrats in both sections would support Fillmore was based on the expectation that Pierce or Douglas, both of whom were tainted with responsibility for the Kansas-Nebraska Act, would get the Democratic nomination. The selection of Buchanan who was supported by anti-Pierce Democrats instead opened up the possibility that national Democrats would get the patronage if he won. On both policy and patronage grounds, that is, Buchanan's nomination destroyed any incentive conservative Democrats might have had to bolt the party.[49]

"*B U C K*" *taking the* "*P O T*".

An 1856 campaign cartoon suggests that Buchanan holds the best cards via his identification with the Union. Courtesy of Dickinson College.

The second was the defeat by House Republicans in July 1856 of Senator Robert Toombs's bill to take a new and fair census in Kansas, convene a constitutional convention, and have it apply for statehood immediately. Historians have correctly pointed out that Republicans acted out of narrow partisan self-interest to keep alive the Bleeding Kansas issue, and thus their action probably helped deter northern Know-Nothings from supporting Fillmore rather than Frémont.[50] Yet Toombs's introduction of the bill, which was actually written by his fellow Georgian, Representative Alexander H. Stephens, may have also shunted conservative Southerners, on whom Fillmore and his men had been counting for four years, into Buchanan's column.

To the extent that historians have explored the intentions of Toombs's proposal, they have interpreted it as an attempt by the congressional Democratic leadership to resolve the Kansas issue, which was damaging the party so badly in the North.[51] Few, if any, have explicitly asked why it was Toombs, who on many occasions during the 1850s seemed as radical a fire-eater as anyone from the South, who introduced such a fair-minded proposal from which Northerners who wished to bar slavery from Kansas stood to benefit. Both Stephens and Toombs were recent converts from Whiggery, and both were far too independent to be labeled loyal Democrats whom the "leadership" could enlist for any purpose. What, in particular, motivated the two Georgians?

Little direct evidence exists, but one possibility is that they wanted to neutralize the charge of Fillmore's Southern supporters that Buchanan favored squatter sovereignty by reemphasizing the Democrats' commitment to a territorial decision only at the statehood phase when a constitution was written. Georgia's Democrats were exceedingly worried about Americans' exploitation of this charge, and in June Stephens wrote a long private letter defending Buchanan from it.[52] Alternatively, Stephens confessed in the same letter that he cared far more about establishing the permanency of popular sovereignty at the statehood stage as a principle for all present and future territories than in securing Kansas as a slave state. Thus he and Toombs may have been attempting to gull Republicans into establishing a fatal precedent.

A still more intriguing possibility exists. The Stephens-Toombs proposal was strikingly akin to the private views Fillmore expressed about the fairest way to settle the Kansas controversy.[53] Could they have been privy to his views, feared he might go public with them, and acted to beat him to the punch, thereby neutralizing his appeal to the so-called National Democrats and conservative Whigs who blamed the Pierce administration for recklessly reigniting sectional strife? No direct evidence exists, but certain clues support such a hypothesis. Both Stephens and Toombs had helped lead Georgia's Union Party between 1850 and 1852, and both had joined with Northern Fillmore Whigs in Congress in trying to create a national Union Party in those years. After 1852, moreover, Toombs remained friendly with Solomon G. Haven, Fillmore's chief lieutenant in Congress and a major proponent of converting the Know-Nothings into the long-sought Union Party. Both Stephens and Toombs vehemently rejected Know-Nothingism because of its secrecy and anti-Catholicism. Once Fillmore accepted the Know-Nothings' nomination, therefore, he was out of the question so far as they were concerned. Even so, it is likely that they sympathized with the goals of a Union Party and were fully aware of the calculations of Fillmore and his friends as to who might join it. In June 1855, for example, Toombs wrote that the only hope for the South was that "Whigs, Democrats, and Know Nothings should come together and combine for the common safety" and "uphold and support that noble band of patriots North who have stood for the Constitution and right against the tempest of fanaticism, folly, and treason which has assailed them." Hodge, Kennedy, or Fillmore himself could have written those words. Similarly, in 1856 Stephens asserted that his goal was to preserve the Union and the Constitution and to assure that "there never will be another sectional or slavery struggle in the United States," sentiments with which Fillmore would have fully agreed. Could it be, therefore, that in offering their Kansas proposal, Stephens and Toombs were trying to undercut Fillmore's appeal as a Union candidate in the South by proving to the so-called "National Democrats" whom Fillmore's friends had long targeted as recruits that the Democratic Party was just as trustworthy a Union Party behind which "Whigs, Democrats, and Know Nothings should come together"? If so, they achieved far more success than historians have previously realized.[54]

The third, totally unexpected, impediment to Fillmore's success was that his nomination by the Americans in February did not automatically assure him the support of all conservative Whigs. This fact points to one of the most intriguing, if unasked, questions about the 1856 campaign. Why was there a rump Whig convention in September that also nominated Fillmore and what does it tell us about the process by which and the reasons why the Whig party disintegrated? Here, answers to these questions can be sketched only briefly.

From the very beginning of the Union Party movement in 1850, a significant minority of conservative, pro-Compromise Whigs from both sections vehemently rejected the idea of displacing the Whig Party with a new organization drawn from both the old parties. Men such as ex-governor Washington Hunt and Senator Hamilton Fish of New York, Edward Everett and Robert C. Winthrop of Massachusetts, Thomas Corwin of Ohio, and William A. Graham of North Carolina typified this group, and their leading voice was the prestigious Whig organ in Washington, the *National Intelligencer*. By 1854 and 1855 these men were appalled by both the Republicans and the Know-Nothings, and they refused to have anything to do with the latter even after Fillmore and his inner circle targeted the order for a conservative takeover. Southern Whigs of this ilk strenuously objected to the proscriptiveness and apparent religious bigotry of Know-Nothings, and Fillmore's willingness to accept the American nomination and particularly Fillmore's nativist speech at Newburgh left them cold.[55]

Among Northerners it seems to have been less the Know-Nothings' anti-Catholicism than considerations of class, culture, and age or generation that offended them. College-educated patricians like Everett and Winthrop regarded the young, working-class men who rushed to the Know-Nothing lodges as riffraff and the initiation rituals as sophomoric mumbo jumbo. Winthrop disgustedly excoriated rank-and-file Know-Nothings as "repulsive," while Everett huffed that "their organized action, in this part of the country, is about an equal mixture of blind machinery, imbecility, and craft." Sheer social snobbery kept some Whigs from having anything to do with the American Party. As one Fillmore American from Massachusetts complained to the candidate in 1856, these diehard conservatives "wear their Whiggery as a badge of aristocracy and parade it rather offensively than otherwise."[56]

Whatever their reasons, old-line Whig conservatives refused to accept the American Party as a new national Union Party, and they regarded Fillmore's nomination by it as a liability, not an asset. Some angrily condemned Fillmore as a traitorous defector from the Whig Party and refused to endorse his candidacy unless Whigs formally sanctioned it at independent conventions of their own. Of these recalcitrants, the most important were Joseph Gales and W. W. Seaton, editors of the Washington *National Intelligencer* to which diehard Whigs around the country looked for direction. Gales and Seaton hated the Know-Nothings, and until September they insisted that their only allegiance was to the Whig Party and complained that "there is no Whig candidate in the field."[57] Others were prepared to vote for Fillmore, but they insisted on maintaining the Whig party as an independent organization.[58] Indeed, while some old-line Whigs like Corwin and Maryland's James Pearce candidly admitted that "the Whig party *as such* is dead & buried" and without prospect of resurrection, others wanted to attach life-support systems to the expiring party in the unrealistic hope that it would revive to fight again another day.[59] Thus local and state Whig meetings and the few remaining Whig newspapers during the Spring and Summer repeatedly spoke of "preserving the organization of the Whig party, that it may be prepared to resume its mission when the ephemeral factions of the day have dissolved" or of keeping "the good old Whig party alive, distinct, and organized, to serve as a nucleus around which all these dispersed conservative republican elements may rally."[60]

Whigs who had followed Fillmore into the American Party realized that these hopes of Whig survival were quixotic, but they were also convinced that old-line Whigs "if properly marshalled [held] the balance of power" in the election.[61] Whig diehards, however, could only be marshaled by other Whigs who had remained clear of the Know-Nothings. For almost a full year prior to Fillmore's nomination, therefore, Kennedy had tried to no avail to persuade his friend Winthrop to rally such Whigs to the American cause, and in 1856 Fillmore personally pressed the same mission on Everett.[62] In the fall of 1856 both Everett and Winthrop would publicly endorse Fillmore, but during the summer they remained reticent while other Whigs awaited some "united action" to "give due expression to the political opinions they still entertain" before committing themselves to any candidate.[63]

During that summer interim, when the eventual course of the supposedly crucial Whig diehards remained uncertain, increasing numbers jumped off the fence and joined the Buchanan camp. By mid-September, prestigious Whigs like James B. Clay, Henry Clay's son, Senator James Jones of Tennessee, Charles Jenkins of Georgia, Senators James Pearce and Thomas Pratt of Maryland, Daniel Barringer of North Carolina, and Rufus Choate of Massachusetts had openly endorsed the Democratic nominee.[64] This trend panicked Fillmore and his supporters, for unless it were checked, what had been a trickle of undecided Whigs in Buchanan's direction could become a torrent. Thus they frantically and pathetically sought the public embrace of equally prominent Whigs like Corwin, Hunt, and Fish of New York, Everett and Winthrop, and the steadfastly standoffish editors of the *National Intelligencer*.[65]

From this confluence of developments in the Spring and Summer emerged the drive to hold what would be the final national Whig convention. Fillmore and his lieutenants did not launch that movement, for they had simply assumed that conservative Whigs would back Fillmore. Rather it was first promoted by Whig papers and local Whig meetings, which insisted on preserving the integrity and independence of the Whig organization. Once it became clear during June and July that Whigs who were contemptuous of Know-Nothingism stood aloof from Fillmore, however, insiders in the Fillmore campaign tried to orchestrate the holding of a Whig convention, which they saw as the last and best hope of stemming Whig defections to Buchanan.

At first even this desperate effort met frustrations because of the shambles into which the Whig Party had been reduced by 1856. With no existing Whig national committee or congressional caucus to set the place and date of such a convention, it was unclear who had the authority and necessary influence to call one. Finally, in April, Kentucky Whigs seized the initiative and called for a national assemblage of Whigs to gather in Louisville in July, a call that the *National Intelligencer* and other Whig papers endorsed.

Yet so muddled were communications among the remaining Whigs that confusion reigned as to whether the date of the convention was 4 July or 30 July.[66] Because of this mix-up and probably as well because of the difficulty Eastern delegates would have in traveling to Louisville, the Kentucky meeting never took place.

Thus two precious months in which old-line Whigs continued to drift and both Buchanan and Frémont made incursions into Whig ranks were lost to Fillmore before the Whig convention met in Baltimore on 17 September 1856. Lest this final chance be squandered, Fillmore and his lieutenants exerted every effort to make sure that trustworthy friends like Francis Granger, Washington Hunt, Graham, Joseph Randolph of New Jersey, and James Townsend of Connecticut attended. As hoped, that gathering of some 160 delegates representing twenty-one states and the District of Columbia gave its nod to Fillmore.[67]

Whereas the disarray displayed by Whigs in arranging a national convention portended the party's imminent demise, the jubilant reaction of Fillmore's friends to this gathering of political fossils shows how deluded they had become by the fall of 1856. "These proceedings," rejoiced one of the delegates from the District of Columbia, "have aroused the Whigs throughout our widespread land, and . . . will lead to the resuscitation of the Old Whig Party." William L. Hodge, who had been in on the Union Party movement from the start and who represented his native Louisiana at the Whig convention, exuded equal enthusiasm and equal dimness. "It was without exception the finest body of men I ever saw assembled on any occasion—staid, sober, solid, respectable—two thirds of them over fifty years of age," he gushed. "Altogether it was a meeting well calculated to 'make its mark' as it undoubtedly will do."[68]

One can imagine Federalists in 1814 saying the same thing about the members and impact of the Hartford Convention. Staid, sober, respectable, and old men do not win popular elections, or at least they had not since the emergence of Andrew Jackson. This gathering, which marked the death rattle of the Whig Party, indeed, makes one think of a witty epitaph for the Whig Party that a Mississippi newspaper editor composed in 1870. "The Whig party died," he wrote, "because of too much respectability and not enough people." But this last Whig national convention reminds one of something else as well. Over twenty-five years ago Lynn Marshall published an article entitled "The Strange Stillbirth of the Whig Party," in which he argued that in the early 1830s the Whig Party stultified itself because it was leader-oriented rather than voter-oriented, because Whigs mistakenly believed they could form a successful party by arranging coalitions of prominent leaders rather than by directly mobilizing voters. Marshall was wrong about the birth of the Whig Party, but his analysis is spectacularly appropriate for its death.[69]

Notes

1. The best account of the election from the perspective of the Democratic Party can be found in Roy F. Nichols, *The Disruption of American Democracy* (New York: Collier Books, 1962), 17–62; the best analysis from the Republican perspective is William E. Gienapp, *The Origins of the Republican Party, 1852–1856* (New York: Oxford University Press, 1987), 239–448.

2. This stricture is no longer fully accurate. Between the time this paper was first delivered at Franklin and Marshall College in September 1991 and its revision, Tyler Anbinder, *Nativism and Slavery: The Northern Know Nothings and the Politics of the 1850s* (New York: Oxford University Press, 1992), was published. Although Anbinder largely ignores the Southern aspect of Fillmore's campaign and the Whiggish origins of the Union Party movement to be described here, he presents the fullest account of the Fillmore campaign now extant and provides additional documentation for many of the assertions made in this essay.

3. Gienapp, *Origins of the Republican Party.*

4. These developments can be traced in a number of accounts. See, for example, Gienapp, *The Origins of the Republican Party,* and Michael F. Holt, *The Political Crisis of the 1850s* (New York: Wiley, 1978).

5. While Anbinder correctly notes that there were other turning points later in the year, he implies that the American campaign was doomed to defeat even earlier than February, namely with the election of the Know-Nothing–turned-Republican Nathaniel P. Banks as Speaker of the House of Representatives in January. Anbinder, *Nativism and Slavery,* 194–202, 218–19.

6. Allan Nevins, *Ordeal of the Union: A House Dividing, 1852–57* (New York: Charles Scribner's Sons, 1947), 468–70.

7. Nichols, *Disruption of American Democracy,* 33.

8. David M. Potter, *The Impending Crisis, 1848–1861,* completed and edited by Don E. Fehrenbacher (New York: Harper and Row, 1967), 255, 261.

9. Anbinder, *Nativism and Slavery,* 233–37; Solomon G. Haven to Millard Fillmore, 2, 28 March, 11 May, 20 July 1856, E. Root to Fillmore, 26 June 1856, Henry Hilliard to Fillmore, 26 June 1856, William A. Graham to Fillmore, 22 July 1856, R. P. Letcher to Fillmore, 13, 27 August 1856, George Robertson to Fillmore, 14 August 1856, Richard H. Day to Fillmore, 14 August 1856, Millard Fillmore Papers, State University of New York at Oswego; Millard Fillmore to William A. Graham, 9 August 1856, William A. Graham Papers, (Southern Historical Collection, University of North Carolina, Chapel Hill).

10. Edward Everett to Millard Fillmore, 9 July 1856 (quotation), S. Sammons to Fillmore, 28 July, 1856, A. B. Ely to Fillmore, 26 August 1856, Fillmore Papers (State University of New York at Oswego); Millard Fillmore to Edward Everett, 12 July 1856, Edward Everett Papers (Massachusetts Historical Society).

11. For examples of Know-Nothing calculations and unrealistic optimism, see Joseph W. Randolph to Millard Fillmore, 28 June 1856, Humphrey Marshall to Fillmore, 10 July 1856, Isaiah D. Fuller to Fillmore, 4 September 1856, W. L Harlan to Fillmore, 12 September 1856, Henry D. Moore to Fillmore, 12 Septem-

ber 1856, William G. Brownlow to Fillmore, 6 October 1856, Fillmore Papers (State University of New York at Oswego); Henry A. Wise to Edward Everett, 11 September 1856, Everett Papers (Massachusetts Historical Society).

12. Gienapp, *Origins of the Republican Party,* especially 239–73.

13. Fillmore ran almost even with Frémont in New Jersey, and Gienapp's tables, *Origins of the Republican Party,* 532–35, indicate that the majority of 1854 and 1855 Know-Nothing voters in New York and Pennsylvania preferred Fillmore to Frémont. In addition, considerable correspondence in the Fillmore Papers, which I shall not cite individually, points to the loyalty of state organizations to Fillmore in those states. Elsewhere, state Know-Nothing councils that sanctioned the separate Know-Nothing movement were replaced by new councils that backed Fillmore.

14. Henry E. Davies to Millard Fillmore, 28 February 1856, Solomon G. Haven to Fillmore, 2 March, 24 April 1856, John P. Kennedy to Fillmore, 18 March 1856, S. Sammons to Fillmore, 18, 23 July 1856, James R. Thompson to Fillmore, 17, 19 September 1856, Horace H. Day to Fillmore, 19 September 1856, Fillmore Papers (State University of New York at Oswego).

15. Charles Ready to William B. Campbell, 12 May 1856, John Bell to Campbell, 29 May 1856, Meredith P. Gentry to Campbell, 12 June 1856, Campbell Family Papers, Perkins Library, Duke University; Anna Ella Carroll to Millard Fillmore, 23 May 1856, Fillmore Papers (State University of New York at Oswego).

16. For the flap over the vice-presidential nomination, see Gienapp, *Origins of the Republican Party,* 383–86; and Anbinder, *Nativism and Slavery,* 229–33.

17. Fillmore was privately initiated into a Know-Nothing lodge in the early spring of 1855 before leaving for Europe. Fillmore to Dorthea L. Dix, 30 October 1856, Dorthea L. Dix Papers, Houghton Library, Harvard University,

18. John Pendleton Kennedy to Millard Fillmore, 18, 28 March 1856, Henry C. Davies to Fillmore, 31 March 1856, Solomon G. Haven to Fillmore, 24 April, 11 May 1856, Fillmore Papers (State University of New York at Oswego); Millard Fillmore to Alexander H. H. Stuart, et al., 21 May 1856, Alexander H. H. Stuart Papers, University of Virginia. The letter in which Fillmore endorsed Know-Nothing principles and which Haven later had published was to Isaac Newton of Philadelphia, a former member of Fillmore's administration, and dated 3 January 1856. See Isaac Newton to Fillmore, 10 January 1855, Fillmore Papers.

19. Fillmore's speeches can be found in the Washington *National Intelligencer,* 24, 26, 27 June 1856 (New York City), 1 July 1856 (Newburgh and Albany). For samples of the delighted reaction, see Solomon G. Haven to Alexander H. H. Stuart, 29 June 1856, Stuart Papers; George Robertson to Millard Fillmore, 3 July 1856, Solomon G. Haven to Fillmore, 4, 15 July 1856, and Henry W. Hilliard to Fillmore, 8 July 1856, Fillmore Papers (State University of New York at Oswego).

20. S. Sammons to Millard Fillmore, 23 July 1856, N. Sargent to Fillmore, 12 October 1856, Fillmore Papers (State University of New York at Oswego); C. J. Albright to Francis P. Blair, 9 August 1856, Blair-Lee Papers (Princeton University); Gienapp, *Origins of the Republican Party,* 367–72; Holt, *Political Crisis of the 1850s,* 179–80; Anbinder, *Nativism and Slavery,* 224–26.

21. Horace H. Day to Millard Fillmore, 4, 5, 9, 10, 12, 27 September 17, 29 October 1856, Fillmore Papers (State University of New York at Oswego).

22. J. Muir to Millard Fillmore, 7 July 1856, C. F. M. Noland to Fillmore, 7 July 1856, Henry Hilliard to Fillmore, 8 July 1856, Fillmore Papers (State University of New York at Oswego).

23. William C. Rives to Millard Fillmore, 16 July 1856, E. C. Cabell to Fillmore, 16 July 1856, Vesparian Ellis to Fillmore, 31 July 1856, Joseph S. Williams to Fillmore, 29 September 1856, Fillmore Papers (State University of New York at Oswego). See also Fillmore's speeches printed in the *National Intelligencer,* cited earlier.

24. Fillmore to William C. Rives, 3 July 1856, Millard Fillmore Papers, Library of Congress, Washington, D.C.; Fillmore to Anna Ella Carroll, 8 September 1856, Anna Ella Carroll Papers (Maryland Historical Society). Examples of Southern pressure on Fillmore to renounce any intention of restoring the Missouri Compromise line are cited in note 22. For examples of Northern pressure on Fillmore to endorse its restoration and guarantee to keep slavery out of Kansas, see Joseph W. Randolph to Fillmore, 28 June 1856, Anna Ella Carroll to Fillmore, 18, 23 August 1856, Amos A. Lawrence to Fillmore, 23 August 1856, Silas Merchant to Fillmore, 23 August 1856, J. M. Brown to Fillmore, 25 August 1856, Fillmore Papers (State University of New York at Oswego).

25. See Fillmore's speeches in the *National Intelligencer,* cited previously, and Anbinder, *Nativism and Slavery,* 220–23.

26. For example, see J. S. Skinner to Millard Fillmore, 12 July 1850, Millard Fillmore Papers (Buffalo and Erie County Historical Society); Charles A. Davis to Daniel Webster, 9 August 1850, Daniel Webster to Peter Harvey, 2 October 1850, Daniel Webster Papers (Dartmouth College).

27. Holt, *Political Crisis of the 1850s,* 91–95; John Pendleton Kennedy to Elizabeth Kennedy, 31 October 1850 (quotation), Kennedy to Robert C. Winthrop, 10 November 1850 (copy), John Pendleton Kennedy Papers, Enoch Pratt Free Library, Baltimore; M. C. Fulton to Howell Cobb, 6 November 1850, in U. B. Phillips, ed., *The Correspondence of Robert Toombs, Alexander H. Stephens, and Howell Cobb,* Annual Report of the American Historical Association for 1911, 2:217–18; C. Prentiss to Thomas Ewing, 8 February 1851, Ewing Family Papers, Library of Congress.

28. John P. Kennedy to Philip C. Pendleton, 12 November 1850, Kennedy to Daniel Webster, 10 July 1851 (copy), Kennedy Papers; C. S. [Charles Stetson?] to Daniel Webster, 28 July 1851, National Union Party to Webster, Newburyport, Massachusetts, 20 October 1851, Webster Papers. Balch's name headed the list of signers of this circular, and subsequent letters from him make it clear he was the initiator of the Newburyport movement.

29. Daniel Lee to Millard Fillmore, 15 November 1852, P. J. Wagner to Fillmore, 6 January 1853, and Benjamin Balch to Fillmore, 31 January 1853, Fillmore Papers (Buffalo and Erie County Historical Society).

30. The correspondence from these men and others interested in a new conservative Union Party to Fillmore in 1853 and 1854 is too voluminous to cite fully, but for examples see John C. Spenser to Fillmore, 5 September 1853, William L. Hodge to Fillmore, 26, 30 September 1853, John P. Kennedy to Fillmore, 26 November 1853, Isaac Newton to Fillmore, 14 October 1853, Alexander H. H. Stuart to Fillmore, 6 December 1853, Daniel Lee to Fillmore, 9 February 1854, and Solomon G. Haven to Fillmore, 18 February 1854, Fillmore Papers (State University of New York at Oswego); John P. Kennedy to Robert C. Winthrop, 4 December 1853, Kennedy Papers.

31. I have found no direct statement from Fillmore admitting his ambition, but such negative evidence is hardly unusual when even men like Henry Clay and Daniel Webster who nakedly hungered for the presidency usually feigned indifference. Fillmore, however, did nothing to discourage his lieutenants from pursuing

their goal of putting him in the White House again, and many of his letters from November 1853 on clearly indicate his interest in a partisan reorganization from which he would benefit.

32. Daniel Ullmann to Millard Fillmore, 5 October 1850, Fillmore Papers (Buffalo and Erie County Historical Society); John P. Kennedy to Robert C. Winthrop, 10 November 1850, 4 December 1853 (copies), Kennedy to J. N. Reynolds, 18 November 1854 (copy), Kennedy to Solomon G. Haven, 29 January 1856, Millard Fillmore to John P. Kennedy, 14 October 1853, Kennedy Papers; Joshua R. Giddings to Milton R. Sutcliffe, 30 December 1850, Milton R. Sutcliffe Papers (Western Reserve Historical Society); James D. Ogden to John O. Sargent, 17, 20 September 1851, John O. Sargent Papers, (Massachusetts Historical Society); John C. Spencer to Fillmore, 5 September 1853, William L. Hodge to Fillmore, 26, 30 September, 6 October 1853, John P. Kennedy to Fillmore, 26 November 1853, John T. Bush to Fillmore, 19 January 1854, Fillmore Papers (State University of New York at Oswego).

33. Samuel Eliot to John O. Sargent, 10 November 1851, Sargent Papers (Massachusetts Historical Society); John P. Kennedy to Robert C. Winthrop, 17 November 1850 (copy), Kennedy Papers; Howell Cobb to Alexander H. Stephens, 3 December 1851, Alexander H. Stephens Papers, Library of Congress; National Union Party [Benjamin Balch] to Daniel Webster, 20 October 1851, Webster Papers; Benjamin Balch to Millard Fillmore, 31 January 1853, Fillmore Papers (Buffalo and Erie County Historical Society).

34. Charles Ready to John Bell, 3 January 1851, John Bell Papers (Library of Congress); James D. Ogden to John O. Sargent, 17, 20, September 1851, Sargent Papers; Charles March to Daniel Webster, 2 December 1851, Webster Papers; William L. Hodge to Fillmore, 6 October 1853, Fillmore Papers (State University of New York at Oswego).

35. C. Prentiss to Thomas Ewing, 8 February 1851, Ewing Family Papers (quotation); Martin Van Buren to Francis P. Blair, 14 December 1850, Blair-Lee Papers; Gideon Welles to Edmund Burke, 3 November 1851, Edmund Burke Papers (Library of Congress).

36. Charles Ready to John Bell, 3 January 1851 (quotation), Thomas A. R. Nelson to Bell, 10 January 1851, Bell Papers; Samuel A. Eliot to John O. Sargent, 10 November 1851, Sargent Papers.

37. William L. Hodge to Millard Fillmore, 6 October 1853, John T. Bush to Fillmore, 6 October 1853, 19 January 1854, Fillmore Papers (State University of New York at Oswego); Fillmore to John P. Kennedy, 14 October, 15 December 1853, Kennedy Papers.

38. The defeat of both Webster and Fillmore at the Whig convention was particularly crushing to proponents of a new party, for hopes had been pinned on them. Some diehards in Georgia and Massachusetts ignored reality and supported Webster tickets even after Webster died, but few went to that extreme.

39. William L. Hodge to Fillmore, 26 September 1853 (quotation), 30 September 1853, Fillmore Papers (State University of New York at Oswego); Fillmore to John Pendleton Kennedy, 15 December 1853, Kennedy to Joseph F. Randolph, 1 December 1855 (copy), Kennedy Papers.

40. Fillmore to John P. Kennedy, 14 October 1853, Kennedy Papers.

41. B. Thompson to Daniel Ullmann, 16 May 1854, Daniel Ullmann Papers (New York Historical Society).

42. Solomon G. Haven to Millard Fillmore, 12 February 1854, Daniel Lee to Fillmore, 9 February 1854, E. R. Jewett to Fillmore, 18 February 1854, Fillmore

Papers (State University Press of New York at Oswego); Millard Fillmore to Edward Everett, 8 February 1854, Edward Everett Papers (Massachusetts Historical Society); Robert C. Winthrop to John Pendleton Kennedy, 31 January, 27 February 1854, Kennedy Papers (Enoch Pratt Free Library, Baltimore).

43. Francis Granger to Millard Fillmore, 19, 24 October 1854, E. R. Jewett to Fillmore, 24 October 1854, Edward Everett to Fillmore, 10 November 1854, William A. Graham to Fillmore, 3 December 1854, Fillmore Papers (State University of New York at Oswego). Technically, the effort of Granger and other New York conservatives was only to reform what they called the National Whig Party in New York State since they believed Sewardites had taken over the regular Whig organization, but they mailed their circular calling the meeting to conservatives across the nation, as the letters from Everett and Graham, among others, attest. Solomon G. Haven, who reported to Fillmore as early as 29 June 1854 that the Know-Nothings wanted Fillmore as their presidential candidate in 1856 was an exception to the delay among Fillmore's inner circle in joining the Know-Nothings. It is likely he joined a lodge in Washington during the summer of 1854. But Kennedy, Stuart, Hall, and Fillmore himself waited to watch events, and Kennedy never joined the order.

44. Millard Fillmore to Edward Everett, 13 December 1854, Everett Papers. For good examples of the awe that Know-Nothing strength evoked from Fillmore's cronies even before the Fall results, see Isaac Hazlehurst to Fillmore, 7 July 1854, and William L. Hodge to Fillmore, 21 July 1854, Fillmore Papers (State University of New York at Oswego).

45. John P. Kennedy to J. N. Reynolds, 18 November 1854 (copy), Kennedy Papers; Solomon G. Haven to Fillmore, 9 December 1854, Fillmore Papers (State University of New York at Oswego); Fillmore to Edward Everett, 13 December, 1854, Everett Papers.

46. Millard Fillmore to Alexander H. H. Stuart, 15 January 1855, Stuart Papers; Solomon G. Haven to Fillmore, 10, 29 January 1855, Isaac Newton to Fillmore, 18 January 1855, Fillmore Papers, Oswego; John P. Kennedy to J. N. Reynolds, 27 February 1855 (copy), Kennedy Papers. Reynolds was a member of the Know-Nothings in New York.

47. Charles M. Conrad [a Louisianan who had been Fillmore's secretary of war] to Fillmore, 28 September, 24 December 1854, Fillmore Papers, Oswego; George S. Bryan to John P. Kennedy, 23 August 1854, Kennedy to J. N. Reynolds, 18 November 1854, 27 February 1855, Kennedy to Robert C. Winthrop, 18 June 1855, Kennedy to Nathan Sargent, 9 July 1855, Kennedy to Joseph F. Randolph, 1 December 1855, copies, Kennedy Papers.

48. John P. Kennedy to J. N. Reynolds, 27 February, 18 November 1855, Kennedy to Nathan Sargent, 9 July 1855, Kennedy to Solomon G. Haven, 29 January 1856, Kennedy to Fillmore, 18 March 1856 (copies), Kennedy Papers; Fillmore's speeches in New York, *National Intelligencer,* 24, 27 June, 1 July 1856.

49. The numerous letters from Hodge and Kennedy cited here made it clear that anger at Pierce's policy and patronage is what made National Democrats potential recruits. See also Nathan K. Hall to Millard Fillmore, 23 March 1856, Fillmore Papers (State University of New York at Oswego). For examples of the voluminous testimony that Buchanan proved far more attractive than Pierce to conservative Whigs and Democrats, see J. B. Norman to William H. English, 23 May 1856, William H. English Papers (Indiana Historical Society Library); Jesse D. Bright to Allen Hamilton, 16 June 1856, Allen Hamilton Papers (Indiana State Library). For a superb contemporary analysis of the reasons anti-Pierce Demo-

crats supported Buchanan, see Alexander H. Stephens to Thomas W. Thomas, 16 June 1856, in Phillips, *Correspondence of Toombs, Stephens, and Cobb,* 367–72.

50. Gienapp, *Origins of the Republican Party,* 349–50; Potter, *The Impending Crisis,* 215.

51. Ibid.

52. Robert Toombs to Thomas W. Thomas, 9 February 1856, Alexander H. Stephens to Thomas W. Thomas, 16 June 1856, and James Buchanan to Howell Cobb, 10 July 1856, in Phillips, *Correspondence of Toombs, Stephens, and Cobb,* 359–61, 367–74.

53. On 8 September 1856, Fillmore wrote Anna Ella Carroll that the best solution for Kansas was quick statehood. "I would therefore repeal its obnoxious laws, provide for a fair representation of the people in a new legislature, secure to the people free and safe ingress and egress to the territory, and protect them when there from all external violence or intrusion, until the population of the territory entitled them to be admitted as a state; then I would let them, that is, the *resident citizens,* form their own constitution, with or without slavery, and admit them into the Union and thus put an end to this most unfortunate controversy." The letter is in the microfilm edition of the Fillmore Papers that I have used throughout.

The key difference between Fillmore's suggestion and Toombs's proposal is that Fillmore would wait until the population of Kansas justified statehood while Toombs would proceed immediately and have the constitutional convention in December 1856. Both called for the admission of the state with or without slavery as its constitution prescribed.

54. Holt, *Political Crisis of the 1850s,* 91–95; Solomon G. Haven to Millard Fillmore, 18 February 1854, Fillmore Papers (State University of New York at Oswego); Robert Toombs to T. Lomas, 6 June 1855, and Alexander H. Stephens to Thomas W. Thomas, 16 June 1856, in Phillips, *Correspondence of Toombs, Stephens, and Cobb,* 350–53, 367–72 (quotation, p. 372).

55. In addition to previously cited letters, see Robert C. Winthrop to William Schouler, 24 January 1851, William Schouler Papers (Massachusetts Historical Society); Edward Everett to William B. Weis, 14 February 1853, Everett to Mrs. Charles Eames, 13 November 1854, 11 August 1855, Henry A. Wise to Everett, 12, 17, 23 August 1856, Everett Papers; William A. Graham to Millard Fillmore, 3 December 1854, Henry E. Davies to Fillmore, 1 October 1855, Charles M. Conrad to Fillmore, 11 April 1856, Edward Everett to Fillmore, 16 July 1856, William L. Hodge to Fillmore, 20 September 1856, Benjamin Ogle Tayloe to Fillmore, 20 September 1856, Fillmore Papers (State University of New York at Oswego); Robert C. Winthrop to John P. Kennedy, 23 August 1855, George S. Bryan to Kennedy, 4 April, 26 May 1856, Kennedy Papers; Hiram T. Craig to William H. English, 24 March 1856, English Papers; James McCallum to John Bell, June 1856, Bell Papers; Daniel M. Barringer to William A. Houck, 6 August 1856 (copy), Daniel M. Barringer Papers, Southern Historical Collection, University of North Carolina, Chapel Hill; Robert C. Winthrop to Hamilton Fish, 13 March, 22 July 1856, Hamilton Fish Papers (Library of Congress); *National Intelligencer,* 7 April, 24 June 1856.

56. Robert C. Winthrop to John P. Kennedy, 3 January 1855 (letterbook copy), Robert C. Winthrop Papers (Massachusetts Historical Society); Edward Everett to William Trescot, 20 January 1856 (copy), Everett Papers; A. B. Ely to Millard Fillmore, 28 August (quotation), 6, 20 September 1856, Fillmore Papers (State University of New York at Oswego).

57. James McCallum to John Bell, June 1856, Bell Papers; report of the Augusta County, Virginia, Whig meeting, *National Intelligencer*, 7 April 1856; Henry A. Wise to Edward Everett, 12, 17, 23 August 1856, Everett Papers; William L. Hodge to Fillmore, 20 September 1856 (quotation), Fillmore Papers (State University of New York at Oswego). Hodge and other Fillmore supporters attributed the refusal of Gales and Seaton to endorse Fillmore in part to the fact that they feared losing Senate printing contracts if they publicly opposed Buchanan.

58. Alexander C. Bullitt to John O. Sargent, 9 July 1856, Sargent Papers; William A. Graham to Fillmore, 22 July 1856, Fillmore Papers (State University of New York at Oswego); New York *Commercial Advertiser*, quoted in *National Intelligencer*, 7 April 1856.

59. James Pearce to John M. Clayton, 15 September 1855, John M. Clayton Papers, Library of Congress, Washington, D.C.; Thomas Corwin to Fillmore, 22 July 1856, Fillmore Papers (SUNY at Oswego).

60. New York *Commercial Advertiser* and Richmond *Whig*, quoted in *National Intelligencer*, 7 April, 24 June 1856. See also the excerpts from the Baltimore *Patriot*, the New York *Evening Mirror*, the Norfolk (Virginia) *Herald*, and the Fayetteville, North Carolina *Observer*, in the latter issue of the *Intelligencer*.

61. William L. Hodge to Fillmore, 21 June 1856, Fillmore Papers, (SUNY at Oswego).

62. Kennedy to Winthrop, 22 April, 18 June 1855 (copies), Winthrop to Kennedy, 20 June 1855, Kennedy Papers; Fillmore to Everett, 12 July 1856, Everett Papers.

63. Baltimore *Patriot*, quoted in *National Intelligencer*, 24 June 1856; for the Everett and Winthrop endorsements of Fillmore, see Everett to William H. Prescot, 12 September 1856 (copy), and Winthrop to Everett, 17 October 1856, Everett Papers.

64. Nevins, *Ordeal of the Union*, 492; numerous references to these endorsements appear in the Fillmore Papers for the summer of 1856, but I shall not cite individual letters.

65. Solomon G. Haven to Fillmore, 20, 28 July 1856, William L. Hodge to Fillmore, 20, 30 September 1856, Anna Ella Carroll to Fillmore, 18, 23 August, 23 September 1856, Benjamin Ogle Tayloe to Fillmore, 20 September 1856, Fillmore Papers (SUNY at Oswego); Fillmore to William L. Hodge, 27 September 1856, Fillmore Papers (Buffalo and Erie County Historical Society).

66. *National Intelligencer*, 21 April, 23, 24 June 1856; William L. Hodge to Fillmore, 21 June 1856, Fillmore Papers (SUNY at Oswego); H. E. Dummer to Richard T. Yates, 9 July 1856, Richard T. Yates Papers (Illinois State Historical Library, Springfield).

67. C. D. Brigham to Fillmore, 9 August 1856, Francis Granger to Fillmore, 9, 11 August 1856, Joseph Randolph to Fillmore, 1 September 1856, James M. Townsend to Fillmore, 15 September 1856, Fillmore Papers (SUNY at Oswego).

68. Hodge to Fillmore, 20 September 1856, William A. Bradley to Fillmore, 26 September 1856, Fillmore Papers (SUNY at Oswego).

69. Jackson *Pilot*, 30 July 1870; Lynn L. Marshall, "The Strange Stillbirth of the Whig Party," *American Historical Review* 72 (January 1967): 445–68.

Dough in the Hands of the Doughface?
James Buchanan and the Untameable Press

MARK W. SUMMERS

POLITICS IS NOT SIMPLY, AS ONE PUNDIT DESCRIBED IT, THE ART of the possible; it is also the art of the plausible. Especially in governments based on the consent of the governed, policy makers can never afford to veer too far from public opinion. Present-day politicians may glance wistfully at the age of the party press, when hireling shills, subsidized by government patronage, defended whatever their leading men did. Perhaps because the way partisanship affected coverage seems so obvious, historians have given short shrift to news management in the years leading up to the Civil War. In this they are mistaken; for a closer examination of James Buchanan's failed administration would suggest that even in the heydey of the organ, the news was far from the controlled substance that the politicians intended it to be.[1]

For all the pamphlets, lithographed cartoons, and Mardi Gras paraphernalia of political campaigning in the 1850s, no party could have done without a press establishment of its own. Newspapers had become indispensable to American life.[2] So great was the demand for dailies that every major city had at least three, and even with the competition, the potential income was immense.[3] The financial power of the press was one gauge of its sway over opinion. "The printing press is more feared this day, among the old rotten aristocracy of Europe, than all the armies of the world," Governor William F. Packer told Pennsylvania editors. Two hundred thousand copies of a newspaper distributed on the streets of Paris would frighten the emperor Napoleon III more than 200,000 soldiers marching down the boulevards.[4] What was true in the Old World was true in the New. It therefore behooved a president to have support among the editorial fraternity.

This, on the face of it, seemed easily enough done. In Buchanan's day, there is no question that most of the press was a party press: hirelings and apologists, trucklers and servitors. Northern villages with hardly enough patronage to sustain one weekly paper were sure to have two, of opposite politics. No lie was too gross, no abuse too coarse for the partisan editor, but, then, his main purpose was not to gather and judge the news of the day, but to further the party. Newspaper proprietors sat on state and national party executive committees, drafted platforms, held seats in the legislature, and lived off the pickings of office: printing contracts, postmasterships, and government advertising.[5] Their names were as familiar as the congressman from their district, and the most famous were more likely to appear in political cartoons than all but a handful of senators.

So when James Buchanan became president in March 1857, the use of the party press was a custom long accepted and long respected. What was different, however, was the scale of the new administration's efforts to fund and curry favor with newspapers across the North, and the test to which party loyalty was put by the policies that Buchanan adopted. How far could presidential action control the news, how far would the organs go in following the leader of their party? Were there, indeed, limits on news management, even among the party presses?

Pennsylvania politics provided a ruthless school for aspiring statesmen. Even by mid-nineteenth-century standards, the Keystone State was notorious for the craft and selfishness of its leading men. To survive in public life for forty years, as Buchanan did, took real skills in managing quarrelsome factions and clashing interests. By 1856, the "Old Public Functionary" was a renowned survivor. That survival he owed in large part to his henchmen in the press, notably John Wien Forney, the ambitious, indefatigable editor of the Philadelphia *Pennsylvanian*. Wielding a massive campaign fund dunned from the businessmen of New York, Forney flooded Pennsylvania with pamphlets for "glorious old Buck" and, said Republicans, filled Philadelphia with freshly minted voters, naturalized on the spot or imported from neighboring states.[6]

Carrying the election, however, was only the first step. Even before the November returns, Buchanan had begun an effort to sustain and support a newspaper community friendly to himself.

That effort was tried most successfully with James Gordon Bennett, whose New York *Herald* had combined sensational coverage of events with conservative politics, to win a large readership. Bennett was worth cultivating and capricious enough to need it. After a long, friendly courtship of Buchanan's candidacy, the *Herald* had jumped ship just as the 1856 campaign began—and clambered aboard that of Republican candidate John C. Frémont. The

Portrait of President James Buchanan. Courtesy of Dickinson College.

conversion was unexpected, especially to any reader familiar with
Bennett's tirades against "Black Republicans," "Nigger Worship-
pers," abolitionists, and other crack-brained "babbling humanitar-
ians." It was also an alliance made to be sundered, since the *Herald*
could only justify its stand by trying to pretend that Frémont was
not the nominee of Republicans at all, but of "popular fusion"
forces! Buchanan had been on excellent terms with Mrs. Bennett,
who had exiled herself to Europe for some years. Whatever her

husband's sympathies might be in 1856, there was no question about his wife's.[7]

So while the campaign that followed showed Bennett at his usual malicious best—so much so that, according to common report, Buchanan had asked why no true friend went up to New York to cut the editor's ears off—he was as ready as ever to be bought or brought over. Weeks before the final returns, the "old dotard, . . . imbecile, miserable, gabbling old granny, who has lost his mind and his memory" had opened overtures to Bennett. The charmed publisher at once wrote back his own hope that, with the curtain rung down on what Buchanan had termed their Comedy of Errors, they might find All's Well That Ends Well; by election day, the *Herald* had shifted into a sullen neutrality.[8]

The election only began the president-elect's flirtation.[9] From then on, there were plenty of favors. The *Herald* received advance copies of state papers and leaks of inside information. Members of the *Herald* entourage were nominated for roving diplomatic appointments, or sent as agents to Mexico and Bordeaux.[10] The Bennetts came to Washington for social functions and dined at the White House. Cabinet members were expected to show like courtesies to the publisher.[11] "I am sure you will have great influence with the President," Mayor Fernando Wood of New York remarked to Bennett, a few months before the inaugural. "There is no doubt of that, because I shall never use it," Bennett shot back—which was about as truthful as anything else he said. There was always plenty of advice from the editor about whom to put in the cabinet, and whom to keep out, and requests for more inside information.[12] And in return, the *Herald* could scarcely find words to praise Buchanan more highly. Indeed, when it became clear that the president might be willing to forget his pledge to stick with one term, if the party would do so, the *Herald* leaped on a bandwagon of its own making and urged his renomination.[13]

Buchanan showed an equal solicitude for a few reporters of national reputation. Foremost among them was Francis J. Grund, correspondent for the Baltimore *Sun* and the Philadelphia *Public Ledger*. As "Observer," Grund's reputation was not of the highest. "The basest Hessian of them all," Senator Jefferson Davis of Mississippi called him. In the 1840s, a hostile source remarked, he "played the part of . . . everything, indeed, 'by turns, and nothing long'." "I can bear your abuse, sir," old Senator Thomas Hart Benton of Missouri had thundered, when Grund tried to make amends, "—but I can't stand your compliment—get out of my way, sir!" Under the Pierce administration, disappointed in his requests

DON'T KNOW WHICH WAY TO GO.

J——s G——n B——t.—I'M CLEAN DAFT WITH THE PUZZLE. IT'S VARY PLAIN TO KEN THE ROADS ALL GANG TO THE SAME PLACE, BUT I WONDER WHICH IS THE NEAREST CUT TO THE FRENCH MISSION.

A cartoon from 1856 satirizes *New York Herald* publisher James Gordon Bennett's indecision about which candidate to support for the presidency. Bennett is seen as looking for appointment as Minister to France, and his preference in the presidential contest will hinge on which candidate is most likely to deliver such a perquisite to him. Courtesy of Dickinson College.

for the consulship to Marseilles (the president had been obliging, but Southerners had forced an indefinite postponement of the nomination), he filled the press with false stories about members of the government. Nor had there been much love lost between the incoming president and the correspondent in past years. In 1848 and again in 1852, when the party's supporters were pressing him for the nomination. "Observer's" abuse had been so gross that the candidate's backers had threatened to horsewhip Grund in the streets. They never did, and by the late 1850s, Grund had found a temporary berth as correspondent of the New York *Herald* and confidant of his old enemy. If hostile reports are to be believed, he also served as eavesdropper and informant, and was so well known as such that Pennsylvanians visiting the capital gave the White House a wide berth lest they run into Grund and have their names taken down. The price for his support, it was said, was the appointment as minister to Vienna. In fact, Buchanan did make him consul at Le Havre in late 1859.[14]

No less useful was Henry Wikoff, a traveling emissary of the government and political intriguer, with twenty years' experience at some of the great courts of Europe, as well as fifteen months in one of its commoner jails. It was Wikoff who handled the early negotiations with Bennett, and continued to carry the editor's views back to the White House to the end of the administration. In return, the president trusted him with foreign assignments and confidential information. Back from a mission to China, he could be spotted on the House floor, "glass in eye, . . . indulging in his favorite occupation of graceful observation—until one of Bennett's enemies had the doorkeeper throw him out.[15]

More important than the *Herald* connection was Buchanan's work to sustain his friends in the party press. The endowment of newspapers was, in fact, a crucial part of the distribution of patronage, for running an organ was not easy work. "It is the most difficult thing in the world to find a man of whom you could say before hand that he would conduct a political paper with ability, and in conformity with a high standard of morals," wrote William Cullen Bryant to Senator Salmon P. Chase. "Sometimes the talent is wanting, sometimes the principles, and sometimes both."[16] Usually, it was the money that was wanting. Party organs were ill-equipped to sustain themselves.

So from the moment a party took power, the clamor for public funding broke forth, from the Elmira *Gazette* to the St. Paul *Pioneer and Democrat*. In Augusta, Maine, the postmaster's right to keep his place was strengthened by his having assumed a third of the loss in publishing the *Age*.[17] "The leading press of the city and I may say of the state, is in a fettered condition and will soon be sold under the hammer," wrote a resident of Iowa City. When the 1857 campaign began, the publishers of the *Crescent and Reporter* were forced to suspend the daily and issue only a weekly. All this might change, if the postmastership went to a man who "will furnish the means" to buy and keep up the paper.[18]

Favors were sought and granted. In Connecticut, for example, the editor of the Bridgeport *Republican Farmer* became Collector of Internal Revenue for his congressional district; the publisher of the New London *Star* was made Surveyor of the Port and published the nation's laws "by authority." So did the Hartford *Times*, while the New Haven *Register*'s proprietor earned $8000 a year as Collector of the Port. The same story might be told in Rome and Raleigh, Vicksburg and Milwaukee.[19]

Most important was the sustaining of a national organ in the capital. This had been traditional since Jefferson's day, and since 1845 the *Union* had served that purpose for Democrats. But while no new establishment needed setting up, the president-elect had to fine-tune the organ and find the financial wind to fill its pipes. This was all the more necessary because of the complicated way in which the two houses of Congress had awarded their printing contracts. Each had chosen a firm of its own; in fact, both of them skimmed a profit off the top and sublet the work to Cornelius Wendell, half-owner of the *Union*. In six years, Wendell collected over two million dollars for himself, by padding the contracts and making a liberal interpretation of the terms governing the quality of materials used. None of this mattered to Democrats, as long as graft was left over to keep the *Union* going. But letting Wendell decide who should edit a Democratic organ was unthinkable: for one thing, he was a Republican. At first, John Appleton had been considered for editor in chief. When Buchanan made him assistant secretary of state, the honor fell to former Congressman William A. Harris of Virginia, who bought Wendell out and promised to see that any printing the *Union* got would be contracted out for Wendell to do. The arrangement could scarcely be improved. With all the binding and printing contracts for the government, having bought out Senate and House printers for $75,000, taking one dollar in every two as clear profit, Wendell had plenty of money not just for one paper but several, and to sustain deserving Democratic politicians as well.[20]

In view of Buchanan's coddling of Pennsylvania newspapers, his dispersal of patronage, his cultivation of the *Herald* and of individual reporters, and the instinctive loyalty of Democratic news-papers, one might assume that he still held a strong advantage. Within a year, however, that advantage was shown for the illusion that it was. What had gone wrong?

There were several reasons for Buchanan's failure, several of them built into the process of dispensing patronage and relying on party papers to influence public opinion.

The settlement of the *Union*'s management reflected one of the obvious pitfalls of using patronage to win over the press. Buchanan had kept control of the foremost party organ, and lost his dedicated friend, John W. Forney, who had put a score of years and thousands of dollars into making Buchanan president. Needy and as passion-ate in his grievances as he was in his hero worship, he had known from the first what his services and editorial talents merited: edito-rial control of the *Union,* with a share in the lucrative printing contracts. Buchanan actually promised it to him without being asked, and Forney was so sure of his reward that he wasted no time in renting and furnishing a house at the capital. Then Southern politicians spoke. They wanted no Northern man heading the party organ, and especially Forney. The president-elect hastily had to withdraw his promise.[21] Other alternatives came to nothing; what-ever Forney may have thought, he was certainly not cabinet mate-rial and not even Buchanan's support could shove the editor into a Senate seat. Forney soon discovered that the administration had nothing for him but leftovers, jobs of little pay and less prestige: the naval office in Philadelphia and the consulate at Liverpool. (Wendell was ready to sweeten the deal with $10,000 from the printing profits, if Forney would only leave the country, an offer that enraged the editor all the more).[22] Drinking more than ever, bathing himself in self-pity, he wrote pleading letters that got in-creasingly less attention. Out of pocket, he quickly became out of patience with what struck him as trifling treatment, "like a com-mon office-beggar," as he complained.[23]

But Forney was no mere office beggar, and that was what made him dangerous. A hustling, determined businessman with long ex-perience at raising money and publishing, he could set up a news-paper of his own and command influence instantly. He did just that, to Buchanan's immediate alarm and over his protests. Unable to buy into the *Pennsylvanian,* Forney established the Philadelphia *Press.* By the time its first issue appeared in August 1857, the cooling between president and editor was unmistakable. Each as-sured the other that nothing had changed; each told third parties something quite different. Buchanan could wish Forney good luck

in his enterprise at the same time that he warned the collector of
the port in Philadelphia to steer clear of it, and voiced suspicions
that the *Press* was working to advance the "Little Giant's"
interests.[24]

Buchanan's failure to satisfy Forney was an extreme example of
a common problem, that there was never enough support to sustain
all the supplicants. The Concord *New Hampshire Patriot* protested
furiously when the Concord *Standard*, "a factious, disorganizing
sheet of two years' standing," was considered for publication of
the laws. But the *Standard's* backers were just as angry at equal
treatment.[25] Hell had no wrath like a newspaper scorned, and its
readiness to make up for lack of government aid with subscribers
made it all the less likely to sustain the administration in unpopular policies.

Even Bennett's support came at an unceasing, ultimately exorbitant price. Though his wife and he did their best to inveigle Buchanan into providing a foreign mission, the idea got nowhere. The
president considered making him consul to Turin, but feared to
offend the secretary of war, whose protégé already held the job
(very likely this was not the job Bennett wanted: his wife, who
meant to live in Paris, wanted her husband near her, and the American minister already there had just died). In the last days of the
administration, the subject of an appointment came before the
cabinet, and was given such a devastating knock that it was hastily
abandoned. By that time, Bennett was no longer pleading; his emis-
saries were carrying veiled threats to the White House. Within
months of Lincoln's accession, the *Herald* began an ugly series of
articles to prove Buchanan a dunderhead, traitor, and the destroyer
of the Union.[26]

All administrations have to live with disappointment—that is,
the disappointment of those who failed to get what they considered
their due. It was not necessarily fatal.

Two other points made it so. The first was built into the very
nature of the party press. However well it could satisfy the faithful,
it had very little power beyond ranks of the faithful. When Southern
senators read extracts from Northern journals, to prove the sedi-
tious designs of the Republicans, Senator Zachariah Chandler of
Michigan reminded them that the quotations came from Democratic papers. Who believed that they spoke for opinion north of
the Mason-Dixon line? "It is fortunate that the republican papers
in Ills. have been violent," Democratic congressman Thomas S.
Harris confided in 1858. "*It has kept our party together,* and with
the accessions we must get, will secure our success."[27]

Perhaps, if the power of both parties' press had been even; but in Northern cities, the weight of editorial opinion was slipping to the Republicans' side, and by Buchanan's administration, that slippage was beginning to tell. Leading Republican newspapers were big and getting bigger. The New York *Tribune* could boast of supplying over 200,000 customers in 1858, and 276,000 in 1859—most of them with its weekly, a distillation and compendium of the dailies. The Chicago *Press and Tribune* doubled its circulation in the last two years of the decade. By contrast, the Democratic organs of the city went from want to beggary. The wealth of Cyrus Hall McCormick not only failed to turn the Chicago *Herald* into a profitable sheet: by July 1860, its circulation was no more than 3,000.[28]

Admittedly, Republicans raised a discordant chorus. Twitted about the free-trade ideas of Republican editor William Cullen Bryant, a Pennsylvania Republican congressman protested any confusion of the editor with the people he claimed to speak for. "The New York *Evening Post* is not an organ in Pennsylvania," he insisted. "We repudiate it; we disclaim it; we spit upon its doctrines." In Chicago, the *Democrat* and the *Tribune* meted out blows to each other, and with all the more bitterness because of the local patronage that neither wanted to share with the other.[29] Yet, for all their internal disagreements, Republican newspapers at least could take a united approach to administration doings. So from Washington came the word, constant and devastating, of corruption in the administration.[30]

What, then, could be said of the influence that Bennett wielded, too rabidly partisan to earn trust in his news, too notoriously fickle to carry weight in his judgments among the politically faithful? Obviously, the New York *Herald* proved an exceptionally mixed blessing. Roger Pryor was not expressing its proprietor's general reputation too harshly when he described Bennett's name as "the execration of both continents."[31] On top of that, the proprietor's reputation for quirkiness and falsehood limited how many people were likely to believe him. All the opposition had to do was print current *Herald* encomiums alongside invective from 1856—as it often did.[32]

But Bennett illustrates the second fatal drawback to the administration news-management strategy: the independence that major metropolitan newspapers could afford. The publisher committed himself to Buchanan personally, perhaps, but on terms of his own choosing. Even when the love fest was at its height, the *Herald*'s correspondents treated as fair game members of Buchanan's cabinet, his inner circle, his most devoted campaign contributors, his Senate champions.[33] Even when friendly to Buchanan, the *Herald* could not direct public opinion very far. Its endorsement of a second term for Buchanan fell entirely flat. Within a fortnight, the *Herald* had to beat a hasty retreat, declaring that under no circumstances would the president accept a new lease on power.

Most of the major metropolitan papers were even less approachable than the *Herald*. With a few exceptions, they flourished in the Republican North, and those not openly leagued with the Republicans at least showed a strong Northern bias in what news they chose to cover. Equally dangerous for a Democratic version of events was a growing sense of professionalism that financial independence permitted among big-city journalists. "We, too, are representatives of the people," Morton McMichael of the Philadelphia *North American* declared to the editorial convention meeting in the capitol at Harrisburg,"—representatives, holding commissions not less honorable, exercising functions not less important, charged with obligations not less weighty, and subject to responsibilities not less grave, than those who, by virtue of popular election, occupy seats in this and the adjoining chamber. In the best and most significant sense we constitute an elective body."[34]

The air of independence, at the very least, sold papers. Papers boasted of it; even the Washington *Union* swore itself "an independent journal," one "ready and anxious to be advised upon all questions of public interest," and "to give expression to the truth, whoever it may hit, damage, or benefit.[35] But the *Union* may have missed the reason why readers so valued at least the illusion of nonpartisanship. Unbiased papers were likely to give the news more completely, and news increasingly was what readers subscribed for. "The true newspaper is chiefly a minute history of the times," the Springfield *Republican* summed up. It was the historian first and "prophet of the people" second.[36]

That outlook was all the more clearly reflected in the growing sense of self-identity manifesting itself among the members of the Washington press corps. Of their own abilities, they had no doubts at all. As the self-proclaimed "'Bohemians' of the Press," they hobnobbed with each other more than they did with the politicians.[37] In Washington, transcribed debates gave way to real news, and to special correspondents, ready to tell what went on behind the fine words.[38] It was an arrangement that no one in power appreciated fully. For one thing, they had a suspicion of reporters in general, and one that was well founded. Regularly, lawmakers rose to denounce the news reports about themselves or to correct errors. But it was also a situation that the administration was wholly unequipped to meet in its own provision of news coverage.

By 1857, then, the administration faced an immense handicap in providing the basic information on which to make the best possible case for its side. The Washington *Union* could set the tone for Democratic opinion. Its funds would never permit it to gather a Democratic version of the news in any comprehensive way. Northern metropolitan papers, virtually none of which were sympathetic to the administration, did that.

Nowhere was the problem of uncontrollable news and adversarial reporting more of a problem than out in Kansas, where the struggle over slavery had culminated in a political travesty. Pro-slavery delegates to the constitutional convention at Lecompton wrote a document effectively assuring the admission of a slave state, whatever the actual voters desired.[39] Bad as the constitution was, Buchanan saw the speedy admission of Kansas as the quickest way of ending the territorial issue and robbing Republicans of their main reason for existing. He submitted the Lecompton Constitution to Congress over loud protest from Northerners of both parties.[40]

Admittedly, then, it would have taken masterminds of propaganda to have transformed Lecompton into something palatable to Northerners of either party. It was equally true that propagandists were already out in Kansas making the most of the administration's discomfiture. With good reason, the Washington *Union* warned readers to trust no telegraphic dispatches out of Kansas. All these were "manufactured . . . only for political effect." From the territory, for example, came ominous news from the Cincinnati *Gazette*'s Lawrence correspondent of an impending battle between James Lane of the free-state government and a company of United States dragoons on Sugar Mound. Another report, to be sure, cited another witness who had seen Lane in at Lawrence on the same day that the battle he was engaged in was supposed to have taken place many miles away; but when the dispatch was trimmed at St. Louis for telegraph dispatch, the Associated Press suppressed that part.[41] But the reason that such dispatches flourished was that the administration went into the battle for news coverage wholly disarmed. Not one single Democratic newspaper had a reporter in Kansas that year; not one administration reporter was present at the Lecompton convention to put proceedings in the best possible light.

The president's faith in the success of Lecompton was not based on what Republican papers would say, of course. With Democrats running Capitol Hill, party regularity would put through the admission of Kansas, just as soon as the rank and file were given the facts—Buchanan's version of the facts. It was a fair assumption, if the party press did its duty.[42] Patronage could help hesitant papers like the Albany *Atlas & Argus* find their voice. And Buchanan's confidence was not wholly misplaced. Southern editors needed no patronage to espouse the administration line. Spoils also held many Northern papers steady, especially those in Pennsylvania.[43] The real surprise was that there should have been any break in the ranks at all.

But there was, a substantial one, for reasons readily apparent. Whatever party leaders thought, Northern Democrats were up in arms against Lecompton from the moment the news reached them; where state political leaders and the administration disagreed, supporting either side ran real risks for party papers. As a result, even newspapers siding with the administration found that they would do so to their peril. Across New England, party organs fell utterly silent, dodged, or came out against the swindle. Not even a legislative endorsement for the president's course could swing more than five of California's twenty-five Democratic newspapers behind the administration—and these among the least significant in the state, customhouse hangers-on all. "The *National* newspaper has done and is daily doing more to weaken Mr. Buchanan here, than . . . all the opposition press could possibly do," wrote a government employee disgustedly.[44]

Douglas himself was proof that some of them did not wait to take their cues from the party press—quite the reverse. When Democrats in Congress went one way and the administration the other, the party press would falter, uncertain of whom to take its own cues from. Forced to choose between their senator and their president, most Illinois papers felt it their duty to go with the former. Many tried to keep some ties with the administration in doing so, but not all.[45]

Patronage, in fact, propped up presses and deprived them of weight simultaneously. A ringing endorsement of the administration was vitiated, to say the least, by the open knowledge that it was a "babbling pensioner," desperate to protect what spoils the administration had already given, or to nose its way in to the trough. No one was surprised when the *Atlas & Argus* editor was rewarded with the Albany postmastership the following July, nor that the Milwaukee *News* preferred to stick with the administration—and its editor to stick in the postmastership. The *Rock Islander* received a ten-dollar advertisement from the post office, hardly enough to explain its alacrity in supporting the administration-backed English bill as a proper party test, but that was how it was explained. Had the Leavenworth *Ledger* been bought up for the administration? one congressman asked his colleague Thomas Harris of Illinois in debate. Harris did not know: how could he keep track, anyhow, he wondered. "They are being bought up so fast that I can hardly keep the run of them."[46] By contrast, an organ that broke with the administration at the obvious risk of its living, earned an immediate (if undeserved) reputation for candor.

The faith that Democrats held in their own journals made the opponents of Lecompton within the ranks all the more dangerous, and there were a surprising number of them. Even in the South, a few newspapers broke ranks. In May, the Richmond *Enquirer* changed hands, and positions, to support Douglas. In Louisville, George Prentice's *Journal* carried on a regular fire against the Lecompton Constitution, and the editor himself had a national following on the lyceum circuit. If anything, the crisis showed how limited patronage's appeal could be, when set against daily circulation. In Detroit, Wilbur F. Storey's vituperative *Free Press* should have had some grounds for standing with the administration: an assistant editor who served as mail agent. Instead, the editor spoke for the state party, and spoke in no uncertain terms against Lecompton, which, to one grumbling regular, showed that it had "turned Black Republican."[47]

Most damaging of all was Forney's breaking ranks. The editor could not have remained a presidential apologist if he had wanted to, not as long as the *Pennsylvanian* carried on its rickety existence. He needed an audience wider than administration loyalists. Reluctant to make an open war, the editor was looking for an opportunity to show that he was his own man. With the Lecompton disaster, he found it. A bad situation Buchanan then aggravated. After withholding the sweets of office for so long, he arranged to send an emissary to Philadelphia with an offer. A post office printing contract worth some $80,000 could be Forney's. All he need do was publish a statement in the *Press* that as a good partisan, he would leave the issue to fellow Democrats to settle and would abide by their decision. At best, the demand for proof in writing of party loyalty was a mortal insult. At worst, it was a transparent bribery attempt, which Forney resented still more.[48]

The former intimacy of the two men gave *Press* attacks special force. So did Forney's freedom from patronage. From Houghton, Pennsylvania, came warnings that the *Press* was "manufacturing a fixed and pervading sentiment" against Lecompton among the Democrats. Even journals that might be counted on the president's side eventually republished its articles. So did Republican newspapers eager to emphasize the disaffection in the enemy camp. Who could be trusted more than "the man who, of all others made James Buchanan President of the United States?"[49] At first cautious in distinguishing between opposition to the president and to Lecompton, Forney grew increasingly sharp-tongued. By the time the House had blocked the admission of Kansas and forced the administration into a face-saving compromise, the *Press* had taken on an edge that few Republican organs could match.[50]

No better illustration could be had of how little patronage could do. Against the *Press*, Buchanan could rely on arguments in the Philadelphia *Pennsylvanian* and the *Argus*. It was hardly a competition at all. The *Argus* barely survived, in spite of Congressman Thomas Florence compelling postmasters, collectors, "and Government pap suckers of every grade," as one contemporary sneered, to subscribe to his paper.[51] Long underfunded, with Forney's departure the *Pennsylvanian* lost more subscribers to the *Press* than patronage could make up for.[52] Unceasingly, publisher W. W. Rice dunned party leaders for help and threatened suspension. The Philadelphia postmaster gave the editor of the *Pennsylvanian* the post of chief clerk, and made Rice himself a mail messenger at $3,600 a year, which was $2,000 more than the job was worth. Wendell provided a share of his profits—$20,000, according to Wendell, less than $10,000 according to Rice—and during the 1860 campaign, Collector of the Port Joseph Baker paid out $2,500 and borrowed $2,500 more on his own name to prop up the *Pennsylvanian*, as well as several hundred dollars more for weekly expenses. It was more even than the lavish profits of the customhouse could afford, as Baker made clear, and he turned to the Democratic campaign committee for reimbursement. And all this aid was never enough.[53]

By contrast, Forney's opposition only made his establishment more robust. Every day the *Press* gathered strength, one correspondent warned Senator Bigler. Republicans actually were beginning to buy it. Even in Buchanan's hometown of Lancaster, subscribers dropped the *Pennsylvanian* in dismaying numbers. According to the New York *Tribune*'s local correspondent, Rice's journal sold no more than one issue where hitherto it had sold twenty—and Forney's two-penny paper was the gainer. A year later, the *Press* could declare its circulation second in the state and first in the city.[54] It was easy for administration supporters to protest by that time that the publisher's lies and gaffes had deprived him of any real following inside the party. "*Forneyism* stinks," one Philadelphian insisted. But the next year, Democrats divided, with Forney wielding his influence in ways surest to bring the state into the Republican column in November.[55]

With Douglas up for reelection that fall, the battle to control the press was waged most bitterly in Illinois; and again, the results provided the president with a lesson of the limits of patronage. Small papers might go where spoils dictated. They could not compete with the major party papers, the Quincy *Herald*, Chicago *Times*, and the Springfield *Illinois State Register*, each of which was ready to stand or fall with the state's senior senator. When one of the editors of the *Register* tried to write an editorial praising the speech of Senator William Bigler of Pennsylvania in the president's defense, it got no farther than the compositor's hands. Before it could be run off, Charles Lanphier, editor in chief and proprietor, spotted it in the composing room and ordered it removed. In the quarrel that followed, the article's author found himself forced to remove as well.[56] From loyalists came pleas for help against "the most bitter and vindictive abuse" from "the factious Press." When "the official axe" fell on local appointees, James Sheahan of the Chicago *Times* had evidence against the new nominees all ready. When Buchanan supporters held a rally in Chicago, they were drowned out by "a posse of ruffians and paid hirelings" from the *Times*.[57] Small-fry administration organs could argue all they pleased, without eliciting a reply. "I think the best policy is not to notice any of these papers," Sheahan wrote Charles Lanphier of the *Register*, "& let their sayings be confined to their own bailiwicks."[58]

Whatever hopes of propitiation the president may have had died quickly. "The Adm. has been considering the propriety of reading us all 'out,' & starting 'Anti' papers in Ills.," Congressman Thomas Harris warned Lanphier in January. "But I think they have concluded that it won't pay."[59] If so, it was a resolve quickly abandoned. By the end of the month, the post office had struck the Chicago *Times* off of its advertising list, and had begun making overtures to Charles Leib to help in forming an organ more to the president's liking. "The Pres. is determined to crush us all," Harris warned.[60]

There were two steps in the crushing: the transfer of government spoils and the establishment of a press more to the president's liking in Chicago. The first job was easier than the second. From Isaac Cook, former part-owner in the Chicago *Times* and manager of the administration cause in Illinois, came demands that the post offices be cleaned out of unfriendly editors. When one of the offenders, Austin Brooks of the Quincy *Herald* was actually confirmed in his place, he gave the best argument for ruthlessness. On hearing the news, he swaggered up to an administration man, just denied a position. "I was *true* to Douglas and *have* been confirmed," he sneered. "You are a *traitor* to him & have not been."[61] After the failure of Lecompton, as hopes of reconciliation dimmed, mistakes like these were corrected (Brooks was out within a month). But in the end, the administration was unable to use the patronage to convert most of the recusants or set up new presses. All they did was provoke the Douglas Democrats further.[62]

In Chicago, Buchanan's most earnest defender, ironically, was Mayor "Long John" Wentworth's Republican paper, the Chicago *Democrat;* Wentworth had old scores to settle with Douglas, and a healthy respect for the danger that the "Little Giant" posed to the Republican Party, a danger that Buchanan's program could never match. But since Wentworth's agreement with the administration stretched no further than their common view of Douglas, and certainly not to admission of Kansas under the Lecompton Constitution, the arrangement was far from satisfactory.[63] When this failed, the alternative of establishing an entirely new paper was explored. In February 1858, several administration men began to organize one in Washington. The Chicago *National Union and Democrat* proved an unqualified disaster. Nothing but patronage could have kept a well-run paper alive. But it was not well-run and by July had caved in to the Douglas Democrats, hoisted their ticket to the masthead, and expired. *"Requiescat in pace!"* the last of its editors snarled. "—which, liberally translated, means 'No one cares a fig about it.'" A German-language administration organ was placed in the hands of Louis Schade, once a Douglas man himself. When it became clear that someone of more professional ability was required, the administration sent Francis J. Grund west. In addition to arranging his own election to an administration excuse for a Democratic state convention at Springfield, Grund was to set up a newspaper of his own and drive Schade out of business. Schade took it badly, threatened to expose everyone concerned, and caned Grund ferociously.[64]

Editors were fired, and reveled in their independence—at least, within the party. "Removed or not removed—our position will not be changed," the Quincy *Herald*'s proprietor announced, after his postmastership was taken away. In Cleveland, the *Plain Dealer*'s editor Joseph W. Gray held the postmastership until June 1858, when his failure to enthuse over Lecompton brought about his dismissal. It did not win the *Plain Dealer* over. Administration men formed a new organ, the *National Democrat.* "This old rum sucker and political renegade,"as Gray called the privileged editor, worked hard among the route agents and postmaster, "levying black mail and subscriptions" to build his paper up at the *Plain Dealer*'s expense. The collector of the port had to pay $500 to the cause; so did the U.S. marshal. But in the end, the rival barely outlived the Buchanan administration and the transfer of spoils.[65]

Heavily subsidized from Wendell's profits, the Washington *Union* was among the least vulnerable of administration organs. And yet by early 1859, it was near collapse. Its daily circulation amounted to some 1,150 subscribers, its weekly to 11,500. With $19,000 a year in outside revenues needed to keep the presses going, Wendell was growing sick at the drain on his printing profits. He wanted out. The most he could arrange was to yield the *Union* to George Bowman, a Democratic editor from the Pennsylvania hinterland. Bowman's credentials as former proprietor of the Bedford *Gazette* and opponent of Buchanan's presidential campaign were not what got him the job; what did was his being superintendent of public printing. If Wendell wanted to continue to do the actual work, he would have to pay $20,000 a year from his profits. Half of these Bowman could put into the *Union,* half into the *Pennsylvanian.* The paper renamed itself the *Constitution* and hired William Browne as editor. Late in 1859, the Democratic Senate made Bowman printer as well.[66]

All the administration got for it was trouble. By early 1860, the *Constitution* sold less than 900 copies of its daily edition and only 1,200 weeklies. After a long struggle, the Republican-controlled House awarded its printing to a Republican and the clerkship to Forney. Bowman and Wendell quarreled. Looking for a practical man to do the printing, the *Constitution*'s proprietor turned to the publisher of the *Congressional Globe.* Wendell threatened vengeance, and could make trouble two ways. First, Bowman still owed him money for the purchase of the newspaper. A writ attaching the office would stop the presses. Second, Wendell knew too much for the administration to offend. It had been his exorbitant profits that had funded Buchanan's organs in Philadelphia and Washington, and he had handled the efforts to bribe congressmen to the president's side during the Lecompton fight. "The exposure will be unpleasant & involve some of our *great* friends," one insider warned Senator Bigler.[67] It did. Wendell had much to tell Congressman John Covode's investigating committee. Among other things, it uncovered the fact that forty-three cents on every dollar of the gross receipts from printing post office blanks were handed over to Rice of the *Pennsylvanian* and later split between him and the owners of the *Argus*.[68]

Not surprisingly, Congress did away with the contracting system for public printing; no less astonishingly, that put the *Constitution* virtually out of business. It expired, indeed, before the president's term did and had no successor. Never again would an administration designate an official Washington organ.

If the administration needed one last proof of the limited power of patronage and news management, it should have found it in ample supply in the presidential campaign of 1860. The *Herald* could be counted on. Bennett was strong for John C. Breckinridge, the administration ticket for president, and even more so for his running mate, Joseph Lane of Oregon, who, he hoped, might make him consul in Paris. "These articles are having a tremendous run," a confidant assured Lane. "They are read and commented upon by men of every class, and every shade of politics." (So they were, but, considering how poorly the ticket ended up doing in New York City, the comment could hardly have been all that favorable.) With postmasterships and customhouse jobs to cling to, most of the Democratic newspapers in Massachusetts found reason to support Breckinridge; the only two sure to go for Douglas were headed by men no longer enjoying the fruits of office.[69]

It certainly demonstrated the power of Boston's collector of the port, when he dismissed a publisher for standing by Douglas, but it also showed the administration's ultimate weakness that the paper refused to fall into line. S. O. Lamb, its editor, had been private secretary to the collector. He resigned rather than give way. In Maine, every Democratic paper but one came out for Douglas; the same was true in Indiana, and in Ohio Breckinridge got one endorsement for Douglas's every ten. Founded in 1858 to speak for the administration, the Chicago *Herald* endorsed Douglas in 1860. "So far as I can learn there are but two papers for us in Illinois," one of the *Herald*'s Breckinridge men wrote, "and they do not amount to much."[70]

The party press could do no other, and still survive. Those holding government posts knew this perfectly well, even if the administration did not. Under the circumstances, the power to reward became an empty one.

Buchanan's experience with the press was not only frustrating. It added to his reputation, already well advanced, of having been faithless to his friends. Forney attested to it regularly. So could the others, used and rejected, as tools of news management. From George Sanderson, proprietor of the Lancaster *Intelligencer,* came imprecations at the man at whose request the paper had been founded in 1849, and for whose benefit it had been run at a loss for the past eight years. "Like an old horse, after being worked almost to death, and his master having no further use for him, I am turned out to starve and die," he complained. " . . . I have hosts of friends here who will resent the ingratitude, and I cannot prevent them." By the summer of 1858, the president's relationship with Rice of the *Pennsylvanian* was poisonous. Begged for the contract to print post office blanks, with profits ranging from $14,000 to $35,000, he responded frostily. "We had a hot time of it," Rice wrote Senator Bigler afterwards.

> I did not get angry until he told me I was not fit to conduct the paper. I said he should have told me that two years ago and I would not be a ruined man as I am at this time and that there was no merit in his opinion in a man being true to him and to the party, but that his worst enemies was taken care of now . . . I see no other course but to sell and if I do not hear from you in a few days I will advertise to sell. A hundred chances to one I shall be closed in less than a month. I have run the length of my tether, my credit destroyed with the paper men and every body else by this decision.[71]

The ultimate legacy, then, of Buchanan's news management was not at all what had been intended. Instead of protecting his reputation, it gave proofs to party regulars of a man weak, treacherous, and ungrateful. Instead of promoting orthodoxy among Democrats, it exacerbated differences. Rather than making his editorial friends strong, it only put off the day that they would die of inanition. And just conceivably, in attempting to attach the press to Lecompton, Buchanan may well have added to the detachment of party papers from political leaders. There was something in the Philadelphia *Press*'s judgment that forcing so many "nauseous doses" on the organs made editors far less likely to take any such medicine in the future.[72] The party press had many years of life left in it, and Buchanan had done for it what he had done for the Union itself and set it well on the road to its doom—and with equally good intentions.

Notes

1. The most thorough study of how patronage affected the press is Culver H. Smith, *The Press, Politics, and Patronage: The American Government's Use of*

Newspapers, 1789–1875 (Athens: University of Georgia Press, 1977). James Pollard, *The Presidents and the Press,* touches on Buchanan's use of the press briefly, arguing that he did not use it at all, which, if one relies solely on John Bassett Moore's eleven volumes of published correspondence *from* Buchanan might seem a reasonable conclusion.

2. For actual numbers, see *Eighth Census: Mortality and Miscellaneous Statistics* (Washington, D.C.: Government Printing Office, 1866), 4:319–22.

3. "S.B.," Springfield *Republican,* 3 December 1859.

4. Philadelphia *Press,* 19 February 1859.

5. Roeliff Brinkerhoff to John Sherman, 3 March 1858, John Sherman Papers, Library of Congress, Washington, D.C. For editors' role in advising appointments, see H.S. McCollum to James Buchanan, 22 December 1856, John Heart to Buchanan, 14 March 1857, Buchanan Papers, HSP, Historical Society of Pennsylvania, Philadelphia, Pa; Washington McLean to William Bigler, 24 November 1856, Bigler Papers, HSP. For their role as dispensers of local political currents, see J. W. Merriam to Horatio King, 21 April 1858, 25 December 1859, Horatio King Papers. For their holding of legislative office, see Chicago *Times,* 22 November 1858.

6. Roy F. Nichols, *The Disruption of American Democracy* (New York: Macmillan, 1948), 42–47. Forney's long, effusive, and occasionally stormy relationship with Buchanan can be traced through Philip S. Klein, *President James Buchanan: A Biography* (University Park: Pennsylvania State University Press, 1962), 133–35, 140–41, 151–54, 195–201.

7. Philip Auchampaugh, "Political Techniques, 1856—Or Why the *Herald* Went for Fremont," *Western Political Quarterly* 1 (September 1948): 243–51; Douglas Fermer, *James Gordon Bennett and the New York Herald: A Study of Editorial Opinion in the Civil War Era, 1854–1867* (New York: St. Martin's Press, 1986), 84–93; Washington *Union,* 24 September 1856.

8. Fermer, *James Gordon Bennett and the New York Herald,* 97; John Bassett Moore, comp. and ed., *The Works of James Buchanan* (New York: Antiquarian Press, 1960), 10:95. The description of Buchanan, from the *Herald,* is quoted in the Springfield *Republican,* 5 November 1859.

9. Bennett to Buchanan, 23, 26 February 1857, Henry Wikoff to Buchanan, 6, 30 December 1856, 3, 4, 9, January 1857, Buchanan Papers, HSP.

10. "Occasional," Philadelphia *Press,* 28 May 1858.

11. "Pioneer," Philadelphia *Press,* 28 January, 25 February 1859; "Occasional," Philadelphia *Press,* 3 January 1860.

12. Henry Wikoff to James Buchanan, 6 December 1856, Albert C. Ramsey to Buchanan, 13 February 1857, Buchanan Papers, HSP.

13. Fermer, *James Gordon Bennett and the New York Herald,* 101–2; Henry Wickoff to Bennett, 27 March 1857, Buchanan Papers, HSP; New York *Herald,* 30, 31 January 1860.

14. Boston *Post,* 22 January 1855; New York *Herald,* 3 October 1863 (obituary); Philadelphia *Press,* 16 June 1858; "Occasional," ibid., 23 June 1858, "A Looker On," ibid., 24 December 1859; James S. Pike to William Pitt Fessenden, 28 September 1859, James Shepherd Pike Papers, Library of Congress, Washington, D.C.

15. "Henry Wikoff," *Dictionary of American Biography,* 10:197–98; "Ezek Richards," Philadelphia *Press,* 2 February 1860.

16. William Cullen Bryant to Salmon P. Chase, 12 May 1851, Chase Papers, HSP.

17. C. J. Ward to James Buchanan, 10 December 1856, James G. Dickie to C. L. Ward, 24 November 1856, Buchanan Papers; Daniel F. Pike to Horatio King, 31 July 1857, N. E. Paine to King, 1 September 1860, King Papers; Henry R. Bass to Elihu Washburne, 13 February 1860, Elihu Washburne Papers, Library of Congress, Washington, D.C.

18. Sam H. Farrall to William Bigler, 27 September 1857, Sam Workman to Bigler, 23 November 1857, 4 May 1858, Bigler Papers. The postmastership stayed right where it was, and the newspaper went under.

19. Philadelphia *Daily News,* 1 March 1858; Lafayette *Daily Journal,* 6 May 1857; David Meerse, "James Buchanan, the Patronage, and the Northern Democratic Party, 1857–1858" (Ph.D. diss., University of Illinois, 1969), 34–40, 210–12.

20. Nichols, *Disruption of American Democracy,* 92, 205–6, 244–46; Charleston *Mercury,* 2, 9 April 1857.

21. H. Rept. 648, "Covode Investigation," 36 Cong., 1 sess., 292–93.

22. H. Rept. 648, "Covode Investigation," 36 Cong., 1 sess., 293–94.

23. Kenneth M. Stampp, *America in 1857: A Nation on the Brink* (New York: Oxford University Press, 1990), 52–53, 79–81; Forney to Buchanan, 6 March, 6 June 1857, Buchanan Papers; Forney to William Bigler, 22, 25 April 1857, Bigler Papers, HSP; Forney to George Plitt, 5 March 1857, Barbee Papers.

24. Stampp, *America in 1857,* 81–82; John W. Forney to Jeremiah Black, 28 June 30 July 1957, Black Papers, Library of Congress, Washington, D.C. Forney to James Buchanan, 12, 20 July 1857, Buchanan to Forney, 18 July 1857, Buchanan to Joseph B. Baker, 9 September 1857, Baker to Buchanan, 14 September 1857, Buchanan Papers, HSP.

25. J. W. Merriam to Horatio King, 17 March, 21 April 1858, Nahum Capen to King, 12 May 1859, King Papers; for similar mishaps in Detroit, see Meerse, "Buchanan, the Patronage, and the Northern Democratic Party," 220–221.

26. Springfield *Republican,* 22 October 1859; Fermer, *James Gordon Bennett and the New York Herald,* 103–5; Moore, *Works of James Buchanan,* 11:192–93. Bennett's ambitions are made clear in Andrew Adams to Joseph Lane, 14 July 1860, Joseph Lane Papers, Lilly Library, Indiana University.

27. *Congressional Globe,* 36 Cong., 1 sess., 34 (7 December 1859); Thomas S. Harris to Charles Lanphier, 15 March 1858, Lanphier Papers.

28. Springfield *Republican,* 11 February 1860; William T. Hutcheson, *Cyrus Hall McCormick: Harvest, 1856–1884* (New York: Appleton-Century, 1935), 42–46; Justin E. Walsh, *To Print the News and Raise Hell! A Biography of Wilbur F. Storey* (Chapel Hill: University of North Carolina, 1963), 142, 150.

29. *Congressional Globe,* 36 Cong., 40 1 sess., (7 December 1859); "Pioneer," Philadelphia *Press,* 24 February 1859; Don E. Fehrenbacher, *Chicago Giant: A Biography of "Long John" Wentworth* (Madison, Wis.: American History Research Center, 1957), 163–64.

30. New York *Evening Post,* 9 June 1858.

31. *Congressional Globe,* 36 Cong., 1 sess., 540 (20 January 1860); see also Philadelphia *Daily News,* 19 July 1861.

32. Springfield *Republican,* 9 April, 5 November 1859.

33. James Gordon Bennett to Buchanan, 23 December 1856, Buchanan Papers; "Pioneer," Philadelphia *Press,* 23 February 1859; John A. Dix to Horatio King, 15 October 1860, King Papers; New York *Herald,* 5, 7 January 1859.

34. Philadelphia *Press,* 18 February 1859.

35. Arthur W. Austin to James Buchanan, 26 May 1857, Buchanan Papers,

HSP; Sacramento *Union,* 19 March 1860; Washington *Union,* 13 July 1858; Springfield *Republican,* 3 December 1859.

36. Sacramento *Union,* 8 February, 19 March 1860; Springfield *Republican,* 28 May 1859; for a similar point, see Philadelphia *Press,* 19 January 1859.

37. Philadelphia *Press,* 26 January 1859; "Ching Foo," Sacramento *Union,* 25 January 1861.

38. "S.B.," Springfield *Republican,* 3 December 1859; Sacramento *Union,* 17 January 1860; Philadelphia *Press,* 21 January 1859, "Occasional," ibid., 25 January 1860.

39. Nichols, *Disruption of American Democracy,* 94–131. The best full account of the territorial crisis remains James A. Rawley, *Race and Politics: "Bleeding Kansas" and the Coming of the Civil War* (Philadelphia: J. B. Lippincott Company, 1969).

40. Robert W. Johannsen, *Stephen A. Douglas* (New York: Oxford University Press, 1973), 582–98; Stampp, *America in 1857,* 283–85; Klein, *President James Buchanan,* 304–8.

41. New York *Tribune,* 9 January, 13 February 1858; Washington *Union,* 28 August 1856, 6 January, 5 February 1858.

42. Washington *Union,* 12 February 1857; William S. Hawley to Stephen A. Douglas, 15 December 1857, Stephen A. Douglas Papers, University of Chicago, Chicago. Similar confidence in the ability of the administration to win the benefit of the doubt can be found in J. W. Merriam to John H. George, 20 December 1857, John H. George Papers, New Hampshire Historical Society, Concord, N.H.

43. Washington *Union,* 14 August 1858; John Hastings to William Bigler, 28 December 1857, Bigler Papers; Washington *Union,* 7, 14, 16, 19, 21 February 1858.

44. Solomon Parsons to Stephen A. Douglas, 15 December 1857, C. J. Whitney to Douglas, 21 March 1858, Douglas Papers, University of Chicago; J. W. Merriam to Horatio King, 28 March 1858, King Papers; Hartford *Courant,* 4, 9 January 1858; Philadelphia *Press,* 14 May 1858; Charles Hampstead to William Bigler, 26 May, 4 June 1859, Bigler Papers.

45. Edward H. N. Patterson to William Bigler, 6 January 1858, Bigler Papers; Chicago *Times* 14, 17 March 1858.

46. Chicago *Times,* 9 November 1858; Washington *Union,* 13 July 1858; Meerse, "Buchanan, the Patronage, and the Northern Democratic Party," 368–69; Lafayette *Daily Journal,* 6 May 1857; *Congressional Globe,* 35 Cong., 1 sess., 893 (26 February 1858). See also Philadelphia *Daily News,* 27 July, 8 October 1858. Milwaukee postmaster John R. Sharpstein might as well not have bothered. The Senate failed to confirm him by one vote.

47. Washington *Union,* 12 March, 16 May 1858; Hartford *Courant,* 5 January 1858; Lafayette *Daily Journal,* 6 May 1857; Walsh, *To Print the News and Raise Hell!,* 106–7; Joseph H. Bagg to William Bigler, 30 December 1857, Bigler Papers. For New York City newspapers, see New York *Tribune,* 24 February 1858.

48. H. Rept. 648, "Covode Investigation," 36 Cong., 1 sess., 291–304; Stampp, *America in 1857,* 288–89, 311–12; Forney, *Anecdotes of Public Men,* 120.

49. R. Bruce Petrikin to William Bigler, 6 January 1858, J. Richter Jones to Bigler, 30 December 1857, G. G. Westcott to Bigler, 11 December 1857, Bigler Papers; Hartford *Courant,* 14 January, 14 September 1858; New York *Tribune,* 4 January, 22 February 1858; "Index," ibid., 3 January 1858; "W. H. F.," ibid., 10 February 1858.

50. John B. Baker to James Buchanan, 26 May 1858, Benjamin H. Brewster to

Buchanan, 7 May 1858, Buchanan Papers, HSP; "Pioneer," Philadelphia *Press,* 11 February 1859.

51. Cleveland *Plain Dealer,* 1 October 1859; Thomas Florence to William Bigler, 30 August 1860, Bigler Papers.

52. Thomas Hastings to William Bigler, 8 August 1857, Bigler Papers.

53. New York *Tribune,* 24 February 1858; W. W. Rice to William Bigler, 20 March, 1 September 1857, n.d. [summer 1858], S. B. Browne to Bigler, 9 June 1859, S. D. Anderson to Bigler, 10 May 1859, J. B. Baker to Bigler, 7 August 1860, Bigler Papers; S. B. Browne to Horatio King, 3 April 1860, King Papers.

54. J. Richter Jones to William Bigler, 30 December 1857, Bigler Papers; "Norman John," New York *Tribune,* 24 February 1858; Philadelphia *Press,* 3 March 1859, 3 January 1860. But not Buchanan, who stopped his subscription in October 1858. See Forney, *Anecdotes of Public Men,* 363–64.

55. Robert Tyler to William Bigler, 17 May 1859, Bigler Papers; "Warrington," Springfield *Republican,* 28 April 1860; Nichols, *Disruption of American Democracy,* 349–50; John F. Coleman, *The Disruption of the Pennsylvania Democracy, 1848–1860* (Harrisburg: Pennsylvania Historical and Museum Commission, 1975), 127–28; John McClernland to Charles S. Lanphier, 26 January 1860, Lanphier Papers.

56. "Pioneer," Philadelphia *Press,* 12 January 1859; Charles N. Pine to William Bigler, 11 June 1858, Joseph S. France to Bigler, 11 January 1858, Bigler Papers; George W. Allen to Charles S. Lanphier, February 1858, Lanphier Papers.

57. N. Weight to William Bigler, 27 April 1858, Isaac Cook to Bigler, 31 March 1858, Bigler Papers; James W. Sheahan to Lanphier, 4 February 1858, Lanphier Papers.

58. James W. Sheahan to Charles S. Lanphier, 23 May 1858, Lanphier Papers.

59. Thomas Harris to Charles S. Lanphier, 1 January 1858, Lanphier Papers.

60. Thomas L. Harris to Charles S. Lanphier, 25, 30 January 1858, Lanphier Papers. For the full and gory details of the factional fight, see Johannsen, *Stephen A. Douglas,* 601–2, 621–44.

61. Isaac Cook to Horatio King, 24 April 1858, King Papers; Cook to William Bigler, 6, 10 May 1858, Charles Leib to Bigler, 11 June 1858, D. M. Boss to Bigler, 3 May 1858, Bigler Papers.

62. Thomas L. Harris to Charles Lanphier, 27 May 1858, Lanphier Papers; to Horatio King, 26 April 1857; Meerse, "Buchanan, the Patronage, and the Northern Democratic Party," 545.

63. James W. Sheahan to Charles S. Lanphier, 19 February 1858, Lanphier Papers; Fehrenbhacher, *Chicago Giant,* 151–53.

64. Matthew Diversey to James Buchanan, 21 July 1859, Bigler Papers; Washington *Union,* 12 March, 20 July 1858; Matthew Diversey to Horatio King, 22 November 1859, King Papers; Chicago *Times,* 24 June 1858; "Occasional," Philadelphia *Press,* 21, 23 June 1858.

65. Chicago *Times,* 30 July 1858; New York *Tribune,* 15 January 1858; Archer M. Shaw, *The Plain Dealer: One Hundred Years in Cleveland* (New York: Knopf, 1942), 116–18; J. W. Gray to Horatio King, 13 June 1859, King Papers; Springfield *Republican,* 15 January, 29 October 1859, 14 January 1860; "Occasional," Philadelphia *Press,* 29 May 1858; J. W. Quiggle to William Bigler, 14 May 1859, Bigler Papers.

66. H. Rept. 648, "Covode Investigation," 36 Cong., 1 sess., 539–46; Springfield *Republican,* 9, 16 April, 7 May 1859; "A Looker-On," Philadelphia *Press,*

24 December 1859, 2, 19 January 1860; Sacramento *Union,* 18 January 1860; "Perley," Boston *Morning Journal,* 20 January 1860.

67. "Perley," Boston *Morning Journal,* 25 January 1860; "Videx," Sacramento *Union,* 25 February 1860; H. M. Phillips to Bigler, 23 January 1860, Bigler Papers.

68. H. Rept. 648, "Covode Investigation," 36 Cong., 1 sess., 19–22, 37.

69. Andrew Adams to Joseph Lane, 14, 21 July 1860, Lane Papers; James E. Hendrickson, *Joe Lane of Oregon: Machine Politics and the Sectional Crisis* (New Haven: Yale University Press, 1967), 228; New York *Tribune,* 27 June 1860; Springfield *Republican* 30 June, 14 July, 11 August 1860.

70. Springfield *Republican,* 7, 14, 28 July, 4, 11 August 1860; New York *Tribune,* 27, 30 June 1860; Thomas L. Smith to Joseph Lane, 2 July 1860, C. N. Pine to Lane, 3 July 1860, Lane Papers; Springfield *Republican,* 14 July 1860.

71. George Sanderson to William Bigler, 21, 23 March 1857, W. W. Rice to Bigler, n.d. [but clearly summer 1858], Bigler Papers.

72. Philadelphia *Press,* 19 January 1859.

"No Bed of Roses": James Buchanan, Abraham Lincoln, and Presidential Leadership in the Civil War Era

William E. Gienapp

"The presidency, even to the most experienced politicians, is no bed of roses," Abraham Lincoln once observed, noting, "No human being can fill that station and escape censure."[1] He was referring to Zachary Taylor's controversy-wracked tenure, but his comment aptly foreshadowed his own experience in the office a decade later. It is safe to say that the position does not hold the same appeal for a president at the end of his administration as it did when he first took the oath of office, but few have been as disillusioned as Lincoln's immediate predecessor, James Buchanan. Deserted by his closest advisers, rejected by a majority of his party, repudiated by the electorate, and subject to a torrent of public ridicule, he felt an enormous relief when his term finally came to an end. As he rode with Lincoln in a carriage to the inauguration ceremony in March 1861, the outgoing president confided to his successor, "If you are as happy in entering the White House as I shall feel on returning [home] to Wheatland, you are a happy man indeed."[2]

Often the capstone of a long career in public life, the presidency brings with it not only significant responsibilities and substantial personal power, but even under the best of circumstances a multitude of problems and headaches as well. Yet for all its trials and tribulations, the presidency remains the focus of the American political system and the most important source of national leadership.

The problem of evaluating presidential leadership has long concerned historians and political scientists. What makes a person a successful president, what constitutes the nature of presidential leadership, and what effect a president has on the course of events are all critical questions. The main conclusion to be drawn from

93

PRESIDENTS BUCHANAN AND LINCOLN ENTERING THE SENATE CHAMBER BEFORE THE INAUGURATION.—[FROM A SKETCH BY OUR SPECIAL ARTIST.]

Leslie's Illustrated Magazine depicts Buchanan's role as Lincoln's escort just prior to the inauguration of the sixteenth

these studies is that there are no hard and fast rules for evaluating presidential performance. Similar action in a different context can often lead to strikingly dissimilar results. Efforts to predict presidential performance, based on some mixture of personality traits and prior experience, have proved misguided and fruitless.

One way to approach the problem of presidential leadership in American history is to compare presidents of the same era. In this regard, James Buchanan and Abraham Lincoln provide a natural comparison. Few presidents have held power in such a critical time as Buchanan and Lincoln; few have made decisions that have had more far-reaching significance for the nation. Under Buchanan, the sectional conflict, long in the making, steadily worsened so that by the time he left office the Union had been sundered by the secession of the Deep South and the nation was on the brink of civil war. Inheriting this crisis, which had been precipitated by his election, Lincoln soon confronted the challenge of leading the republic safely through a costly civil war to preserve the Union. The purpose of such a comparison is not to extol Lincoln at Buchanan's expense, but instead to examine the dimensions of presidential leadership in the Civil War era and to probe the sources of presidential success and failure.

In evaluating presidential performance, historians have given the two men strikingly different grades. Lincoln invariably is included in the highest category, and most put him at the very top of the list, ranking him as the greatest president in American history. Buchanan, in contrast, has fared much more poorly. In the 1982 Murray-Blessing poll, the most extensive of these surveys, he was ranked a failure, with only Nixon, Grant, and Harding below him.[3]

Yet if prior experience was any guide, Buchanan should have easily outshone Lincoln as chief executive. Indeed, few men have entered the presidency after such long and varied public service. Active in public life for more than four decades, the Pennsylvania leader had been a member of both houses of Congress, held several diplomatic posts, served in the cabinet as secretary of state under James K. Polk, and had been a serious candidate for his party's presidential nomination for over a decade. Indeed, his long and wide-ranging experience, coupled with his reputation for caution and moderation, played a large role in gaining him the 1856 Democratic nomination. In 1852, the party had nominated a dark horse, Franklin Pierce, to head its national ticket. Pierce had proven woefully inadequate for the task at hand, and not wanting to make the same mistake again, the delegates in 1856 turned instead to Buchanan, a veteran party wheelhorse. Following Buchanan's victory in November, Democrats were confident that he would avoid

HARPER'S WEEKLY.

A JOURNAL OF CIVILIZATION

VOL. V.—No. 220.]　　　NEW YORK, SATURDAY, MARCH 16, 1861.　　　[PRICE FIVE CENTS.

THE INAUGURAL PROCESSION AT WASHINGTON PASSING THE GATE OF THE CAPITOL GROUNDS.—FROM A SKETCH BY OUR SPECIAL ARTIST.—[SEE PAGE 165.]

Harper's Weekly **portrays the inaugural procession, 4 March 1861. Courtesy of Dickinson College.**

Pierce's mistakes and successfully guide the party and the nation through the sectional crisis.[4] The normally astute Alexander H. Stephens of Georgia, for one, predicted that with Buchanan's election "there will never be another sectional or slavery struggle in the United States, at least in our day."[5]

Abraham Lincoln, on the other hand, was one of the least experienced presidents in American history. He had served several terms in the Illinois legislature, but his entire federal experience was limited to one undistinguished term in the 1840s in the House of Representatives. Failing to obtain an appointive position in Illinois under Taylor, he had never held an executive office, and had been out of public office for more than a decade prior to his nomination for the presidency. He had made two unsuccessful attempts, in 1855 and again in 1858, to obtain a seat in the United States Senate. For a variety of reasons, however, the delegates at the 1860 Republican national convention believed that he was the strongest candidate they could run, and that none of the other leading contenders could be elected. Dismissing the possibility of secession, the delegates and party leaders gave little consideration to Lincoln's qualifications or his ability to lead the country. Republicans concluded that Lincoln had the best chance of winning and that was sufficient.[6]

Upon entering the presidency, Buchanan and Lincoln each faced one overriding challenge. For Buchanan, it was to dampen the sectional conflict, reassure Southerners, and check the growth of the suddenly robust Republican Party. In 1856 the antislavery Republican Party, which seemed close to death at the start of the year, had nearly triumphed in its first national campaign. John C. Frémont, the party's presidential candidate, had surprisingly run first in the North, carrying all the free states but five, and had nearly been elected. Moreover, despite his strength in the South, Buchanan was a minority president, as 55 percent of the voters had supported either Frémont or former president Millard Fillmore, the candidate of the American Party.[7] With the sectional Republican Party having come so close to winning, it was imperative that the new president defuse the controversy over the expansion of slavery. Buchanan needed to pursue policies that would retain the Democratic Party's regular supporters, prevent the Republicans from gaining a disproportionate share of new voters, and keep the Fillmore voters in the free states out of the Republican ranks. Large gains by the Republicans among new voters and former Know-Nothings would produce a Republican victory in 1860, and with it the likely disruption of the Union.

Nor was Buchanan blind to this political situation. On the contrary, he discerned precisely the challenge before him. Soon after his election, he declared that his goal as president would be "to arrest, if possible, the agitation of the slavery question at the North, and to destroy sectional parties. Should a kind Providence enable me to succeed in my efforts to restore harmony to the Union, I shall feel that I have not lived in vain."[8]

Assuming office four years later, Lincoln confronted a considerably more difficult problem: to preserve the Union. By the time he was inaugurated, seven Southern states—the entire Deep South—had seceded from the Union and established a rival government, the Confederate States of America. Unwilling to recognize the legality of secession, Lincoln tried to continue the existing stalemate over Fort Sumter in Charleston harbor, but his decision to send a relief expedition to the besieged federal garrison led instead to war. In response to the attack on Fort Sumter, Lincoln adopted the policy of using whatever military force was necessary to restore the Union. Like Confederate leaders, he initially anticipated that the war would be short and require only limited use of force, but by the time the conflict ended four years later, it had cost over 620,000 American lives and billions of dollars. Presiding over the government during the greatest crisis in the nation's history, a crisis entirely without precedent, Lincoln had to feel his way as he went, adopting means and altering policies as he thought best. Still, his fundamental goal remained to preserve the Union without destroying democracy in the process.

In setting up their respective administrations, Buchanan and Lincoln confronted the thorny problem of selecting a cabinet. Lincoln's cabinet was easily the more distinguished of the two, but Buchanan's cabinet was not a collection of nonentities. It contained two reasonably talented members, Howell Cobb in the Treasury Department and Jeremiah S. Black as attorney general, and if the other members were of no particular merit, only Secretary of War John Floyd was totally incompetent. Since Lincoln appointed all of his major rivals for the 1860 Republican nomination to his cabinet—probably in part so he could keep an eye on them—its members were considerably more prestigious. It had two outstanding members in Secretary of State William H. Seward and Secretary of the Treasury Salmon P. Chase; only Caleb B. Smith in the Interior Department was a nonentity. One member, the incompetent Secretary of War Simon Cameron, became enmeshed in charges of corruption and eventually departed. Thus Cameron balanced Floyd,

THE CABINET COUNCIL.

Buchanan and his cabinet, ca. 1857. From *Leslie's Illustrated Magazine*. Courtesy of Dickinson College.

and each was replaced by a far abler man, Joseph Holt in Buchanan's cabinet and Edwin Stanton under Lincoln.

A distinguished cabinet, however, is no guarantee of a successful presidency; a mediocre cabinet, as Andrew Jackson's presidency shows, does not inevitably preclude presidential achievement. While the two cabinets varied in ability, more critical was the relationship between each president and his department heads. The cabinet played a quite different role in the two administrations. Under Lincoln, the cabinet was never a policy-making body. From the beginning of his administration, Lincoln intended to be his own man and to rely on his cabinet more to administer policy than to determine it, especially with respect to the war. Secretary of the Navy Gideon Welles reported that cabinet meetings were "infrequent, irregular, and without system." Seward was frequently absent, preferring to deal with the president privately, and Secretary of War Stanton, fearing leaks, refused to discuss matters concerning the war in the presence of other members. The self-righteous Chase, convinced that his talents eclipsed all other members of the administration, including the president, was especially irritated by this state of affairs. "We . . . are called members of the Cabinet," he complained, "but are in reality only separate heads of departments, meeting now and then for talk on whatever happens to come uppermost, not for grave consultation on matters concerning the salvation of the country."[9]

Confident in his own ability to decide on the correct policy, Lincoln never felt bound by the prevailing opinion in the cabinet. In its first meeting, a majority of the cabinet voted to abandon Fort Sumter, yet Lincoln reserved judgment. On April Fool's Day, when Seward offered to be the premier of the administration and assume the burden of leadership, Lincoln tactfully but firmly rebuked his secretary's pretensions by affirming that *he* intended to fulfill that responsibility.[10] Critical decisions such as army commands and military strategy were not made by the cabinet. Nor was the decision to issue the Emancipation Proclamation, the most crucial decision Lincoln made in the entire war, a collective one. When he presented the subject to his cabinet on 22 July 1862, Lincoln prefaced the discussion by telling its members: "I have got you together to hear what I have written down. I do not wish your advice about the main matter—for that I have determined for myself. . . . If there is anything in the expressions I use, or in any other minor matter, which anyone of you thinks had best be changed, I shall be glad to receive the suggestions."[11]

With the exception of Chase, Lincoln remained on good personal terms with his cabinet members, but he relied on them as advisers only selectively. He sought their advice on matters germane to their department, and usually deferred to their judgment, but on other questions consulted them sporadically if at all. Welles confessed that "of the policy of the administration, if there be one, I am not advised beyond what is published and known to all." Chase fumed that if he wanted to know what was going on elsewhere in the administration, he had to send a clerk to get a copy of the New York *Herald*.[12] After his early misjudgment, Seward became a loyal supporter and Lincoln's most intimate official advisor. Jealous of Seward's influence, Welles grumbled that the secretary of state spent "a considerable portion of every day with the President, patronizing and instructing him, hearing and telling anecdotes, relating interesting details of occurrences in the Senate, and inculcating his political party notions."[13] Yet there was no doubt that with Seward, as the other members of the cabinet, Lincoln kept the upper hand and retained the final authority for himself.

In Buchanan's administration, in contrast, decision-making was a collaborative effort, achieved only after long discussion in the cabinet. Buchanan's style of administrative leadership was the search for consensus. This approach to decision-making meant that the makeup of Buchanan's cabinet, which might have been adequate under different circumstances, was seriously flawed. First of all, the most important post—secretary of state—was occupied by Lewis Cass, who was never particularly dynamic in his best days, and who by now was seventy-five years old and verging on senility. Cass was selected primarily because he posed no threat to any ambitious party leader, either inside or outside the administration. Moreover, as an experienced diplomat Buchanan intended to take the lead in guiding foreign policy, which rendered Cass's role superfluous. In cabinet deliberations, however, the secretary of state, as the leading member, should have played a key role, both in forging a consensus and in steering the administration away from any disastrous decisions. Lethargic and mentally unalert, Cass failed to provide such direction or weigh in with any authority. Buchanan's initial choice for the post—Robert Walker, his colleague from the Polk cabinet—would have been a far superior choice. In particular, Walker, though from Mississippi, was a shrewd politician with national ambitions and would have served as a forceful counterbalance against the overweening Southern influence in the cabinet and among Buchanan's unofficial advisers. Cass played that role only once, when in a public relations ploy he suddenly resigned in December 1860 in protest over the administration's policy toward Fort Sumter—but by then Buchanan's presidency had been wrecked.

More disastrous still was the fact that Buchanan's cabinet represented only a narrow range of opinion within the Democratic Party. A bachelor who savored good food and could hold his liquor, Buchanan intended to make his department heads and their wives the center of his society. He viewed the cabinet as akin to a family, and thus, except for Cass, who was simply a figurehead, he appointed men with whom he felt personally comfortable. But the cabinet was excessively pro-Southern in its orientation, and its discussions were often dominated by Howell Cobb of Georgia and Jacob Thompson of Mississippi. Black, the most prominent member from the free states, tended to take a narrow, legalistic approach to problems and nurtured an intense hatred of abolitionism, which he simplistically identified with the Republican Party.[14]

Conspicuously absent from the cabinet was any supporter of Stephen A. Douglas. Harboring a strong personal dislike for the Illinois senator, Buchanan spitefully excluded him from the administration's counsels and did not consult with him to any great extent concerning the distribution of patronage, even in his own state. The most popular Democrat in the country and the odds-on favorite to be the party's presidential nominee in 1860, Douglas was simply too important and too popular to be ignored. Moreover, as the most important Northern Democrat, he represented precisely that wing of the party that had to be placated and sustained if the Republican challenge was to be beaten back. If Democratic strength in the North eroded any further, the Republicans would control all the free states and be able to elect a president without any support in the South. It was imperative that Northern Democrats have a voice in the administration, yet they were effectively shut out.[15] Isaac Toucey lacked any weight, Cass was in his dotage, and Black was out of touch with Northern public opinion on the slavery issue.

The pro-Southern orientation of Buchanan's administration was reinforced by his unofficial advisers. Along with Cobb, Senator John Slidell of Louisiana, Senator Jesse Bright of Indiana, and Governor Henry Wise of Virginia were Buchanan's closest friends. They declined to join the administration but continued to give the president advice. None was particularly useful in this regard. Despite his New York origins, Slidell was an ardent proslavery sectionalist, Wise was erratic and impulsive, and Bright was a petty and vindictive political hack who was only nominally a free-state man. His sympathies lay with the South (he owned a plantation and slaves in Kentucky), and he was consumed with jealousy of Douglas, whom he considered his rival for leadership of the party in the Northwest. The thought that Bright could supplant Douglas as the favorite of the western Democrats was laughable. Indeed, it did not take an astute political observer to recognize that Bright's power had sharply declined in Indiana because of his proslavery views, and that he would be fortunate to retain control of his state, let alone the Northwest. During the war, he was expelled from the Senate for disloyalty, but by then his political power had been broken. Of one mind, Buchanan's advisers gave him similar advice until the secession crisis, and with his desire for harmony and consensus always uppermost, he lacked the independence of mind to disregard their advice.

In contrast to Lincoln's dominance, Buchanan's role in his administration was much more circumspect. In this regard, the cases of John Floyd and Simon Cameron provide an instructive comparison. Evidence of mismanagement, favoritism, and corruption came to light during each man's tenure in the War Department. Realizing that Floyd's actions had further discredited the administration, Buchanan wanted him to resign but shrank from insisting on it when the secretary refused. Floyd remained in the cabinet against the president's wishes until he could find a principled pretext for leaving. Lincoln's handling of Cameron, who was a powerful Pennsylvania Republican, if not more honorable, was at least more effective. He forced the reluctant Cameron to resign, but softened the blow by appointing him minister to Russia, the kind of position presidents dream about, since it carried a certain amount of prestige but offered little opportunity to embarrass the administration.

The process of collaborative decision-making gave the impression that Buchanan was simply a tool of his cabinet. In a famous story, Cobb, when once asked by a friend why he appeared worried, replied: "Oh, it's nothing much; only Buck is opposing the Administration."[16] The idea that Buchanan was controlled by his cabinet is a stereotype. True, Buchanan was not especially forceful in imposing his ideas on his administration, but he did not have to be, for throughout most of the term his advisors were not only unified but their views were in accord with Buchanan's own inclinations.[17] Nonetheless, Buchanan did not take a strong lead in establishing policy, he shut himself off from dissenting points of view, including those within his own party, and he was remarkably stubborn in adhering to policies even after their disastrous consequences had been demonstrated.

The harmony of Buchanan's cabinet collapsed in the secession crisis. The president's advisers were bitterly divided between secessionists, headed by Cobb and Thompson, and Unionists, led by Black. Caught between these two groups, Buchanan vacillated, although from the outset he consistently refused to recognize the legality of secession. The deep divisions among Buchanan's counselors eventually led to the breakup and reorganization of the cabinet. Cobb was the first member to leave; he was soon followed by Thompson and Floyd. Buchanan was particularly shaken by Cobb's departure, since he was especially fond of the jovial Georgian. Harkening back to the ideas of an earlier era, Buchanan viewed politics in terms of personal allegiances, and thus he felt personally betrayed by the resignation of the Southern members of the cabinet. When Black also threatened to resign unless the president adopt a stronger Unionist position concerning secession, Buchanan abjectly capitulated and allowed Black to rewrite his reply to the South Carolina commissioners. "I cannot part with you," the distraught president told Black, who now emerged as the dominant personality in the cabinet. For the remainder of his term Buchanan was no longer in effective control of his administration.[18]

In all of these areas, Lincoln provided a more impressive exam-

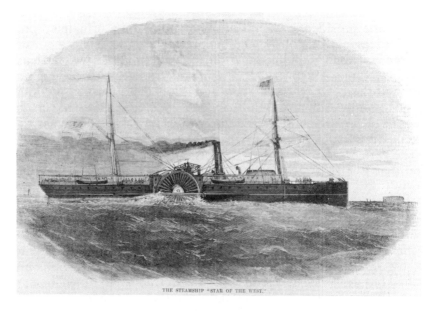

THE STEAMSHIP "STAR OF THE WEST."

Contemporary portrait of the steamship *Star of the West*, an unarmed merchant vessel dispatched to Fort Sumter on 5 January 1861, providing reinforcements and provisions for Major Robert Anderson's beleaguered force in Charleston harbor. On 9 January the ship was repulsed with cannon fire from South Carolina shore batteries and returned to New York. From *Leslie's Illustrated Magazine.* Courtesy of Dickinson College.

ple of presidential leadership. Lacking an inner circle of advisers and political cronies, he exposed himself to a wide range of opinion, took the lead in establishing policies on matters that he considered presidential responsibility, delegated authority effectively to subordinates, and displayed remarkable flexibility on questions of policy. His cabinet represented all the major factions in the party and contained the full spectrum of Republican opinion, from the radical Salmon P. Chase to the ultraconservative Gideon Welles. Nor did Lincoln allow personal feelings to determine his decisions. Lincoln was "a very poor hater," a longtime Illinois associate remarked, and he was always ready to work with anyone who agreed with him on a particular issue, whatever their other differences, including men he did not like personally.[19] He kept Chase in the cabinet until 1864, despite their increasingly icy relations, because of the secretary's valuable service to the Union. His philosophy was well summarized by his advice in the 1850s to Whigs who resisted joining with abolitionists in opposing the Kansas-Nebraska Act: "Stand with anybody that stands RIGHT. Stand with him while he is right and PART with him when he goes wrong."[20] Jealousy and touchy dignity, which held sway over Buchanan, had no influence with Lincoln.

The two presidents also presented contrasting styles of leadership in the areas of foreign affairs. Buchanan was an activist president in foreign affairs, both in his involvement with diplomacy and in his efforts to promote American expansion. Ignoring the sectional tensions that had checked the expansionist impulse, Buchanan sought to acquire Cuba, a key objective of slavery expansionists; was insufficiently vigilant against filibustering expeditions; and negotiated a one-sided treaty with a political faction in Mexico that established a protectorate over that country's northern provinces and authorized unilateral American military intervention. A coalition of Southern moderates and Northern Republicans rejected this treaty, which clearly was intended to lead to the annexation of additional Mexican territory.[21] Buchanan's reckless foreign policy reflected the same blindness that undermined his domestic program: his failure to comprehend the nature and intensity of Northern fears of the slave power, and his failure to see that the balance of political power in the country was shifting away from the South. A letter he wrote shortly after he was elected discussing his objectives as president starkly revealed his political blinders. "If I can be instrumental in settling the slavery question . . . and then add Cuba to the Union," he wrote without comprehending that these goals were totally incompatible, "I shall be willing to give up the ghost."[22]

Lincoln lacked Buchanan's diplomatic training and took little interest in foreign affairs. Instead, he left the conduct of diplomacy largely in the hands of his able secretary of state, William Henry Seward. Occasionally Lincoln took a more active role, as for example when he toned down the language of Seward's instructions to Charles Francis Adams, the American minister to Great Britain, following the outbreak of war, but such action was unusual. After a rocky beginning, when Seward proposed fighting a war against a European power as the means to reunite the country, the secretary soon won the president's confidence.[23]

Lincoln's style of presidential leadership on foreign affairs was not inherently superior to Buchanan's. Indeed, with a secretary of state such as Cass it was essential that the president be actively involved in the affairs of the department. Instead, Buchanan's frustrations grew out of the fact that his policies were ill-advised.

Lincoln devoted his attention instead to military affairs. He took an active role in the conduct of the war, both in the selection of

Cartoon from 1861 shows the new Republican president, Abraham Lincoln, vigorously engaging secessionists, while former President James Buchanan, in devil's horns, slinks off stage, muttering, "I am glad I'm out. Just in time!" Courtesy of Dickinson College.

commanders and in the determination of strategy. While prodding his often sluggish generals forward, he did not hesitate to intervene as commander in chief and counteract their plans. A good example was when he detached part of George B. McClellan's army during the ill-fated peninsular campaign to protect the capital at Washington. Lincoln was a much more activist president on military affairs than on foreign affairs and on most domestic policies. His activity did not stem from any extensive military experience, which was limited to a brief service in the Illinois militia during the Black Hawk War. Instead, it reflected the sobering effect of the Union military's disastrous performance at the beginning of the war, and his understanding that the responsibility and the blame would rest with him as commander in chief. Lincoln soon lost faith in Winfield Scott, an imposing military figure but now well past his prime, and discovered that Henry Halleck, whom he brought to Washington in 1862 to advise him, was useless in such matters.[24] Instead, he soon came to rely on himself, carefully listening to advice from his generals but making decisions himself. This process began after the Battle of Bull Run and continued throughout the war. Lincoln's intervention varied according to his faith in the commanding general. He was less active in dealing with Grant and Sherman, who shared his fundamental strategic outlook, than he was with more laggard generals such as McClellan and Don Carlos Buell.[25]

Lincoln was also a more effective party leader than Buchanan. Political parties in the nineteenth century were held together by the glue of patronage: "to the victor belong the spoils," a New York politician once commented. Consequently, both Buchanan and Lincoln devoted considerable attention to these appointments. On occasion Lincoln pretended to be above such sordid political details, as for example when he told a group of Pennsylvania party leaders, "You know I was never a contriver; I don't know much about how things are done in politics."[26] Nothing was further from the truth. David Donald has argued that "the secret of Lincoln's success is simple: he was an astute and dexterous operator of the political machine." Neither president had enough offices to satisfy every office seeker, but Lincoln made much more effective use of the patronage because under his policy of "justice to all" he included all party factions in his appointments.[27]

Buchanan, by contrast, refused to recognize the Douglasites from the beginning, and once Douglas had broken with the administration over the attempt to admit Kansas under the proslavery Lecompton Constitution, Buchanan and his advisers waged an all-out war on the Illinois senator's supporters. Douglas loyalists were abruptly removed from federal office and opponents appointed in their place. This wholesale war on the Douglasites and anti-Lecompton Democrats was especially marked in Illinois, where the administration supported a separate pro-Lecompton Democratic state ticket in 1858 in a vain effort to defeat Douglas. While grounded in fundamental differences of principle, the bitter Douglas-Buchanan feud became increasingly personal, for which the president deserves most of the blame. With the Democratic Party on the defensive in the free states, such internecine warfare was suicidal, as the Democratic debacle in the 1858 Northern congressional elections revealed. In the aftermath of these elections, which decimated the party's regular Northern wing in Congress, the most important task confronting Buchanan was to heal the breach with Douglas. Buchanan, however, refused to take any step in this direction; indeed, he watched approvingly while short-sighted party leaders in the Senate stripped the Illinois senator of his committee chairmanship, which added more fuel to the popular perception of a personal vendetta against Douglas.[28]

Lincoln constantly had to adjudicate disputes among various Republican factions in the different states, but at no time did he single out his critics for political annihilation. Even after Chase left the cabinet following his clumsy attempt to challenge the president for the 1864 nomination, Lincoln did not purge the federal bureaucracy of Chase's allies; indeed, he eventually appointed Chase chief justice of the Supreme Court. Similarly, Lincoln was caught up in the increasingly bitter fight in Maryland between Henry Winter Davis and Montgomery Blair, yet he retained the support of both men. Blair remained loyal even after Lincoln dropped him from the Cabinet in 1864. Despite Davis's vituperative denunciation of the president for refusing to sign the Wade-Davis bill on Reconstruction in 1864, Lincoln, sensing the shifting tide in the state's politics, extended greater recognition to the radicals in Maryland appointments.[29] Lincoln's adroit handling of party critics stands in bold contrast to Buchanan's efforts to purge anti-Lecompton Democrats.

On taking office, Buchanan realized that the most critical problem confronting him was the situation in Kansas. He made an excellent appointment in selecting Robert Walker as the new governor of the territory. Buchanan's powers of persuasion never shown more brightly, for the ambitious Walker did not want the job, which had been a political graveyard for everyone who held it. Before Walker went to Kansas, he and Buchanan agreed any state constitution would be submitted for approval by the bona fide residents of the territory. Had Buchanan adhered to this policy it would have defused the Kansas crisis. Shortly after he took up his new post, Walker concluded that the cause of slavery was futile in the territory. Consequently, he soon came under fire from Southern leaders in Washington, and under heavy pressure Buchanan abandoned his governor, with disastrous results for himself and his party.[30]

Lincoln, in contrast, could take the political pounding. He stood up to an avalanche of criticism after rescinding John C. Frémont's emancipation edict in Missouri in 1861. He refused to let the radicals force his hand on emancipation in 1862 or on his policy of reconstruction in 1864. He resisted the growing popular cry for peace negotiations in 1864 and effectively deflected the issue by permitting unofficial peace commissioners to go to Richmond, a move that exposed the unwillingness of Jefferson Davis to consider anything less than Southern independence.[31] After endorsing a premature military campaign that resulted in the Union rout at Bull Run, he relied more on his own judgment in strategic matters, a tendency that was reinforced by Henry Halleck's refusal to take responsibility or give advice. He made some unfortunate appointments to army commands, but in the end he found the generals he needed to win the war. He endured personal slights, social humiliation, unprecedented ridicule, and vicious criticism without losing faith in himself or the Union cause.

Neither party was completely united when each man took office, and these divisions worsened over time. But under Buchanan the Democratic Party was torn to shreds by the Lecompton issue and the mounting hostility between Southern Democrats and the Douglasites. Far from ending the feud and healing the breach, Buchanan contributed to it by waging an all-out war against anti-Lecompton Democrats in the North and removing them from office. While more was involved in this division than Buchanan's personal feelings, only he had the power to heal this division. A magnanimous gesture, an appeal for party unity, and some plain talk to Southern Democrats was essential. Instead, the president responded by nurturing petty grievances, voicing a determination to destroy his party opponents, and promoting blatantly pro-Southern policies. The result was the rupture of the party at the 1860 Charleston convention, an outcome orchestrated by Buchanan's advisers on the scene, headed by Slidell and Bright.[32] In the end, the Democrats ran two presidential candidates in 1860, Douglas, who represented the Northern wing of the party, and Vice-President John C. Breckinridge of Kentucky, who was nominated by Southern

Democrats. Buchanan ended his term a thoroughly repudiated president. Deserted by his Southern friends, he had no influence in Congress, even among Democrats, and was openly ridiculed. Few presidents have left office with less influence over their party than Buchanan. By his retirement he was truly a man without a party, rejected by virtually everyone and without prestige or influence.[33]

Lincoln also confronted a deepening division in his party, especially over the issues of slavery, war policy, and reconstruction. As the war dragged on, the Radicals became more vociferous in their condemnation of the president and his policies. But Lincoln handled this division much more effectively. With an eye to party harmony, he granted the Radicals honesty of purpose. As he told his secretary, John Hay, "They are nearer to me than the other side, in thought and sentiment, though bitterly hostile to me personally. They are utterly lawless—the unhandiest devils in the world to deal with—but after all their faces are set Zionwards."[34] Moreover, time and again he effectively outmaneuvered the Radicals and defeated their efforts to dictate policy. As agitation to make emancipation a Union war aim intensified in the party, Lincoln undercut the Radicals by approving the First and then the Second Confiscation Act. Although he signed the second act, which provided for the emancipation of any slave owned by a disloyal master, Lincoln ignored the law and continued to pursue his own policy on slavery. Radicals might fume privately, or grumble about Lincoln's lack of purpose, but they were powerless to check him. Few participated in the movement to nominate a separate ticket in 1864, and any hope to prevent Lincoln's nomination at the Union convention quickly ended with the election of so many federal officeholders, all loyal Lincoln men, as delegates. Despite more than three years of criticism that he was too indecisive and not up to the task before him, Lincoln was easily renominated by the Republican convention in 1864. Lincoln's ability to keep policy in his own hands, to retain the support of the federal bureaucracy, and easily win renomination were all testimony to his effective party leadership. A number of Republicans were unhappy with Lincoln, but they could not prevent his renomination.[35]

Another critical component of presidential leadership is relations with Congress. In dealing with the legislative branch, neither Buchanan nor Lincoln was an activist president in the modern sense of the term. While they recommended general policies, they generally did not submit legislation to Congress.

Lincoln's philosophy harked back to the principles of the Whig

Party. "My political education strongly inclines me against a very free use of any . . . means, by the Executive, to control the legislation of the country," he affirmed in a speech as president-elect. "As a rule, I think it better that congress should originate, as well as perfect its measures, without external bias."[36] Thus, while he was a firm believer in using government power to promote economic development, he showed little interest in the precise form of economic legislation passed during the war, leaving it largely to Congress to frame such important legislation as the Homestead Act, the Land Grant College Act, the protective tariff, and the national banking laws. Indeed, he largely relied on Chase to deal with Congress on matters of taxes, bonds, and banking. Once, when the secretary of the treasury sought his advice on a financial matter, Lincoln replied with less than complete candor, "You understand these things. I do not."[37] Only Chase's insistence that the outcome in Congress hinged on presidential action induced Lincoln to lobby personally for passage of the National Banking Act of 1863.

Lincoln's most active role in legislative matters occurred on the issue of slavery. Again, this reflected Lincoln's basic belief that the question of emancipation and Union war aims was his responsibility as commander in chief, and not that of Congress, since the Constitution gave Congress no jurisdiction over slavery in the states. As Lincoln expressed his constitutional view on one occasion, "I conceive that I may in an emergency do things on military grounds which cannot be done constitutionally by Congress."[38] In his annual message in 1861, Lincoln urged Congress to adopt a plan to finance gradual emancipation in the border states. When Congress failed to act on the matter, Lincoln sent specific legislation to Congress. In the summer of that year, when Congress passed the Second Confiscation Act, Lincoln forced a modification of the act by threatening to veto it until Congress passed an explanatory resolution meeting his objections, which it did. (Though he then signed the bill, he sent the veto message he had drafted to Congress anyway.)[39] Finally, following his reelection, he threw all of his influence behind the drive to gain the last few votes needed in the House of Representatives to pass the proposed Thirteenth Amendment abolishing slavery. He made lavish use of the patronage to win the votes of a handful of Northern Democrats, which enabled the amendment to pass and be sent to the states for ratification. Never before as president had Lincoln taken such an active and concerted role in securing legislation.[40]

Buchanan was even less active, viewing the president's responsibility as simply to approve or disapprove laws Congress passed. The most concerted intervention by his administration was during the unsuccessful struggle to get Congress to approve the Lecompton Constitution and in the ensuing negotiations to find a way out of the stalemate that produced the English bill. Buchanan was more energetic, however, in using the veto. Lincoln vetoed only one important piece of legislation during his presidency, the Wade-Davis bill, which he believed infringed on his power as president to establish a program of reconstruction. Buchanan, on the other hand, vetoed several pieces of legislation that would have economically benefited the North, including a homestead bill, a bill to expedite overland mail to California, and a bill to grant public land to support agricultural colleges. These vetoes, done at the behest of Southern politicians, further weakened the Democratic Party in the free states and did nothing to shore up the president's sagging popularity.[41]

Neither president enjoyed especially harmonious relations with Congress, but again Buchanan fared worse. His problems began with his ill-fated decision to endorse the Lecompton Constitution, which would have made Kansas a slave state. Douglas broke with the president and led a small number of Northern representatives into open rebellion. His anger roused by this challenge to his leadership, Buchanan refused any compromise and vowed to force Lecompton, as he phrased it, "naked through the House."[42] He pulled out all the stops to secure the votes in the House to admit Kansas under the Lecompton Constitution, including allegations of outright bribery. Rarely had Washington witnessed such a titanic struggle or more aggressive intervention in congressional affairs by the executive branch. Yet in the end Buchanan's humiliation was complete. The Lecompton Constitution was rejected, the unscrupulous lobbying campaign was soon exposed to public eyes, and a majority of Northern Democrats in Congress was estranged from the administration.

Buchanan's relations with Congress reached the nadir in the secession crisis. Disowned by a majority of his party and repudiated by the recent national election, Buchanan could have salvaged his leadership only by decisive action. With his cabinet deeply divided, such a response from the indecisive chief executive was impossible. Instead, he destroyed whatever credibility he had left by adopting the constitutional position that secession was illegal but he had no power to coerce a state.[43] He left it to Congress to decide whether new legislation was required to deal with secession. Only Congress, he insisted, could "authorize the employment of military

OLD MOTHER BUCHANAN AT WHEATLAND.

Cartoon during the secession crisis depicts Buchanan as a feckless granny, unable to cope with the secession of South Carolina and its ramifications. Courtesy of Dickinson College.

force." The president had "no authority to decided what shall be the relations between the Federal Government and South Carolina." In his memoirs, he emphasized the Congress had refused to pass any legislation to call up volunteers or employ force, but the truth was Buchanan did not want such legislation enacted.[44] Buchanan's goal was simply to hang on for the remainder of his term, refuse to recognize secession, and turn the problem over to Lincoln. "It was his policy to preserve the peace if possible," Secretary of War Joseph Holt explained, "and hand over the Government intact to his sucessor."[45]

Because of his hesitant response to secession, false charges of the president's complicity in disunion and treason soon began to circulate. Buchanan found himself virtually without political support: Republicans dismissed him as a weakling and a coward and called for his impeachment, Douglas Democrats wanted nothing to do with him, and his Southern allies quickly deserted him, leaving him a bitter and broken man. According to one supporter, the harried president was "execrated now by four-fifths of the people of all parties."[46] In this situation, Congress went out of its way to affirm publicly its lack of confidence in the chief executive, routinely voting down various laws to deal with the crisis and refusing to consider his appointments to fill federal vacancies caused by the resignation of secessionists.

Lincoln also found Congress a trial. Once a senator came to the White House and launched into a vituperative denunciation of the president and his policies and ended with the warning, "Sir you are within one mile of Hell!" To which a smiling Lincoln replied, "Yes, . . . it is just one mile to the Capitol!"[47] Determined to respond vigorously and conduct the war according to policies he set, he refused to allow himself to be hamstrung by the lack of congressional authorization, and he had no illusions about the role of Congress in waging the war. With the outbreak of hostilities, he called Congress into special session to meet on 4 July, thereby giving himself a free hand for more than two months. Lincoln took full advantage of this period, taking a series of steps by executive edict that clearly exceeded his legal authority. Lincoln felt he had to act decisively, which was true, but it is clear he also did not want any interference by Congress. When Congress convened, it had little choice but to ratify Lincoln's actions after the fact. Indeed, it was not just coincidence that Lincoln's most decisive assertions of presidential power normally occurred when Congress was not in session.[48]

Still, Lincoln's relations with the legislative branch never descended to the level of the Buchanan years. This more harmonious relationship reflected in part the fact that Lincoln was much more tactful and flexible in his approach. As a minority president and the Republicans' first chief executive, Lincoln was also more sensitive about maintaining party unity. He shrewdly steered a middle ground between the conservatives and Radicals in his party, satisfying neither fully but keeping both united in their opposition to the Democrats. Had he lived, he would have reached some accommodation with his party critics over the question of Reconstruction. Relations between the president and Congress no doubt would have been strained at times, but they never would have reached the paralysis of the final months of Buchanan's administration, or during the presidency of Lincoln's successor, Andrew Johnson.

A striking example of Lincoln's astuteness and his ability to outmaneuver his congressional critics was the cabinet crisis in December 1862. Egged on by Chase's allegations that Lincoln was controlled by Seward, who purportedly opposed a vigorous prosecution of the war, and that the rest of the cabinet was ignored, a committee of Republican senators came to the White House to demand a shake-up of the cabinet. Aware of the origins of this movement, Lincoln arranged for the delegation to meet with him in the presence of the entire cabinet except for Seward. With his cabinet colleagues as witnesses, Chase was forced to declare that the cabinet was in basic agreement on war policy, thus directly contradicting what he had been telling members of Congress privately. Seward had already submitted his resignation, and the next day an embarrassed Chase hesitantly offered his. Drawing on his backwoods heritage, Lincoln explained, "Now I can ride; I have got a pumpkin in each end of my bag."[49] He rejected both resignations, thereby stymieing the Congressional movement to reorganize the cabinet. The crisis ended with Lincoln in firm control of his cabinet and free of congressional dictation. As Leonard Swett, who had observed Lincoln closely for many years in Illinois, remarked, "He handled and moved men remotely as we do pieces upon a chess-board."[50]

Contrast this outcome with Buchanan's famous interview with Stephen A. Douglas prior to the assembling of Congress in December 1857. Cognizant that the proslavery Lecompton Constitution threatened to annihilate the Democratic Party in the free states, Douglas urged Buchanan not to endorse the constitution, which represented the wishes of only a small minority of the residents of Kansas. Far from seeking some understanding with the Illinois senator, Buchanan threatened to end his political career if he did not go along with the administration on this question. He not too subtly reminded Douglas that those Democrats who opposed Andrew Jackson on the bank issue had been destroyed. Unwilling to be read out of the Democratic Party by a man he considered his inferior, Douglas as he reached for his hat defiantly shot back, "Mr. President, I wish you to remember that General Jackson is dead."[51] The situation required more than false bravado and meaningless threats on the president's part; its outcome amply demonstrated the inadequacy of Buchanan's leadership.

Neither Lincoln nor Buchanan had extensive dealings with the judiciary, but a famous example from each man's presidency highlights their different approaches to presidential leadership. Buchanan's most celebrated dealing with the Supreme Court occurred in the Dred Scott case, when he surreptitiously intervened to get Justice Robert Grier of Pennsylvania to join the Southern majority in issuing a broad decision. Privately informed of the Court's pending decision, Buchanan announced in his inaugural address that the Court would soon render its decision. "To their decision, in

common with all good citizens," he proclaimed with affected igno-
rance, "I shall cheerfully submit, whatever this may be."[52]

Buchanan's intervention was improper, but the real failure of his
leadership on this matter was not that he exceeded his authority--
so did Lincoln on many more occasions, with not nearly as much
damage to his reputation—but the ends to which he used this
power. Buchanan naively believed that a Supreme Court decision
upholding the extreme Southern position on the legality of slavery
in the territories would settle the sectional conflict. Instead, the
Dred Scott decision was one of the most ill-conceived decisions
the Court has ever rendered in its long history, for which Buchanan
bears partial responsibility. It angered the North, intensified the
sectional conflict, weakened popular sovereignty, which was the
only remaining moderate solution to the problem of slavery expansion, and gave nothing of substance to the South. It neither
strengthened slavery nor enhanced Southern power. Moreover, it
reinforced the growing Northern belief in a slave power; if Buchanan's role in the decision had been known at the time, the
outcry in the North would have been even stronger.[53]

During the Civil War, the Supreme Court generally refrained
from interfering with the Lincoln administration's war policies. Its
celebrated decision in *ex parte Milligan,* striking down military
trials of civilians accused of antiwar activities, was not rendered
until after the war was over. The most famous clash between Lincoln and the judiciary occurred at the beginning of the war, when
Chief Justice Roger Taney, sitting on the circuit court, ruled in the
case of *ex parte Merryman* that Lincoln's suspension of the writ
of habeas corpus in Maryland was illegal. Lincoln did not shrink
from this challenge or hide behind subordinates. Convinced that
this was an executive power and that it was necessary to prevent
disloyal activity, he instructed his military commanders to disregard Taney's ruling and reaffirmed his expansive view of presidential powers in wartime. Lincoln's action was an ominous precedent
that could be used by future presidents far less well intentioned
and far more abusive of presidential power than he. But Northern
public opinion was generally supportive of his action because of
the extraordinary nature of the threat to the government.[54]

Another major source of presidential power is public opinion.
As the only member of the federal government elected by all the
people, the president is in a unique position to shape and mobilize
public opinion; his relationship with the people can provide a great
reservoir of power in any clash with the legislative branch. Buchanan proved hopelessly inept at this aspect of governing, dis-

playing a lack of ability to read the public mood and no talent to rouse popular support. Lincoln, in contrast, was a master in these matters.

Adept at using his voluminous private correspondence to gain support, Buchanan had never displayed particular talent as a public speaker or literary stylist. He had received a good education and was an extremely successful lawyer, yet he lacked the ability to elevate his thought out of the ordinary channels. He produced no ringing documents defending his administration's policies, and indeed, in four decades of public service, never coined a memorable phrase or voiced a memorable statement. His failures in this regard were apparent in the struggle over the Lecompton Constitution, and again in the secession crisis. Buchanan was woefully incapable of mobilizing Northern public opinion behind his policy on secession. If ever a president needed to stake out a clear and forceful position and rally public sentiment behind it, it was then; if ever a president failed utterly, it was then.

While he was largely self-educated, having by his calculation less than a year of formal schooling, Abraham Lincoln was an accomplished literary craftsman. He was also a superb debater, well versed in appealing to the ordinary folk. His speeches and writings possess an eloquence few presidents have ever approached. Time and again during the war, in his public documents, he displayed unrivaled ability to rouse the popular emotions by placing the struggle in its broadest context and rooting it in the most basic American values. In his special message to Congress on 4 July 1861, he described the war as part of the larger struggle for democracy and opportunity throughout the world: "This is essentially a People's contest. On the side of the Union, it is a struggle for maintaining in the world, that form, and substance of government, whose leading object is, to elevate the condition of men—to lift artificial weights from all shoulders—to clear the paths of laudable pursuit for all—to afford all, an unfettered start, and a fair chance, in the race of life."[55] His letter to James Conkling on emancipation and to Erastus Corning on civil liberties demonstrated his fundamental decency and good sense. The Gettysburg Address, the most famous presidential speech ever delivered, concisely stated the meaning of the war, and the Second Inaugural, given on the eve of victory, was remarkable for its humility and its compassion. Lincoln's ability to reach out to the common people of his society, from whose ranks he had risen, was displayed throughout his presidency, and provided him a solid base of popular support. In fact, Lincoln was probably more popular with the people than he was with the leaders of his party, as his easy renomination in 1864 demonstrated.

In every regard, Lincoln proved a superior president to Buchanan. He was an extraordinary politician, able to work with men of diverse viewpoints on a broad range of issues. He displayed an uncanny feel for public opinion and was unrivaled in his ability to shape and influence popular feelings. He had the ability to assess character, to weigh alternatives, and to clearly perceive the consequences of his actions. He did not blind himself to political reality or surround himself with individuals who thought like he did on all matters. While he preferred harmony to conflict, he did not believe it was possible to establish an effective administration on the ideal of consensus.

Like other strong presidents, Lincoln took an expansive view of his powers. Whether he would have been as active a president had the war not occurred is doubtful since he grounded his claim of special powers on his role as a commander in chief. The powers Lincoln exercised were breathtaking in their extent and significance. He spent money without congressional authorization, suspended the writ of habeas corpus throughout the Union, authorized military trials of civilians, proclaimed a blockade, initiated a program of reconstruction, dictated the terms for peace, and abolished slavery by presidential edict. He walked the thin line between failing to respond vigorously and abuse of power with remarkable deftness. Exercising unprecedented power, he was neither corrupted by it nor viewed it as an end in itself.

After a number of disappointments, his domestic and military policies finally bore fruit and the Union prevailed in the war. The Union was saved and slavery abolished, two accomplishments that have enshrined Lincoln in the national memory. Lincoln was fortunate that the military tide turned before the 1864 election. Had he left office in 1862 or even 1863, historians undoubtedly would rank him a failure.

Buchanan enjoyed no similar success. A useful and talented subordinate when guided by a strong hand like James K. Polk's, Buchanan was far less effective as the leader of a national administration. Buchanan displayed three fundamental shortcomings as president. First, he disliked conflict and confrontation, and thus selected his cabinet on grounds of personal compatibility rather than ability, usefulness, or representativeness. Second, he sought to rule by consensus in a period when party consensus was impossible. His conception of the administration, in which the president was the first among equals, was a severe handicap to devising effec-

OUR NATIONAL BIRD AS IT APPEARED WHEN HANDED TO JAMES BUCHANAN MARCH 4 1857.

THE IDENTICAL BIRD AS IT APPEARED A.D. 1861.

Satirical cartoon about the state of the Union that suggests Buchanan utterly failed in his cardinal responsibility as president of the United States. Courtesy of Dickinson College.

tive policies, a shortcoming exacerbated by his unwillingness to consider dissenting points of view. Effective presidents must handle conflict and confront divergent viewpoints. As his popularity dropped, Buchanan psychologically withdrew into his narrow circle of advisers and cronies; he wailed bitterly over the desertion of some of his closest friends and political allies.

But Buchanan was hurt most of all by the policies he followed. He manifested little comprehension of public opinion, lacked the ability to shape and mobilize popular sentiment, and repeatedly failed to anticipate correctly the consequences of his actions. Buchanan's obliviousness to political reality is difficult to explain, primarily because it was so unrelenting. But beyond his indecisive nature, his close personal friendships with Southerners, his moral indifference to the institution of slavery, and his emotional dependence on his friends, several other factors can be cited. He came from Pennsylvania, a state where antislavery sentiment was weak, which hindered his developing a sound understanding of the antislavery movement. Instead, he persisted in lumping abolitionism with other, more moderate forms of antislavery sentiment. This basic misperception was compounded by his absence from the country in 1854 and 1855; as a result, he had no appreciation of the depth of feeling involved in the protest against the Kansas-Nebraska Act or any comprehension of the nature of the Republican Party and the reasons for its success. Furthermore, he had not been a candidate for a popularly elected office for a quarter of a century when he ran for president, a fact that lessened his understanding of public opinion and the electorate. He owed his political success much more to his ties to party leaders than to any popular base of support. In many ways, by the time he became president at the age of sixty-five, he was a political anachronism. He looked back to an earlier era of American politics, when antislavery was disreputable, sectionalism was condemned, and the Northern majority was ready to make concessions to the South for the sake of the Union. He never appreciated how much the political situation had changed during the past few years.

While Buchanan adhered to an unremarkable view of the powers of his office, his failure stemmed less from his conception of presidential power than from his blindness to political reality. As president, he demonstrated cardinal shortcomings as a political leader. He was unable to judge character and to assess accurately men's usefulness. Remarkably sensitive to Southern fears, he betrayed not the slightest comprehension of Northern public opinion and lacked the ability to shape and mobilize opinion in either section. And finally, he lacked the ability to clearly weigh the consequences of actions and policies.

The result of these shortcomings was a series of political disasters, the cumulative effect of which was to wreck his party and his presidency. Few presidents have done more in four years to bring the opposing party to power. Aided by the proslavery Dred Scott decision, in which Buchanan played a direct and improper role; the unprecedented level of graft and corruption that marred his term in office; the administration's economic policies, which alienated important groups in the North; the Lecompton struggle, which inflamed sectional passions and reinvigorated the slavery-extension issue; and the split of the Democratic Party, which Buchanan's policies precipitated and his small-mindedness continued, the Republican Party carried the 1860 presidential election. This was precisely the result he had pledged to prevent on taking office. When he left Washington and returned to Wheatland in March 1861, the dark clouds of the sectional storm had gathered, and civil war was only a few weeks away.

Notes

1. Roy Basler et al., *The Collected Works of Abraham Lincoln*, 8 vols. (New Brunswick, N.J.: Rutgers University Press, 1953), 2:89.

2. Quoted in Philip S. Klein, *President James Buchanan: A Biography* (University Park: Pennsylvania State University Press, 1962), 402.

3. Robert K. Murray and Tim H. Blessing, "The Presidential Performance Study: A Progress Report," *Journal of American History* 70 (December 1983): 535–55. Earlier, more limited polls reached the same conclusion.

4. Roy F. Nichols, *The Disruption of American Democracy* (New York: Macmillan, 1948), 2–50.

5. Quoted in Elbert B. Smith, *The Presidency of James Buchanan* (Lawrence: University Press of Kansas, 1975), 17.

6. William B. Hesseltine, ed., *Three against Lincoln: Murat Halstead Reports the Caucuses of 1860* (Baton Rouge: Louisiana State University Press, 1960), 141–77; Don E. Fehrenbacher, "The Republican Decision at Chicago," in Norman A. Graebner, ed., *Politics and the Crisis of 1860* (Urbana: University of Illinois Press, 1961), 32–60; Kenneth M. Stampp, "The Republican National Convention of 1860," in *The Imperiled Union: Essays on the Background of the Civil War* (New York: Oxford University Press, 1980) 136–62.

7. William E. Gienapp, *The Origins of the Republican Party, 1852–1856* (New York: Oxford University Press, 1985), 375–448.

8. Quoted in Smith, *Presidency of Buchanan,* 17.

9. Quoted in David H. Donald, ed., *Inside Lincoln's Cabinet: The Civil War Diaries of Salmon P. Chase* (New York: Longman's, Green, 1954), 16–17.

10. Basler et al., *Collected Works,* 4:316.

11. David H. Donald, *Lincoln Reconsidered,* (2d ed. New York: Knopf, 1972), 201.

12. Ibid., 16; Allan Nevins, *The Statesmanship in the Civil War,* (rev. ed. New York: Collier, 1962), 121.

13. Donald, *Inside Lincoln's Cabinet,* 16.

14. Nichols, *Disruption,* 52–93.

15. Robert W. Johannsen, *Stephen A. Douglas* (New York: Oxford University Press, 1973), 551–52.

16. Quoted in Allan Nevins, *The Emergence of Lincoln,* 2 vols. (New York: 1950), 1:246.

17. Smith, *Presidency of Buchanan,* 19–22.

18. Klein, *Buchanan,* 380–81, 387 (quotation on p. 381).

19. Leonard Swett quoted in Paul Angle, ed., *Herndon's Life of Lincoln* (Cleveland, Ohio: World Publishing, 1942), 431.

20. Basler et al., *Collected Works,* 2:273.

21. David M. Potter, *The Impending Crisis, 1848–1861* (New York: Harper and Row, 1976), 195–96; Howard L. Wilson, "President Buchanan's Proposed Intervention in Mexico," *American Historical Review* 5 (July 1900): 687–701.

22. Quoted in Smith, *Presidency of Buchanan,* 65.

23. Glyndon G. Van Deusen, *William Henry Seward* (New York: Oxford University Press, 1967), 297–98, 337–40, 378.

24. Tyler Dennett, ed., *Lincoln and the Civil War in the Diaries and Letters of John Hay* (New York: Dodd, Mead, 1939), 176, 167.

25. T. Harry Williams, *Lincoln and His Generals* (New York: Knopf, 1952); Joseph T. Glatthaar, *Partners in Command: The Relationships between Leaders in the Civil War* (New York: Free Press, 1994), 51–94, 135–62, 191–224.

26. Quoted in Donald, *Lincoln Reconsidered,* 66.

27. Ibid., 65.

28. Johannsen, *Douglas,* 602, 624–29, 646–55, 678–85; Nichols, *Disruption,* 210–15.

29. Harry J. Carman and Reinhard H. Luthin, *Lincoln and the Patronage* (New York: Columbia University Press, 1943), 229–67; Jean H. Baker, *The Politics of Continuity: Maryland Political Parties from 1858 to 1870* (Baltimore: Johns Hopkins University Press, 1973), 91–96, 101–2, 142–45.

30. See Kenneth M. Stampp, *America in 1857: A Nation on the Brink* (New York: Oxford University Press, 1990), 141–81, 266–322; Nichols, *Disruption*, 96–131, 153–76.

31. Basler et al., *Collected Works*, 7:435, 451; James M. McPherson, *Battle Cry of Freedom: The Civil War Era* (New York: Oxford University Press, 1988), 760–72; Edward Chase Kirkland, *The Peacemakers of 1864* (reprinted ed. New York: AMS Press, 1969), 85–96.

32. Nichols, *Disruption*, 294–309; Nevins, *Emergence of Lincoln*, 2:203–28.

33. For examples of the abuse Buchanan received in the Northern press, see Kenneth M. Stampp, *And the War Came: The North and the Secession Crisis, 1860–1861* (Baton Rouge: Louisiana State University Press, 1950), 53–54, 70–71, 95.

34. Quoted in Dennett, *Lincoln in the Civil War*, 108.

35. William Frank Zornow, *Lincoln and the Party Divided* (Norman: University of Oklahoma Press, 1954), 3–104.

36. Basler et al., *Collected Works*, 4:214.

37. Quoted in Frederick Blue, *Salmon P. Chase: A Life in Politics* (Kent, Ohio: Kent State University Press, 1987), 171.

38. Quoted in Dennett, *Lincoln in the Civil War*, 204.

39. James G. Randall, *Constitutional Problems under Lincoln,* (rev. ed. Urbana: University of Illinois Press, 1951), 88, 276–80.

40. James G. Randall, *Lincoln the President*, 4 vols. (New York: Dodd, Mead, 1945–55), 4:307–13 (vol. 4 completed by Richard N. Current); Allan G. Bogue, *The Congressman's Civil War* (New York: Cambridge University Press, 1989), 49–50, 161. The administration's not entirely savory lobbying efforts are detailed in John H. Cox and LaWanda Cox, *Politics, Principle, and Prejudice, 1865–1866: Dilemma of Reconstruction America* (New York: Cambridge University Press, 1963), 2–30.

41. Klein, *Buchanan*, 346–47; Nevins, *Emergence of Lincoln*, 1:450, 2:191, 194–95.

42. Quoted in Potter, *Impending Crisis*, 323.

43. Stampp, *And the War Came*, 53–57, 60.

44. Ibid., 81, 104, 111; Potter, *Impending Crisis*, 521–22n.

45. Quoted in Stampp, *And the War Came*, 103.

46. Sidney Webster quoted in ibid., 73.

47. Randall, *Lincoln the President*, 3:132.

48. Ibid., 3:140.

49. Quoted in John Nicolay and John Hay, *Abraham Lincoln*, 10 vols. (New York: The Century Company, 1886–90), 6:271.

50. Quoted in Donald, *Lincoln Reconsidered*, 67.

51. Quoted in Nevins, *Emergence of Lincoln*, 253.

52. Quoted in Potter, *Impending Crisis*, 287.

53. Ibid., 273–74, 287–89.

54. Harold M. Hyman, *A More Perfect Union: The Impact of the Civil War and Reconstruction on the Constitution* (New York: Knopf, 1973), 81–99.

55. Basler et al., *Collected Works*, 4:438.

James Buchanan, the Neutrality Laws, and American Invasions of Nicaragua

ROBERT E. MAY

WHEN IT COMES TO RATINGS OF AMERICAN CHIEF EXECUTIVES, President James Buchanan occupies a lowly rank. Though there are dissenting voices such as that of biographer Philip Shriver Klein,[1] historians long ago reached a consensus that Pennsylvania's only president did his country a terrible disservice by promoting policies that aggravated the sectional crisis of the 1850s: he imposed on the Supreme Court for the Dred Scott decision and he tried to impose the Lecompton Constitution on a free-soil majority in Kansas. His patronage mistakes and inability to suppress corruption within his cabinet, moreover, facilitated the Republican Party triumph that triggered Southern secession. Once faced with disunion, the conventional wisdom has it, Buchanan ducked responsibility by an unmanly dumping of the mess onto the laps of his country's congressmen and, ultimately, his successor in the White House.[2] Buchanan, we are reminded ad infinitum, was no General Jackson!

Historians, as Robert K. Murray and Tim H. Blessing recognize in their study of presidential ratings, are far less likely to consider foreign policies crucial when assessing nineteenth-century presidents than in evaluations of their twentieth-century successors: world power status following the Spanish-American War heightened the salience of diplomatic concerns and meant that American decision making would have increased impact on other nations. Certainly this observation applies to James Buchanan's administration, given its relationship to the seminal domestic event in American history—the Civil War. Unlike many successors, and even some earlier chief executives such as James Monroe and James K. Polk, whose names are connected with foreign affairs, Buchanan is remembered primarily for his domestic policies. Nevertheless, Buchanan's conduct of diplomacy is not, and has not been, irrelevant to assessments of his presidential record. Today, I would like you to ponder this "other" side of the Buchanan administration.

123

Does analysis of Buchanan's diplomacy contribute to his poor standing? Or does consideration of Buchanan's foreign policies—and they were *his* policies since scholars agree that he thoroughly dominated Secretary of State Lewis Cass—revise the stereotype of a catastrophic presidency?[3]

This is not an easy question to answer. Some modern scholars echo Louis Martin Sears's now ancient pronouncement that Buchanan's diplomacy proved "a moderate success." Philip Klein's biography praises the president's handling of U.S. relations with Great Britain. He lauds Buchanan's success in persuading the British to give up their Bay Islands colony and Mosquito Protectorate in Central America and to renounce the right to search U.S. vessels on the high seas. He also credits Buchanan with a miscellany of other diplomatic triumphs, including a satisfactory resolution of U.S. claims against Paraguay, the protection of naturalized Americans traveling abroad against conscription into the French army, and treaties that facilitated U.S. trade with three continents. Consequent journal articles by Foster M. Farley and Robert Ralph Davis, Jr., confirmed Klein's assessment. Farley commended Buchanan for resisting Anglo-French blandishments to involve the United States in military campaigns in China. Davis offered statistical evidence that Buchanan took energetic and effective action against the African slave trade.[4] However, reviews of Buchanan's foreign relations are mixed. Blistering indictments in Elbert B. Smith's *The Presidency of James Buchanan* and other works help fetter Buchanan in the presidential cellar.

Though scholars fault the president's diplomacy on several counts, their most consistent charge is that Buchanan's foreign policies mirrored his flawed domestic course. That is, just as slave-power managers manipulated his domestic policy decisions, so they controlled his conduct of foreign relations. The same president bent on forcing slavery on Kansas tried to impose a slave Cuba on the United States. The same president who challenged ethical boundaries by contacting Supreme Court justices prior to the Dred Scott decision abused federal statutes and international law by tolerating Southern filibusters against Central America. Smith notes that Buchanan would have spent much more to purchase Cuba from Spain than Alaska—which would have been free territory—from Russia. He also contends that Buchanan showed far more determination to make British ships leave suspected American slavers alone than to prevent the hated trade itself.[5]

But is it possible that Buchanan's critics have too hastily pro-

THE "OSTEND DOCTRINE".
Practical Democrats carrying out the principle.

Buchanan gained the presidency partly because of his prior advocacy of U.S. acquisition of Cuba, by force if necessary, in the Ostend manifesto—a paper which he co-authored with two other U.S. diplomats while he was U.S. minister to Great Britain. In this cartoon, Buchanan antagonists satirized his position by suggesting that Buchanan had virtually legitimized robbery in the manifesto. Courtesy of Dickinson College.

jected the president's domestic policies upon his conduct of foreign relations? I would like to suggest that this indeed is the case.

To demonstrate my point, I have examined one of the charges raised against Buchanan's diplomacy—that his administration favored and even abetted American filibustering expeditions, especially Southern filibusters against Nicaragua. William Walker, a Tennessean, conquered Nicaragua in 1855–56 and reestablished slavery there, before being evicted in the early months of the Buchanan administration. Through virtually the entire Buchanan presidency, Walker mounted new expeditions to reconquer Nicaragua. Several of these eluded U.S. authorities and reached Central America. Finally, Walker was executed in Honduras in September 1860.

Buchanan spent many hours pondering diplomatic initiatives in his library at Wheatland. *Leslie's Illustrated Magazine* **offered its readers a glimpse of the environment in which the president worked. Courtesy of Dickinson College.**

President Buchanan never endorsed filibustering publicly. His third annual message complained that Mexican authorities had peremptorily executed filibuster Henry Crabb and his cohorts for their invasion of Sonora without benefit of a jury trial. But this hardly meant that the president approved of Crabb's endeavor. Rather, Buchanan's messages to Congress and a 30 October 1858 proclamation to the American people, pronounced *against* filibustering with striking consistency. Buchanan noted that filibuster invasions threatened U.S. access to its own Pacific coast because they interrupted transit routes across Panama and Nicaragua. He suggested that if filibusters refrained from hostile acts, Americans could dominate Central America anyway through peaceful emigration. From the president's perspective, filibustering was immoral. He told the nation that its practitioners were "lawless" men who committed "ravages" against foreign people and violations of international law, which brought America's "character as a nation" into doubt and eroded U.S. influence over Latin republics. Warning that filibusters were usurping Congress's war-making powers, Buchanan opined that filibustering "violates the principles of Christianity, morality, and humanity, held sacred by all civilized nations and by none more than by people of the United States. Disguise it as we may, such a military expedition is an invitation to reckless . . . men to enlist under the banner of any adventurer to rob, plunder, and murder the unoffending citizens of neighboring states, who have never done them harm." As late as his fourth annual message, Buchanan was suggesting that it "ought to be the prayer of every Christian and patriot" that filibusters never again depart American shores. Still, expedition after expedition departed U.S. territory during the Buchanan presidency. Perhaps the president's critique was designed as meaningless rhetoric. British diplomat Charles Wyke informed his government, "President Buchanan by word of mouth always condemned Walker's Expeditions, and yet his Government imbued with Southern ideas, took no effectual means to prevent Vessel after Vessel crowded with armed men from leaving their Ports." Pursuing such logic, one scholar contends, "William Walker was proslave, and in dealing with him Buchanan stayed barely within the boundaries of propriety."[6]

It is hardly surprising that historians have taken Buchanan to task for accommodating filibusters, since many of his contemporaries, especially antislavery Republicans, voiced identical suspicions. John Bigelow wrote to William Cullen Bryant that it was "well understood that the Genl's expedition was countenanced in every practicable way by the administration," and a New York *Times* reporter thought there "every reason to believe that the administration favors Walker." "I have no doubt in my mind of the collusion of the administration with the Filibusters," a U.S. Army officer concluded in a private letter mailed from Fort Leavenworth in the Kansas Territory. Latin American and European observers, if anything, were even more convinced than Republicans of Buchanan's duplicity. America's minister to France felt compelled to inform Cass that "ill-natured suspicions" were circulating in Paris that Walker "has the sympathies of the Government." The U.S. commissioner to distant Paraguay, similarly, reported to the Department of State that Paraguay's secretary of foreign relations seemed "agreeably surprized" [*sic*] to hear that "the *Filibusteros* were not in power" in Washington. Convictions of a Buchanan-filibuster link waxed strongest in the republics of Central America. In September 1858, the presidents of Nicaragua and Costa Rica issued a document that became known as the "Rivas Manifesto." It charged that Walker, under the "patronage" of the U.S. government, intended to conquer all Central America, and called upon England, France, and Sardinia to ensure Central America's sovereignty.[7] However, perceptions sometimes belie reality. And the accusation of Buchanan's complicity in filibustering does not withstand close scrutiny of the documentary record.

What are the specific charges in the case of President James Buchanan, filibuster accomplice? Most revolve around one incident—Buchanan's reaction when U.S. naval officer Hiram Paulding quashed William Walker's first reinvasion of Nicaragua. Walker and some two hundred men departed Mobile, Alabama, 14 November 1857, on the steamer *Fashion.* The ship landed "Colonel" Frank Anderson and his company of about fifty men at the mouth of the Colorado river, a southern branch of Nicaragua's San Juan River, before proceeding northward up Nicaragua's eastern coast to Punta Arenas, a spit of land opposite San Juan del Norte—then also known as Greytown. Walker and the remaining filibusters disembarked on the morning of 25 November and established a camp on shore. Paulding, commander of the U.S. Home Squadron, arrived off Punta Arenas on 6 December. Two days later, the commodore ordered marines and sailors ashore to deploy in line of battle around Walker's camp, and trained his squadron's guns on the encircled filibusters. When Paulding demanded Walker's surrender, the filibuster had to comply. Paulding permitted Walker to return to the United States aboard a mail steamer, on the understanding that Walker would turn himself in to the U.S. marshal at New York City when the ship arrived at that port. With the exception of a handful of men who escaped, Paulding sent the filibusters who surrendered with Walker to Norfolk, Virginia, aboard the sloop of war *Saratoga,* a vessel just recalled from its Central American station. On 23–24 December, U.S. Navy Captain Joshua R. Sands took Anderson and forty-four followers into custody. Anderson had succeeded in seizing several vessels, ascending the San Juan, and capturing a fort, before learning of Walker's surrender and deciding that it would be futile to continue his campaign. In January, Paulding personally brought Anderson's party to Key West aboard his flagship *Wabash,* and then turned over his captives to the U.S. marshal on assignment there. While at Key West, Paulding received orders from the Department of the Navy to proceed to New York City. Paulding arrived at New York in February. By that time, Congress and the nation's press had already spent several weeks in heated debate over whether he had done the right thing. For a while filibustering crowded Kansas off the national agenda.[8]

Though Paulding's seizure of Walker earned so much goodwill from Nicaragua that the Nicaraguan government rushed to thank him officially and later offered him a sword and tract of land in

William Walker, filibuster who sought glory in Nicaragua. Courtesy of Robert May.

token of its appreciation (and also sent an official message of thanks to the U.S. Department of State),[9] Buchanan released Walker from federal custody in late December[10] and scolded Paulding when he addressed the incident that January in a message to the Senate. The president acknowledged that Nicaragua had benefited from Paulding's intervention, and described the commodore as a "gallant officer" who had acted from "pure and patriotic motives and in the sincere conviction that he was promoting the interest and vindicating the honor of his country." However, Buchanan sandwiched these plaudits between censures of Paulding for committing a hostile act on foreign soil. By exceeding his instructions and engaging in an act of war in Nicaraguan territory, the president declared, Paulding had committed a "grave error." "Obedience to law and conformity to instructions are the best and safest guides for all officers, civil and military," Buchanan lectured the Senate and, implicitly, the absent Paulding, "and when they transcend these limits and act upon their own personal responsibility evil consequences almost inevitably follow." Buchanan explained that he had released Walker because his seizure had been illegal. The next month, Buchanan's secretary of the navy, Isaac Toucey, detached Paulding from command of the Home Squadron. When Toucey issued orders to Paulding's successor, Commodore James M. McIntosh, they included admonitions that his vessels restrict endeavors against ongoing filibusters to interception at sea.[11]

Buchanan's chiding Paulding, the removal of Paulding from command of the Home Squadron, and the orders to McIntosh alone might have condemned Pennsylvania's only president to filibustering infamy. Diplomatic historian Richard W. Van Alstyne derided the president's instructions to McIntosh as "a study in Executive humor." However, it is also known that Walker informed Paulding prior to his surrender that the president had been "fully advised of my intention to return to Nicaragua"—which implied prior consent. Walker further drove the nail into Buchanan's historiographical coffin by charging, following his release from custody, that the administration turned against him because he had rejected its last-minute request that he divert operations from Nicaragua to Mexico.[12] At any rate, many scholars believe that the Paulding affair provides ample proof either that Buchanan supported filibustering or that he was too weak to take a consistent position against it. Some of Buchanan's critics suggest that his policies in the Paulding affair constituted a reluctant concession to pressure from the slave states. Others agree with Elbert Smith that Buchanan operated from proslavery instincts to begin with.[13]

But was Buchanan's antifilibustering rhetoric as insincere as such accounts would lead us to infer? By the time Buchanan took his presidential oath, he had already compiled a two-decades-long antifilibustering résumé. While U.S. senator, he had called for prosecution of Americans who filibustered into Mexican Texas and British Canada. While secretary of state, he had opposed John C. Frémont's semiofficial intrusion into Mexican California prior to the Mexican War, and then taken action against American filibuster plots involving Mexico, Venezuela, and Cuba as that conflict drew to its close. In fact, he even passed on to the Spanish government information given in confidence to the Polk administration about an incipient filibustering expedition that was being timed to coincide with a revolutionary uprising in Cuba. This information allowed Spanish authorities to crush the revolt in its preliminary phase. While minister to Great Britain, he had lodged an official complaint against charges in the English press that the American government secretly encouraged filibustering.[14]

It is my contention: (1) that Buchanan made a conscientious effort to stop Walker's November 1857 invasion of Nicaragua; (2) that Buchanan's message to the Senate faulting Paulding derived from the president's comprehension of constitutional and international law and historical precedent rather than from blighted hopes for Walker's success; (3) that Buchanan did not relieve Paulding from command as punishment for his interference with Walker; (4) that Buchanan's course in the Paulding affair, rather than appeasing proslavery interests, actually diminished his support in the South; and (5) that Buchanan continued to resist filibustering, with modest success, for the balance of his term.

Long before Walker's *Fashion* steamed out of Mobile Bay bound for Nicaragua, Buchanan and his cabinet knew that a new expedition was in the works. Walker announced publicly, and apparently asserted directly to Buchanan during an interview at the White House on 12 June, that he still considered himself Nicaragua's president. Throughout the summer and fall, the American press carried reports of Walker's preparations for the new strike. Information about Walker's intentions also reached the administration from its district attorneys, the diplomatic corps in Washington, and other sources. Representatives of Central American states fed news and rumors of Walker's doings to the Department of State, and solicited federal intervention against the filibusters.[15]

Rather than encourage Walker, Buchanan acted aggressively to ensure that the filibuster never departed American shores. On 18 September 1857, noting that he was acting under explicit instructions from the president, Secretary of State Cass sent a circular to nineteen U.S. attorneys, fourteen U.S. marshals, and eleven collectors of customs at points on or near the coast from Maine to Texas, alerting them to reports of pending filibuster expeditions and demanding that they "use all due diligence" and employ "all legitimate means" to prevent any infractions of the nation's principal antifilibustering legislation, the Neutrality Act of 1818. When it became evident that Walker had selected the New Orleans–Mobile area for his embarkation point, Cass rushed additional antifilibustering instructions to the appropriate officials. "Take all proper measures under the law and your instructions to arrest the parties to the expedition. If necessary, you are authorized to employ a steamer for this purpose, and to place on board the marshal with a sufficient *posse*," Cass telegraphed U.S. District Attorney Franklin H. Clack in New Orleans.[16]

Buchanan took nothing for granted. Rather than assume that the State Department's orders would stop Walker, he also put the U. S. Navy on alert and strengthened its forces in Central America. Should the filibusters manage to defy federal authorities in the nation's ports, Buchanan hoped that the navy would intercept them at sea. Noting that he was obeying a directive from the president, Secretary of the Navy Isaac Toucey sent a copy of the State Department's antifilibustering circular to Commodore Paulding (then on station at Aspinwall, New Granada), other U.S. naval officers in Central America, and the commandants of seven U.S. navy yards. Toucey told his recipients to regard the instructions contained in the circular as addressed to themselves. On 3 November, Toucey ordered Lieutenant John J. Almy, commanding the U.S. steamer *Fulton* at Washington, D.C., to proceed to Chiriqui, Panama, "at the earliest practicable moment" to reinforce Paulding's squadron. After Walker departed Mobile, the administration ordered Captain Joshua R. Sands to take his steam frigate *Susquehanna* from Key West to San Juan del Norte, also to join the Home Squadron.[17]

Works implying or asserting Buchanan's complicity in the *Fashion* expedition do the president's record a tremendous disservice. The State Department's orders caused federal authorities in New Orleans to arrest Walker on 10 November. It was federal district judge Theodore McCaleb, not the president, who set Walker's bond so low that the filibuster decided to jump bail, travel secretly to Mobile, and launch his expedition. (Perhaps McCaleb took into account that Walker had *not* jumped bail three years earlier in a

STEAMSHIPS--SHIPS.

Mobile and Nicaragua Steamship COMPANY.

The steamship FASHION Capt. Cough-lin, will ply as a regular packet between Mobile and St. Juan del Nicaragua. Her next departure from Mobile will take place between the 1st and 5th of December, next.

☞ Another Steamship will be added to the line in a short time. For further particulars apply to

JULIUS HESSEE & CO.

nov15

This advertisement, printed on the first page of the *Mobile Daily Register*, 25 November 1857, indicates: (1) that after landing in Nicaragua, William Walker intended to send his ship back to Mobile for reinforcements; and (2) that Walker virtually proclaimed his intentions to the press while presenting his ship as engaged in legitimate commerce. The Buchanan administration, acting on such information, took steps to guarantee that no reinforcements reached Walker from the United States. Courtesy of Robert May.

similar proceeding following the filibuster's expedition to Lower California.) Had Buchanan telegraphed McCaleb to increase Walker's bond, it would have constituted tampering with the judiciary—the very sin he has been accused of in relation to the Dred Scott case. It was federal officials at Mobile, not the president, who failed to detect Walker and munitions aboard the *Fashion* and provided it clearance to Nicaragua. There is absolutely no evidence of any implicit understanding between the Buchanan administration and its officials in the field that the president expected laxity in the enforcement of the Neutrality Act. Rather, those officials who allowed Walker to escape experienced the president's wrath. When Secretary of the Treasury Howell Cobb informed the collector of customs at Mobile that he had been "instructed by the President to say to you that your conduct in this matter does not meet his approval" and that he had better see to it that there be no recurrence of his error, the collector responded that he felt "keenly the rebuke," that he had lacked sufficient evidence to detain the *Fashion,* and that he had never encouraged filibustering by word or deed. If there had been any prior arrangements for laxity, no one clued in Lieutenant Almy. Putting in at Mobile on his way to Nicaragua in October, Almy was taken aback when the U.S. district attorney informed him that local public opinion believed that the administration "winked" at filibustering. "Being just from Washington," Almy reported to the Navy Department, "I stated that I knew that the government was utterly opposed to such expeditions, and had most decidedly set its face against them." Nor did anyone clue in Frederick Chatard, captain of the U.S. war sloop *Saratoga* and the naval officer on station off Punta Arenas at the moment when Walker's ship arrived on the scene. Thoroughly surprised when the *Fashion* slipped by the *Saratoga* and docked at Punta Arenas before he could react, Chatard sent two pathetic pleas for help to Paulding at Aspinwall, which reveal clearly both that Chatard knew that he was expected to stop Walker and that he felt humiliated by his impotence at the crucial moment:

> I so completely failed by stupidity in doing, at least, what I could have done, made the steamer heave to: but somehow or other I was spell bound, and so my officers seemed to be. . . . As we all stupidly gazed at her, expecting her to anchor any moment, not dreaming she would run up to Scott's wharf, but having a full head of steam on, she quickly arrived there—and, before my boat with a Lieut could get to her, her passengers had all landed, armed to the teeth, with revolvers, rifles and bowie knives, 150 in number—what could I do?[18]

Soon afterward, Paulding heeded Chatard's summons and rectified the lapse.

Had Buchanan desired Walker's success, he surely would not have done everything in his power to guarantee that no reinforcements would follow the filibuster to Nicaragua. Following Walker's departure from Mobile, Buchanan undercut his presidential pretensions by accepting the credentials of Antonio José de Irisarri, who had been designated minister to the United States by the government in power in Nicaragua. This move lessened the likelihood that naive Americans could be persuaded to enlist in Walker's service, thinking that the filibuster remained Nicaragua's legitimate president. The administration also sent a barrage of new antifilibustering instructions to federal officials in port cities and rushed another sloop of war to Central America under orders to prevent filibuster landings. Federal authorities paid heed to the president. In Mobile Bay, a U.S. revenue cutter intercepted a suspect vessel and subjected it to inspection. In port, U.S. officials denied clearance to Greytown for the schooner *Queen of the South,* a vessel belonging to the same proprietor as the *Fashion.* In Charleston, South Carolina, the U.S. district attorney put a suspected filibuster recruiter under arrest.[19]

Buchanan's critics have certainly misconstrued his response to Paulding's apprehension of Walker. Buchanan's January 1858 message to the Senate chastising the commodore hardly constituted an endorsement of filibustering. Rather, the president, an attorney by career who was well versed in international law, genuinely felt that Paulding had infringed an accepted axiom of the law of nations—that states lacked the power to arrest offenders against their laws within the territory of another nation, but that they could effect such arrests upon the high seas. Previous administrations, including George Washington's, had consistently taken the position that federal courts lacked jurisdiction over crimes committed by American citizens on foreign soil. In August 1848, long before William Walker invaded anything, Buchanan, then secretary of state, had answered a Mexican request for U.S. troops to repress an uprising in Yucatán by saying that the president "does not possess the power to employ the army beyond the limits of the United States, in aid of a foreign country, without the sanction of the Treaty or war making power." By the same logic, in 1857 Buchanan believed that he lacked the authority to inject U.S. naval forces into Nicaraguan territory, without either a treaty with Nicaragua authorizing such action or a congressional declaration of war against Nicaragua. Cass had signed a draft treaty with Irissari on

16 November (less than a week after his reception of the minister), by which Nicaragua and the United States would jointly guarantee the security of the Nicaraguan transit route, which included San Juan del Norte. However, this agreement had not been ratified at the time of Paulding's intervention and, in fact, it never went into effect.[20]

Historians would better comprehend Buchanan's position if they avoided the trap of assuming that his relief of Paulding signaled retribution for the commodore's apprehension of Walker. Prior to the incident, the navy had adopted a policy of limiting cruises to two years, and putting officers on paid leave following their cruises. Paulding had assumed command of the Home Squadron in November 1855, and he was relieved from command in 1858 because his cruise was up. Naval officers at the time understood what historians later overlooked. As commander Thornton A. Jenkins put it in a private letter, "McIntosh is Flag [Officer] of the Home Squadron. . . . Paulding's term is said to be over, under the new two year rule." Actually, the administration was rather pleased with the way that the whole thing worked out. In a March 1858 dispatch to the U.S. minister in Nicaragua, Cass expressed satisfaction with the bloodless removal of the filibusters, even though it had been effected "not in a manner strictly legal."[21]

Were Buchanan doing the South's bidding, he would have done what multitudes of Southerners, including some of the most prominent politicians in the region, demanded—that he rectify Paulding's lapse by sending Walker back to Nicaragua on a U.S. warship! Indeed, many Southerners expected Buchanan to do just that. The Charleston *Mercury*'s correspondent in Washington claimed that there was "no question" but that Buchanan would have Paulding court-martialed "and that WALKER and his men will be sent back at the expense of the Government." In the same vein, a Georgia Superior Court judge wrote Alexander H. Stephens that if "they do not send him back and make complete restitution they ought to be ashamed to look one another in the face." Walker himself anticipated that public pressure would force the administration to send him back. Instead, Buchanan sacrificed some of his Southern support by not only denying Walker government conveyance to Nicaragua, but allowing federal prosecutions of the filibuster to proceed unimpeded. That a New Orleans jury in May 1858 voted 10–2 to acquit Walker on charges of violating the Neutrality Act can hardly be attributed to the president. To many Southerners, Buchanan had proved that he supported slavery's containment rather than its expansion. Such charges hardly perturbed the presi-

JAMES BUCHANAN AND THE NEUTRALITY LAWS   137

dent, since he assumed that his *pro-Northern* antifilibustering policy would compensate for lost support in the South with new
approval above the Mason-Dixon line. Buchanan took great delight
that his most prominent rival had joined the chorus denouncing
Paulding. "Douglas has alienated . . . the North upon the Filibuster
question," he noted with satisfaction in a private letter.[22]

Buchanan continued to resist filibustering to the end of his presidential term. His October 1858 proclamation exposed the illegality
of Walker's recruiting subterfuges, and told the American people
that they had a civic responsibility to help federal officials enforce
the neutrality laws. Documents pertaining to the *Susan* expedition
of December 1858, part of yet another effort by Walker to reconquer Nicaragua, reveal Buchanan's cabinet members sending
a secret agent to Mobile to beef up law enforcement efforts there,
urging the collector of customs to deny clearance to suspicious
vessels rather than risk a recurrence of the previous year's events,
and promising to provide the collector with legal defense if the
filibusters carried through on their threat to sue the collector for
denying clearance to their vessel. While these precautions failed
to prevent the expedition's departure, they did force the filibusters
to use a much smaller vessel and to leave many men behind. The
ship crashed on a coral reef long before reaching Nicaragua
waters.[23]

Buchanan's cabinet never doubted that their antifilibustering efforts accorded with the chief executive's wishes. Secretary of the
Treasury Cobb wrote Buchanan in October 1859, after the administration denied clearance to a suspected filibuster vessel in New
York City and a U.S. marshal, backed by a company of U.S. artil-
lery, broke up an encampment of filibuster recruits below New
Orleans, "You will be gratified to learn that the Walker expedition
has in all probability been frustrated by the energy of our officers."
And Buchanan had cause for pride in the strides that his administration had made in its efforts against filibustering. By the time
Walker attempted his last invasion of Nicaragua in 1860, Americans had generally lost interest in his doings and no longer anticipated his success. Buchanan told Congress, on the eve of the Civil
War: "I . . . congratulate you upon the public sentiment which
now exists against the crime of setting on foot military expeditions
within the limits of the United States . . . to make war upon the
people of unoffending States with whom we are at peace. In this
respect a happy change has been effected since the commencement
of my Administration."[24]

To rescue Buchanan's record on filibustering, I must emphasize, is not to argue that he could not have done even more to prevent illegal expeditions. Buchanan's strict legalism caused him to blend antifilibustering instructions with strictures that federal civilian authorities and naval officers take care to avoid interference with ships and persons engaged in legitimate trade, travel, and emigration. For instance, Secretary Cobb told the federal collector at Mobile, within a single dispatch, both that he ought to avoid any "violation of the private rights of our citizens" when considering whether to clear a ship, and that he should deny clearance if "well grounded suspicions" existed. Such orders put a tremendous burden upon port authorities, district attorneys, and naval commanders, many of whom would have preferred far less discretionary responsibility and who lodged requests that the administration provide clearer directives. Flag Officer McIntosh even posed this hypothetical situation to the secretary of the navy in order to force the administration's hand:

> Suppose I was to meet a vessel at sea, from New-Orleans or Mobile, for instance, bound to Nicaragua, having a proper clearance from the Collector, list of passengers, and with all other papers regularly made out,—her passengers professing to be gone peaceably to reside in Nicaragua, or to the Pacific, but I find on board such persons as are well-known to be leading "filibusters["] or others, connected with former expeditions,—the men are found to bear arms, although no demonstration had been made during the passage to form them into companies . . . would the Collector's clearance and the other papers warrant my permitting the vessel to pass, or would the fact of these well-known "filibust[ers"] being on board warrant my sending her back[?] . . .

But there was never any doubt that the administration wanted filibustering stopped. McIntosh acknowledged having read Buchanan's antifilibustering proclamation and promised that he would commit his "best energies" toward complying with the president's wishes. He even took umbrage at reports that Nicaraguan officials were so unimpressed by the navy's interference with Walker that they were looking to Great Britain for protection. Undoubtedly a president more inclined toward bending the laws—say, an Abraham Lincoln—would have risked mistakes and ruled that *any* suspicions, rather than "well-grounded suspicions" only, warranted denials of clearance and interceptions at sea. That Buchanan refused to go that far hardly convicts him as an accomplice to filibustering.[25]

In the end, I think the mystery has less to do with Buchanan's stand on filibustering than why some historians missed the mark so widely when they addressed this question. For the portrait of a profilibuster president defies logic as well as evidence. Throughout his presidential term, Buchanan heard from countless informants that the filibusters jeopardized one of his primary diplomatic objectives—the reduction of Anglo-French power in the Central American Isthmus. As the U.S. minister to Guatemala and Honduras put it, Walker's expeditions gave British diplomats the opportunity to tell Central Americans that the Buchanan administration could not "restrain the filibustering spirit of the [American] masses, and that protection withdrawn by England from Central America, would leave it the prey of bucaneering swarms of marauding filibusters, who would descend from the seaboard of the United States, seize upon their Governments, lay waste their country, and desecrate their religion." During Buchanan's very first weeks in office, the U.S. minister to Mexico reported that Henry Crabb's pending filibuster would likely subvert a growing movement in Chihuahua and Sonora for annexation to the United States. Also in 1857, New Granada asked Great Britain and France to establish a protectorate over its territory as insurance against American filibusters. In 1858–59, the United States found itself in a war crisis with England over British boardings of American merchant ships in efforts to search out filibusters. In 1858–59, the Department of State learned about and protested Anglo-French plans to land troops in Central America for purposes of repressing filibusters as well as a draft British-Nicaraguan treaty that would have given the British permission to take such action. In the waning moments of Buchanan's presidency, Britain delayed its planned cession of the Bay Islands to Honduras because of renewed fears of American filibusters. The transfer ceremonies, which should have occurred before Buchanan left office, were deferred until 1 June 1861.[26]

This matter of logic, in turn, leads me full circle back to my initial premise—that perhaps historians have been too quick to project Buchanan's domestic policies and tolerance for slavery as an institution upon his diplomacy. My findings correlate with Robert R. Davis's discoveries about Buchanan's energy against the African slave trade. Of course, it is also possible, as David Meerse suggested some time ago in an article about Buchanan's patronage policy, that historians have exaggerated the pro-Southern character of the president's domestic course.[27] If it is indeed true that Buchanan has been unfairly judged a tool of the South, then surely the time has arrived when we may reevaluate his place in history. While we may never be able to carry Buchanan many steps out of the presidential cellar, we can at least acquit him of the charge that he was a mere lackey of the slave power.

Notes

1. Philip S. Klein, *President James Buchanan: A Biography* (University Park: Pennsylvania State University Press, 1962); Michael J. Birkner, "A Conversation with Philip S. Klein," *Pennsylvania History* 56 (October 1989): 243–73. For another favorable assessment, see Philip Gerald Auchampaugh, *James Buchanan and His Cabinet on the Eve of Secession* (Lancaster, Pa.: privately printed, 1926).

2. Attempts to rank U.S. presidents consistently include James Buchanan among the five worst presidents in American history. Robert K. Murray and Tim H. Blessing, *Greatness in the White House: Rating the Presidents, Washington through Carter* (University Park, Pa.: Pennsylvania State University Press, 1988), 14–17. It is impossible to list all the major studies highly critical of Buchanan's presidency. For several such works, see Elbert B. Smith, *The Presidency of James Buchanan* (Lawrence: University Press of Kansas, 1975); Mark W. Summers, *The Plundering Generation: Corruption and the Crisis of the Union, 1849–1861* (New York: Oxford University Press, 1987), 239–60; James A. Rawley, *Race and Politics: "Bleeding Kansas" and the Coming of the Civil War* (Philadelphia: J. B. Lippincott, 1969), 182–88, 223–38; Roy Franklin Nichols, *The Disruption of American Democracy* (New York: Macmillan, 1948); Allan Nevins, *The Emergence of Lincoln,* vol. 1, *Douglas, Buchanan, and Party Chaos, 1857–1859* (New York: Charles Scribner's Sons, 1950), 168–72, 239–47, 254–55, 269–70.

3. Murray and Blessing, *Greatness in the White House,* 68. For Buchanan's controlling Cass, see Auchampaugh, *Buchanan,* 35; Klein, *President James Buchanan,* 267, 268, 275–76; Nichols, *Disruption,* 79–80, 90; Frank B. Woodford, *Lewis Cass: The Last Jeffersonian* (New Brunswick, N.J.: Rutgers University Press, 1950), 315–16.

4. Louis Martin Sears, *A History of American Foreign Relations,* rev. ed. (New York: Thomas Y. Crowell, 1935), 306; Klein, *President James Buchanan,* 317–27; Foster M. Farley, "William B. Reed: President Buchanan's Minister to China, 1857–1858," *Pennsylvania History* 37 (July 1970): 269–80; Robert Ralph Davis, Jr., "James Buchanan and the Suppression of the Slave Trade, 1859–1861," *Pennsylvania History* 33 (October 1966): 446–59.

5. Smith, *Presidency of James Buchanan,* 68–80; Donathon C. Olliff, *Reforma Mexico and the United States: A Search for Alternatives to Annexation, 1854–1861* (University: University of Alabama Press, 1981); Samuel Flagg Bemis, *A Diplomatic History of the United States,* 4th ed. (New York: Holt, Rinehart and Winston, 1955), 321–23, 333; Nevins, *Emergence of Lincoln,* 446–49; Paul A. Varg, *United States Foreign Relations, 1820–1860* (East Lansing: Michigan State University Press, 1979), 216–18; Tyler Dennett, *Americans in Eastern Asia* (New York: Barnes and Noble, 1941), 292–346; James E. Southerland, "John Forsyth and the Frustrated 1857 Mexican Loan and Land Grab," *West Georgia College Studies in the Social Sciences* 11 (June 1972): 18–25; James W. Cortada, *Two Nations over Time: Spain and the United States, 1776–1977* (Westport, Conn.: Greenwood Press, 1978), 75–76. Varg and Nevins both argue that Buchanan's attempt to buy Cuba was solely a bid for domestic political capital—that Buchanan knew from the start that Spain would refuse to sell the island.

6. James Buchanan Inaugural Address, 4 March 1857, First Annual Message,

8 December 1857, Message to Congress of 7 January 1858, Proclamation, 30 October 1858, Third Annual Message, 19 December 1859, Fourth Annual Message, 3 December 1860, all in James D. Richardson, ed., *A Compilation of the Messages and Papers of the Presidents, 1789–1908* (New York: Bureau of National Literature and Art, 1908), 5:435–36, 447–48, 466–69, 496–97, 565, 649; Sir Charles L. Wyke to Lord John Russell, 17 January 1861, Great Britain, F.O. 39/12, Consular Despatches from Honduras, microfilm copy; Smith, *Presidency of James Buchanan,* 79.

7. John Bigelow to William Cullen Bryant, 28 December 1857 (copy), John Bigelow Papers, New York Public Library, New York; New York *Times,* 25 October 1859; George Washington Hazzard to J. D. Howland, 25 January 1858, George Washington Hazzard Papers, United States Military Academy Library, West Point, N.Y.; Charles Sumner to the Dutchess of Argyll, 12 January 1858, in Beverly Wilson Palmer, ed., *The Selected Letters of Charles Sumner* (Boston: Northeastern University Press, 1990), 1:489–90; John Y. Mason to Lewis Cass, 12 December 1857, James B. Bowlin to Lewis Cass, 29 December 1858, in, respectively, William R. Manning, ed., *Diplomatic Correspondence of the United States: Inter-American Affairs, 1831–1860* (Washington, D.C., 1932–39), vol. 6, *Dominican Republic, Ecuador, France,* 674–75, and vol. 10, *The Netherlands, Paraguay, Peru,* 188; London *Times,* 4 January 1859; Karl Bermann, *Under the Big Stick: Nicaragua and the United States since 1848* (Boston: South End Press, 1986), 97.

8. William Walker to Hiram Paulding, 30 November 1857 [copy], Hiram Paulding to Isaiah Rynders, 11 December 1857 (copy), Hiram Paulding to Isaac Toucey, 14, 15, 18 December 1858, 15, 25 January, February (no exact date) 1858, Frank P. Anderson to Joshua R. Sands, 20, 23 December 1857, Joshua R. Sands to Frank P. Anderson, 22 December 1857 (copies), Joshua R. Sands to Hiram Paulding, 28 December 1857 (copy), all in Letters Received by the Secretary of the Navy from Commanding Officers of Squadrons (hereafter, Squadron Letters), Record Group (hereafter, RG) 45, M89, Roll 97, National Archives, Washington, D.C.; William O. Scroggs, *Filibusters and Financiers: The Story of William Walker and His Associates* (New York: Macmillan, 1916), 324–32; Charles H. Brown, *Agents of Manifest Destiny: The Lives and Times of the Filibusters* (Chapel Hill: University of North Carolina Press, 1980), 414–18; Robert E. May, *The Southern Dream of a Caribbean Empire, 1854–1861* (Baton Rouge: Louisiana State University Press, 1973), 114–26. Charges were filed against the filibusters whom Paulding brought to Key West. The U.S. district judge at Key West remanded the filibusters to the custody of the U.S. marshal there, under orders that they be taken to New Orleans to be tried. The U.S. attorney at New Orleans dismissed charges against the men in the ranks, but proceeded with indictments against four officers, as well as one against Walker himself. Following a trial, which transpired between 31 May and 2 June, a jury voted 10–2 for acquittal of Anderson and Walker. Deciding that further proceedings would be fruitless, the district attorney entered a *nolle prosequi* in the case. Thomas J. Semmes to Jeremiah S. Black, 3 February, 7 June 1858, RG 60, Letters Received, Louisiana, NA.

9. Hiram Paulding to Isaac Toucey, 15 January 1858, Squadron Letters, M89, Roll 97, NA; Antonio José de Irisarri to Lewis Cass, 30 December 1857, Luis Molina to Jeremiah S. Black, 3 January 1860, in Manning, *Diplomatic Correspondence,* 4:638–39, 963–64. Paulding's 15 January dispatch reported that prior to his leaving Nicaragua, General Máximó Jérez had boarded his ship "and in the name of His Excellency the President of Nicaragua, thanked me for the service rendered to his country." Following Walker's expulsion from Nicaragua earlier

in 1857, that country's conservative and liberal factions had established a provisional government headed by a duumvirate, with Jérez provisional president representing the liberals and General Thomás Martínez representing the conservatives. In November, Nicaragua's Constituent Assembly chose Martínez as sole executive. Brown, *Agents*, 419–20; Bermann, *Under the Big Stick*, 96.

10. Richardson, *Messages and Papers*, 5:467; Charleston *Mercury*, 1 January 1858. Walker kept his word and turned himself in to the U.S. marshal for the Southern District of New York, Isaiah Rynders—who coincidentally had been a pro-Walker activist for some time. Rynders took Walker to Washington, arriving at the capital on the evening of 29 December and proceeding immediately to the Department of State. After a brief discussion, Secretary of State Cass dismissed Walker from custody. Scroggs, *Filibusters*, 174, 238, 333–34.

11. Richardson, *Messages and Papers*, 5:466–69; Hiram Paulding to Isaac Toucey, February (no exact date) 1858, Squadron Letters, M89, Roll 97, NA; Isaac Toucey to James M. McIntosh, 5 May 1858, Bauer, *New American State Papers: Naval Affairs*, 2:170.

12. Richard W. Van Alstyne, *American Diplomacy in Action*, rev. ed. (Stanford, Calif.: Stanford University Press, 1947), 706; Report dated Mobile, Ala., 26 January 1858, in Pittsburg *Post*, 27 January 1858; William Walker to the Mobile *Register*, 19 July 1858, in Jackson *Semi-Weekly Mississippian*, 27 July 1858; Brown, *Agents*, 424–25; Scroggs, *Filibusters*, 339. Walker claimed that Secretary of War John B. Floyd told filibuster general Charles Frederick Henningsen in an October 1857 private interview that while Buchanan opposed an expedition to Nicaragua, he would support Walker's joining forces with Ignacio Comonfort, then provisional president of Mexico. Once established in Mexico, the filibusters were to seize Cuba. Walker also claimed that Buchanan opposed his Nicaragua plans as revenge against former U.S. Senator Pierre Soulé. Soulé, who was very involved in Walker's Nicaragua movement, had thrown his influence against the administration-sponsored efforts of the Louisiana Tehuantepec Company to procure transit concessions from the Mexican government.

Walker's charges correlated with Buchanan's well-known interest in annexing Cuba as well as the state of U.S.–Mexican relations at the time. In October and November 1857, the administration learned that Comonfort, who earlier had rejected Buchanan's efforts to buy Mexican territory, might be willing to approve a cession. Mexico's government was bankrupt, and Comonfort faced serious opposition from both liberals and conservatives. Thus Buchanan had a vested interest in shoring up Comonfort's regime. Oliff, *Reforma Mexico*, 86–96; May, *Southern Dream*, 163–89.

13. Van Alstyne, *American Diplomacy*, 706; Samuel Flagg Bemis, *A Diplomatic History of the United States*, 4th ed. (New York: Holt, Rinehart and Winston, 1955), 329–30; Smith, *Presidency of James Buchanan*, 72–73; Bermann, *Under the Big Stick*, 89–91; David F. Long, *Gold Braid and Foreign Relations: Diplomatic Activities of U.S. Naval Officers, 1798–1883* (Annapolis, Md.: Naval Institute Press, 1988), 135; John H. Schroeder, *Shaping a Maritime Empire: The Commercial and Diplomatic Role of the American Navy, 1829–1861* (Westport, Conn.: Greenwood Press, 1985), 131; Kenneth J. Hagan, *This People's Navy: The Making of American Sea Power* (New York: Free Press, 1991); Roger Bruns and Bryan Kennedy, "El Presidente Gringo: William Walker and the Conquest of Nicaragua," in Robert James Maddox, ed. *Annual Editions: American History* (Guilford, Conn.: Dushkin Publishing Group, 1991), 1:151–52. For accounts that credit Buchanan with taking a firm position against filibustering, see Varg, *United States*

Foreign Relations, 253–54; Scroggs, *Filibusters,* 349–52; Nevins, *Emergence of Lincoln,* 1:287.

14. Klein, *President James Buchanan,* 146–47; Frederick Merk, *The Monroe Doctrine and American Expansionism, 1843–1849* (1966; New York: Vintage Books, 1972), 119–20; James Buchanan to Romulus Saunders, 17 June 1848, James Buchanan to Robert Rantoul, 23 June 1848, James Buchanan Circular, 30 August 1848, James Buchanan to Nathan Clifford, 10 October 1848, in John Bassett Moore, comp. and ed., *The Works of James Buchanan* (Philadelphia: J. B. Lippincott Company, 1908–11), 8:90–102, 105, 192–95, 216, 9:362–66; Basil Rauch, *American Interest in Cuba, 1848–1855* (New York: Columbia University Press), 74–80.

15. William Walker to Ambrose Dudley Mann, 16 July 1857, William Walker Miscellaneous Papers, Library of Congress, Washington, D.C.; Brown, *Agents,* 410, 413; *Harper's Weekly,* 22 August 1857; Natchez *Daily Courier,* 21 October 1857; Greensboro, *Alabama Beacon,* 23, 30 October 1857; T. B. Childress to Lewis Cass, 30 October 1857, James Conner to Lewis Cass, 10 November 1857, in H. Doc. 24, 35 Cong., 1 sess., 9–10, 13–14; Antonio José de Irisarri and Luis Molina to Lewis Cass, 14 September 1857, Antonio José de Irisarri to Lewis Cass, 8, 16 October 1857, in Manning *Diplomatic Correspondence,* 4:601, 609–10, 610–11, Lewis Cass to Lord [Francis] Napier, 20 October 1857, in Manning *Diplomatic Correspondence,* 7:176; George P. Ihrie to Samuel Cooper, 30 September 1857, Records of the Adjutant General's Office, Letters Received, M567, Roll 581, NA.

16. Department of State Circular, 18 September 1857, Lewis Cass to Joseph M. Kennedy, 13 November 1857, Lewis Cass to Franklin H. Clack, 13 November 1857, Lewis Cass to F. H. Hatch, 14 November 1857 (all telegraphs) in H. Doc. 24, 35 Cong., 1 sess., 4–5, 22.

17. Isaac Toucey to Frederick Chatard, 2 October 1857, Isaac Toucey to Hiram Paulding, 3 October 1857, in H. Doc. 24, 35 Cong., 1 sess., 49, 50; Isaac Toucey to John J. Almy, 3 October 1857, Isaac Toucey to Joshua R. Sands, 16 November 1857, in K. Jack Bauer, ed., *The New American State Papers: Naval Affairs* (Wilmington, Del.: Scholarly Resources, 1981), 2:166.

18. Joseph M. Kennedy to Jeremiah S. Black, 25 November 1857, RG 60, Department of Justice, Attorney General Papers, Letters Received, Louisiana, NA; A. J. Requier to Lewis Cass, 16 November 1857, Lewis Cass to Franklin H. Clark, 19 November 1857, Thaddeus Sanford to Lewis Cass, 14 November 1857, Howell Cobb to Thaddeus Sanford, 27 November 1857, Thaddeus Sanford to Howell Cobb, 7 December 1857, John J. Almy to Isaac Toucey, 26, 29 October 1857, in H. Doc. 24, 35 Cong., 1 sess., 23, 25, 39–44, 54–55; Frederick Chatard to Hiram Paulding, 27 November, 1 December 1857, Squadron Letters, RG 45, M89, Roll 97, NA. Buchanan had no cause to anticipate halfhearted enforcement of the neutrality laws by his officials on the Gulf Coast, since they had written Washington both that they had received the administration's instructions and that they would be vigilant. Joseph M. Kennedy to Lewis Cass, 30 September 1857, F. H. Hatch to Lewis Cass, 1 October 1857, in H. Doc. 24, 35 Cong., 1 sess., 7. Lieutenant Almy's journal and a dispatch from Paulding to Toucey provides evidence that those two naval officers had every intention of stopping filibusters. John J. Almy Journal, 10 November 1857, New York Public Library, New York; Hiram Paulding to Isaac Toucey, 17 November 1857.

19. Cincinnati *Daily Enquirer,* 18 November 1857; Lewis Cass to the Collector of Customs at Mobile, 2 December 1857 (telegraph), Lewis Cass to Thomas J.

Semmes, 16 December 1857, Thaddeus Sanford to Howell Cobb, 16 December 1857, Howell Cobb to H. Stuart, 26 December 1857, Lewis Cass to the Collector of Customs at New Orleans, 2 January 1858 (telegraph), James Conner to Lewis Cass, 7 December 1857, in H. Doc. 24, 35 Cong., 1 sess., 28–31, 35, 38, 45–46; William (?) G. McGregor to Thaddeus Sanford, 27 November 1857, RG 26, Department of Transportation: Records of the United States Coast Guard, "Weekly Reports from the Commander of Revenue Cutter Rt. McClelland," NA. Meanwhile, precautions continued off Nicaragua's coast. Lieutenant Almy established a one-ship blockade off the outlet of the Colorado River, which he maintained until Christmas, to intercept filibusters setting out during the interim between Walker's arrest and receipt of the news in the United States. Almy Journal, 15 December 1857.

20. Henry Wheaton, *Elements of International Law: The Literal Reproduction of the Edition of 1866 by Richard Henry Dana,* ed. George Grafton Wilson (Oxford: Clarendon Press, 1936), 114; William Edward Hall, *A Treatise on International Law,* ed. J. B. Atlay, 6th ed. (London: Henry Frowde, 1909), 49, 215; Opinion of Attorney General William Bradford, 6 July 1795, in Benjamin F. Hall and others, comps., *Official Opinions of the Attorneys General of the United States* . . . (Washington, D.C.: U.S. Government Printing Office, 1852–1906), 1:58–59; John C. Calhoun to Edward Everett, 25 September 1844, in John Bassett Moore, comp., *A Digest of International Law* (Washington, D.C.: U.S. Government Printing Office, 1906), 2:225; William L. Marcy to José de Marcoleta, 22 August 1855, Antonio José de Irissari to Lewis Cass, 17 November 1857, in Manning, *Diplomatic Correspondence,* 4:70–71, 629–30; Klein, *President James Buchanan,* 83. Walker's supporters in Congress disputed Buchanan's construction of international law and presidential powers. Nicaragua's government, moreover, took the position that Walker was a pirate, and that Paulding's act was therefore justified since international law permitted the seizure of pirates from thinly peopled areas like the Nicaraguan coast near Punta Arenas. See Henry Bartholomew Cox, *War, Foreign Affairs, and Constitutional Power: 1829–1901* (Cambridge, Mass.: Ballinger, 1984), 236–41; Antonio José de Irisarri to Lewis Cass, 30 December 1857, in Manning, *Diplomatic Correspondence,* 4:638–39.

21. H. Doc. 11, 35 Cong., 1 sess., 584; Louis N. Feipel, "The Navy and Filibustering in the Fifties," *United States Naval Institute Proceedings* 44 (April–July, 1918): 1529; Thornton A. Jenkins to Samuel Francis Du Pont, 22 January 1858, Samuel Francis Du Pont Papers, Hagley Museum and Library, Wilmington, Del.; Lewis Cass to Mirabeau B. Lamar, 2 January 1858, in Manning, *Diplomatic Correspondence,* 4:107.

22. Charleston *Mercury,* 1 January 1858; Thomas W. Thomas to Alexander H. Stephens, 7 February 1858, in Ulrich Bonnell Phillips, ed., *The Correspondence of Robert Toombs, Alexander H. Stephens, and Howell Cobb* (Washington, D.C.: AHA Annual Report for 1911, 1913), 2:430; William Walker to Callender Irvine Fayssoux, 5, 9 January 1858, Callender I. Fayssoux Collection of William Walker Papers, Tulane University Library, New Orleans; May, *Southern Dream,* 114–26; Brown, *Agents,* 427; James Buchanan to Joseph B. Baker, 11 January 1858, in Moore, *Works,* 177. It is significant that Georgia congressman A. R. Wright, who in a December 1857 private letter called Buchanan the "soundest man in all the North," turned against the president over the Walker-Paulding affair and wrote in another private letter that he now had "confidence" in the Douglas Democrats. A. R. Wright to Frank (?), 18 December 1857 and undated letter (copies), Augustus R. Wright Papers, Library of Congress, Washington, D.C.

23. Richardson, *Messages and Papers*, 5:496–97; Henry Wilson to Jeremiah S. Black, 4 December 1858, RG 60, Letters Received, Alabama, NA; H. Doc. 25, 35 Cong., 2 sess., 3–22; Brown, *Agents*, 428–32.

24. Howell Cobb to James Buchanan, 7 October 1859, in Phillips, *Correspondence*, 447; Fourth Annual Message, 3 December 1860, in Richardson, *Messages and Papers*, 5:649.

25. Howell Cobb to Thaddeus Sanford, 29 April 1858, in H. Doc. 25, 35 Cong., 2 sess., 3–4; James McIntosh to Isaac Toucey, 7 May 1858, Squadron Letters, M89, Roll 98, NA; James McIntosh to Mirabeau B. Lamar, 27 November 1858, in Manning, *Diplomatic Correspondence*, 4:727n. See also Thaddeus Sanford to Howell Cobb, 20 April 1858, in H. Doc. 25, 35 Cong., 2 sess., 3; Thaddeus Sanford to Lewis Cass, 14 November, 7 December 1857, John J. Almy to Isaac Toucey, 7 October 1857, Isaac Toucey to John J. Almy, 12 October 1857, in H. Doc. 24, 35 Cong., 1 sess., 39–40, 42–44, 51–52; Frederick Chatard to Hiram Paulding, 1 December 1857, Squadron Letters, M89, Roll 97, NA.

26. Beverly L. Clarke to Lewis Cass, 15 October 1859, Pedro Zeledón to Mirabeau B. Lamar, 9 May 1859, Mirabeau B. Lamar to Lewis Cass, 29 May 1859, in Manning, *Diplomatic Correspondence*, 4:783–84, 746–54, John Forsyth to Lewis Cass, 24 April 1857, ibid., 9 (Mexico): 915–16; "Minute of a conversation between John Y. Mason . . . and Count Walewski. . . ," ibid., 6 (Dominican Republic, Ecuador, France): 695–97, Lewis Cass to George M. Dallas, 26 November, 3 December 1858, Squadron Letters, M89, Roll 98, J. C. Long to Isaac Toucey, 28 January 1859, Roll 39, NA; Frederick Rogers to Edmund Hammond, 31 July 1860, Great Britain, F.O. 39/9, Consular Despatches from Honduras (microfilm), C. H. Darling to the Duke of Newcastle, 24 June 1861, ibid., F.O. 39/13.

27. David Meerse, "Buchanan's Patronage Policy: An Attempt to Achieve Political Strength," *Pennsylvania History* 40 (January 1973): 37–57.

James Buchanan, the Election of 1860, and the Demise of Jacksonian Politics

PETER KNUPFER

THE PRESIDENTIAL ELECTION OF 1860 WAS THE MOST CRITICAL election in the nation's history, for it set the stage for the great transformations in American politics during the Civil War era. Historians agree that without slavery there would have been no Civil War; and it is just as certain that without the Republican Party there would have been no war either. It is understandable, then, that the unique conditions that produced and shaped the early Republican Party in the 1850s have received such searching attention from scholars. The odd four-cornered campaign of 1860, coming after ten years of rising sectional tension, seemed suited to the peculiar political situation in the late 1850s. The opposition to the new Republican Party fragmented early in the year, putting three additional candidates in the field against Abraham Lincoln. An atmosphere of crisis, fear, and violence gripped the country, as voters made up their minds in the shadow of John Brown's body and Southern threats of secession should Lincoln be elected. Sectional blocs paralyzed Congress. In his landmark study of the events leading up to the election, Roy Franklin Nichols remarks that "the chaotic political situation . . . of 1860 was unique in the annals of the nation. Never before or since has it been duplicated. Only in that fateful year has the stage been occupied by four parties of relatively equal potentiality, and only then was the election followed by civil disorder serious enough to threaten national security."[1]

The election marked the end of James Buchanan's administration and with it, the old Jacksonian or "second" party system. That previous alignment of political forces had been based on a firm consensus among the country's leaders that sectional questions must remain beyond the reach of national political parties and institutions. The intersectional diplomacy of compromise and evasion practiced by the parties from 1819 to 1850 had successfully accom-

146

plished this objective by placing the value of a union between slave and free states above all other considerations. The party leaders of the Jackson period perfected a powerful set of political tools to implement this policy. The political culture and institutions of the second party system encouraged high voter turnouts and intense partisan activity within a framework of national organizations and issues. The voters' interests and affections turned toward national ends and away from underlying sectional pressures.[2]

The election of 1860 showed unmistakable signs that this system was undergoing fundamental and far-reaching changes. Old issues took on an ominously sectional cast, while new issues, such as the responsibility of the federal government for deciding the status of slavery in the western territories, official corruption, enhanced federal involvement in the economy, and a greater awareness of the government's extended role in maintaining domestic order, broke with traditional limitations on the scope and reach of political controversy. The outward manifestation of the impending development of a new party system was the emergence of the Republican Party, an avowedly sectional organization, from the fragments of the old Whig and nativist American parties. In particular, the disruption of the Democratic Party and the triumph of the Republicans revealed a conscious determination by a majority of the electorate to obtain a final settlement of the slavery question through, if necessary, a changed political universe. As an epilogue to the election of 1856, the campaign of 1860 affirmed the depth of conviction behind this decision. It completed the Republican effort to build a powerful electoral foundation for national prominence and justified the new party's decision to adopt a more comprehensive platform that committed the federal government to a form of economic activism far beyond the dreams of the most ardent Whig. And as a prelude to the Civil War party system, the election released the parties from the previous requirement that they attain "nationality" by developing a bisectional coalition and invited them to adopt new styles of campaigning and a host of new issues.

The administrations of Millard Fillmore, Franklin Pierce, and James Buchanan all had dedicated themselves to preserving the Union against sectional pressures, and each president used tried and true strategies to carry that mission forward. These self-described conservatives openly aligned themselves with the Jacksonian generation and sought to preserve the customs and institutions that it had created and fostered. The extent to which these administrations defended and strengthened these institutions and the customs that undergirded them would be the measure of the public's confidence that the government could still contain and control violent issues like slavery. So the power of federal and state patronage, the rhetoric of Union saving, the continued efforts at sectional compromise, the purchase and deployment of the party press, the application of mass political organizing techniques and party discipline to hold voters to the party standard and suppress sectional militants were exercised with increasing desperation and futility to arrest the corrosion of the old party system. In describing the issue before the country as "Union or disunion," the conservative politicians of the 1850s—whether Whig, American, or Democratic—had in effect put the Jacksonian political system on trial. Their Republican opponents were well aware of this, and in their drive for power sought to identify themselves with a conservative, Union-loving sentiment. But the Republicans could not escape the image of being the party of innovation, for they not only needed to prove that the existing arrangement of parties was betraying the vision of the founding generation, they also had to depart from the Jacksonian consensus on the nature of national parties and the importance of avoiding the slavery issue.

The only way that Republicans could accomplish this object was to exploit the mistakes of their opponents and depart from the normal principles and practices of the Jacksonian system. This would be possible if large blocs of voters were so dissatisfied with the political condition of the country, or were new enough to politics to be but in the beginning stages of their civic lives, that these voters would be open to a new party. In sum, the realignment of the 1850s required a special set of social conditions that would magnify the voters' normal skepticism of parties and politicians. The challenge, as Michael Holt has pointed out, was to attack their opponents as corrupt tools of Southern politicians while simultaneously invigorating an increasingly cynical electorate's faith that parties could still be effective shields of the republic.[3] The policies of the Buchanan administration would provide the spark for the Republicans, the infusion of new voters into the electorate would provide the powder, and the presidential campaign of 1860 would see the resulting explosion as the final demise of Jacksonian politics. The Republicans would take advantage of the "old public functionary's" dilemmas by connecting Buchanan's patronage and Kansas policies to the "old fogyism" of the president's political age, and thereby enhance their appeal to new voters while still proclaiming their own conservatism as champions of the original, antislavery intent of the founding generation. Such rhetoric suggests that the campaign of 1860 would reveal the rise of a new political generation advocating new issues and willing to depart from the usages of the recent past. There was widespread recognition that the political cycle was going through a fateful turn, and the people associated such changes not only with the demise of old issues and exhaustion of old policies, but also with a change in the makeup of their leaders.

Understanding the nature of this generational influence in the political conflict of the late 1850s requires us to define a "political generation" and make important distinctions about the demographic and historical influences that create political generations. Although a political generation can theoretically be defined by the existence of a generation gap in the demographic structure of the electorate, it need not be. The existence of generational rhetoric— of appeals to age-related sentiments in the popular mind—can indicate that a leadership associated with traditional political customs has become vulnerable to charges of being out of date. The public has, in effect, conflated policy with the age group of the policy makers and drawn some plausible conclusions—the age of the leadership becomes an issue and the dynamics of public discourse change as a result. As Marvin Rintala has put it, "a political generation is seen as a group of individuals who have undergone the same basic historical experiences during their formative years [ages 17– 25]. Such a generation would find political communication with earlier and later generations difficult, if not impossible."[4]

A political generation is not a compact unit; its members disagree intensely with each other. The shared historical experience of a political generation can be simply a set of civic rhythms that anchor their political attitudes and behavior to a predictable order in political life. Many defenders of the Jacksonian system in the 1850s arrived at political maturity with the formation of the two major parties. As children of the Era of Good Feelings, they entered politics with weaker preconceptions about how they might position themselves in the emerging party alignments of the 1830s. In effect, the parties socialized them to politics, functioning much as the family would in the transmission of political attitudes, and breeding in these men a particularly fierce attachment to the power and importance of political parties.[5] In the case of the 1850s, despite the deep animosity of Whigs and Democrats, the remnants of these parties late in the decade repeatedly called on the public to recall the basic consensus on which they had operated since 1828—the idea, agreed to by all parties, that the party system must restrain the natural inclination to thrust new and dangerous questions such as slavery into national politics. Such appeals ac-

quired an almost religious tone. Thus, Stephen A. Douglas tire-
lessly promoted the idea that the Compromise of 1850 had been a
catholic, wholesome agreement between the Whigs and the Democrats to restore the Jacksonian consensus on nonintervention in
the territories. In an explicitly religious metaphor that would have
drawn a chuckle from the latitudinarian Henry Clay, Douglas kept
referring to the great Trinity of old fogyism—"Clay was the great
leader, with Webster on his right and Cass on his left" (the latter
two switched sides in a later version)—that had immaculately con-
ceived, with Douglas's willing assistance, the Compromise of 1850
to suppress the Free-Soil Agitation. By 1860, conservatives of the
old school were still plying these topics, calling on voters to return
to the standard of Jackson, Clay, and Webster and support a party
of "the Union as it is."[6]

Douglas had attempted for years to rally his forces around his
claim that the repeal of the Missouri Compromise was consistent
with the practices and beliefs of the Jacksonians. But by 1860 it
was becoming clear that, as the most prominent representative of
Young America, he too had departed from the ways of the old
school, and that popular sovereignty forced him to do so. Old-
line Whigs could make common cause against him with Buchanan
Democrats and Republicans, by arguing that the act was an incen-
diary and impulsive inducement to renewed sectional agitation.[7]

These preliminary comments about the nature of political generations and generational politics suggest that we should supple-
ment the current interpretations of the realignment of the 1850s
and especially of the triumph of the Republicans with an explanation that accounts for generational themes in the politics of the late
1850s. Much of the current literature on the political crisis of the
1850s has centered on the extent to which the sectional quarrel
over slavery's status in the republic was responsible first for the
demise of the Whig party by 1854, then for the emergence of the
Republicans, and finally for the disruption of the Democratic Party
late in the decade. Scholars tend to depict the transformation of the
party system as a matter of altered voting allegiances and shifting
policies in its aftermath. The massive defections of Whigs and
antislavery Democrats to the Republican Party contrasted with the
ability of the regular Democratic organization to retain a core of
supporters well into the Civil War. Although the social demography
of the electorate plays a vital role in conventional analysis of re-
alignments, its makeup is limited largely to economic and ethno-
religious characteristics of the population, largely because the
census data permit extended longitudinal analysis. Political prac-

tices and customs remained relatively constant in this view—the great change was the introduction of new issues such as slavery and the shift in the parties' geographical constituencies along a sectional axis. In general, the literature seems to support the conclusion that aside from the changes just noted, the voters and their leaders continued to respect the basic usages, customs, and practices of the Jacksonian political system even as they denounced abuses and sought relief from a leadership associated with that era.[8]

Although the end of the second party system did not inaugurate an entirely new set of political styles, structures, and customs, the very fact of its occurrence raises questions about the nature of political change in a realigning phase. The rending of party loyalties was accompanied by a rising chorus against parties, politics as usual, corruption, and moral decline.[9] Certainly these themes can be detected in public discourse during more peaceful times. But because they occurred during such an abrupt and permanent shift in traditional party loyalties, they assume a special significance in our attempts to understand the political history of the period. The intrusion of sectional questions into the party battles of the 1850s was at the heart of the crisis that precipitated realignment, but sectional questions were hardly new to American politics. Nor was corruption a particularly underworked theme. What gave these problems special significance was the failure of the system's leaders to adjust and control them. The continued agitation of the slavery question would convince voters that a system designed to "remove" issues from political controversy was in fact intensifying those very problems and that a different approach was needed.

It is arguable that the election of 1860 marked a crucial turning point in the evolution of the civic culture. As scholars of realignment have noted, permanent shifts in the parties' constituencies entail a widespread reaction against the recent past.[10] The consequent deterioration of party loyalties leaves the electorate receptive to the appeals of new parties, new leaders, and new issues. Further accelerating this trend in the 1850s was the relative youthfulness of the electorate. Recent research indicates that fresh infusions of young, unattached voters swelled the ranks of the upstart Know-Nothing movement and offered the Republicans a tempting target late in the decade. The Know-Nothings rebelled against party wire-pullers and brokered conventions and mobilized gangs of nativist mechanics and workers in the urban and commercial centers of the East and the Ohio River valley. When the Order transformed itself into a generic political party, reverted to the shopworn rhetoric of sectional compromise, and abandoned its unique organization and reform agenda, the defections to the Republicans mounted.[11] Although the demographic profile of the electorate in the 1850s does not disclose what we would call a generation gap, the fate of the Know-Nothings, the campaign style and tactics of the Republicans, and the failures of the Buchanan administration gave the impression that one political generation was in decline, while another was beginning to emerge. As Dale Baum has noted in his study of the formation of the Civil War party system in Massachusetts, "new voters"—those who have previously abstained or who were voting for the first time—were crucial to the onset of the new party system. And the political parties that effectively recruited these voters would in turn seek to hold them to the standard and firmly entrench their loyalty to the party for the rest of their civil lives.[12]

Buchanan was a typical member of the Jacksonian political generation. His understanding of the way politics worked, of the function of political parties, of the nature of the Union and the policies needed to preserve it were inculcated through a party system that rewarded him with increasingly powerful positions and influence. An apostate from Federalism, Buchanan signed on early to the Democratic movement in his home state and rode it to power. Throughout his long career he helped to wield the state party's patronage to reward loyalty and deter dissent. The Democratic Party came to represent, in his eyes, the Union itself; it was a coalition of free and slave interests whose survival depended on the suppression of sectional conflict. The driving force of the Democratic Party had always been the preservation of the Union and, indeed, the party could not survive in its present form without sectional tensions that it could direct to its own purposes. Ever since the creation of the party, sectional pressures welled up from its Northern and Southern wings; the party effectively contained these pressures at the state level, permitting its leaders to use sectional fidelity as a test of party loyalty without carrying it into the national convention. As sectional issues became more acute in the late 1840s and broke into the national organizations with the advent of the territorial question, politicians like Buchanan resorted to familiar methods to limit the damage. Buchanan supported the extension of the Missouri Compromise line to the Pacific and opposed popular sovereignty as the party's program. By the time that he entered the White House, Buchanan was already fully trained in the system's strategy for handling sectional questions. Firmly believing, along with most politicians of his generation, that slavery's ultimate fate was beyond the reach of ordinary politics, Buchanan saw only mischief and peril in the agitation of the issue.

Buchanan's policies contributed mightily, if unintentionally, to the decomposition of party loyalties and the growing sense that the old party system had decayed beyond repair. Buchanan entered office when sectional issues were well developed and the Republican Party had already become a formidable force in national politics. His predecessor, Franklin Pierce, had been a weak president, lacking in national experience and subservient to the demands of party leaders undisciplined by the threat of a powerful opposition.[13] Buchanan, on the other hand, acting on the assumptions and customs that had undergirded Jacksonian politics, sought first and foremost to preserve the national Democratic Party intact and to suppress further agitation of the slavery question. "Should I be elected," Buchanan told a close associate in Pennsylvania, "my efforts shall be directed towards strengthening and extending the Democratic party & putting down the slavery agitation."[14] This strategy, as Walter Dean Burnham has pointed out, "seems to have been foredoomed to failure. It reckoned without the implications of accelerating cultural, demographic, and economic divergences along regional lines. The system as a whole tended to be dominated by political elites who represented a declining sector of the national socioeconomic system. Elites who represented the values and interests of dynamically evolving sectors at first resented, and later rose in rebellion against, that traditional dominance."[15] Buchanan made himself a symbol of the declining Jacksonian generation, and thereby helped to sharpen the public's perception that a generational change was in the offing. In sum, the policies associated with his administration assumed not just a sectional, pro-Southern cast in the public mind; they also could be attached to the traditional outlook and usages of a party system in disrepute. Such a realization on the part of large blocs of voters could set the stage for the adoption of new political ideas, customs, and organizations.

Just as the Republicans and the Democrats employed the rhetorical devices of a "slave power conspiracy" and "Black Republicanism" to encapsulate for the voters a constellation of policies and attributes they assigned to their opponents, so did Buchanan and his fellow holdovers from the Jackson generation unwittingly contribute to the shrill discourse of the 1850s a new label—"old fogyism"—that would be powerful ammunition in the 1860 campaign. The sixty-five-year-old Buchanan, the "old public functionary," consciously associated himself with the previous generation and

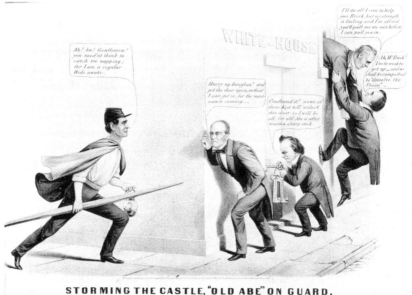

STORMING THE CASTLE, "OLD ABE" ON GUARD.

Cartoon from the presidential campaign of 1860 offers a pro-Lincoln perspective. Buchanan is shown trying, fruitlessly, to assist John C. Breckinridge into the White House. Published by Currier and Ives. Courtesy of Dickinson College.

bewailed the decline of politics since its heyday. As a result, he helped intensify the reaction against the policies of his age and pave the way for a new party system to emerge. Addressing Breckinridge supporters in July 1860, he proclaimed himself "the last survivor of a race of men who were in their day the faithful guardians of the Constitution & the Union." Breckinridge's generation now inherited this duty, and "I am happy to believe, that they will prove themselves to be worthy of this momentous trust. . . . May the kind Providence which has watched over our Country from the beginning restore the ancient friendship & harmony among the different members of the Confederacy & render the Constitution & the Union perpetual!"[16]

Buchanan's policies and his handling of the Democrats' intraparty feuds offered convincing proof that old-style politics as usual had sunk to new lows. The new president surrounded himself with an uninspiring cabinet of Southerners, Northern doughfaces, and aging party wheelhorses, none of them trailblazers in politics. He had little or no understanding of the party's antislavery wing. "The most serious defect in the Buchanan Cabinet was its lack of a young, articulate representative of the northern Democracy— someone who could express its views on Kansas policy and the meaning of popular sovereignty, and prevent the administration from appearing to be wholly a body of southerners and doughfaces," concludes a recent analysis.[17]

Nestled among such men, Buchanan lurched into the minefield of sectional politics. He endorsed the pro-Southern Dred Scott decision and sought to force a proslavery constitution on Kansas against the clear wishes of Kansans and of a large segment of his own party led by Senator Stephen A. Douglas of Illinois. He pursued an assertively pro-Southern foreign policy aimed at acquiring potential slave territories in the Caribbean. His messages spewed out a continuous stream of invective against abolitionists and antislavery elements, which alienated important sectors of Northern public opinion. Buchanan believed that by defending the South he was preserving the Union; he did not see slavery as a cancer on the body politic. His understanding of what was good for the South rested on a conception of sectional politics carried over from a period that wanted to integrate regional economies into a diverse national polity. He expected that such developments would continue the process of ending, not expanding, slavery.

That Southern militants used his policies for more aggressive purposes was undoubtedly true, and that Republicans and many Northerners assessed the situation from that vantage point was also true. No wonder Buchanan's response to the sectional crisis was so confused, so legalistic, so supremely confident in its insularity. Jacksonian politicians acted on the assumption that aside from civil war, the only way for slavery's fate to be determined was outside the political system. Slavery, like industrialism, was beyond the power of the federal government to control. It resulted from historic economic and geographical conditions that mere politicians could only minimally influence through legislation. In Buchanan's mind, then, even the proslavery decisions of the Supreme Court and of Congress would ultimately do little to change the course of things unless by threatening slavery they precipitated a civil war. Their benefit would be to assure Southerners of their constitutional rights and maintain the old Union. Northerners needed to recognize this, he believed. They had time on their side, if they were only willing to be patient and ignore the emotional appeals of abolitionists and the insults of disunionists.[18]

These policies handed Republicans a ready-made issue. In his celebrated debates with Stephen Douglas, Lincoln repeatedly attacked the Democratic Party for its constant resuscitation of the slavery issue. Appealing to the public's weariness with sectional strife, Lincoln urged that the country settle the question of slavery extension now.[19] Further temporizing by leaders who were indifferent to the spread of the institution and who couched their carelessness in a cloud of legalistic rationalizations only conceded the future of the country to slaveholders who did care about it. "Both the Whig and the Democratic parties were engaged for years in attempting to suppress the discussion of the question of Slavery," Horace Greeley replied to conservative demands that the country evade the territorial question, "and what they failed to bring about does not seem very likely to be accomplished by a few respectable elderly gentlemen from various parts of the country or even by their distinguished and excellent candidates for the Presidency." Indeed, "there is a very earnest and almost universal desire for a decision respecting them. . . . We think the decision of all sensible people, belonging to the present geological epoch, will be that the matter had better be adjudicated and settled now, so that we can afterward attend to other business without danger of being interrupted and disturbed by this."[20]

Buchanan's handling of party affairs and the federal patronage worsened matters. Ever since the split with Douglas over Lecompton the administration and its friends in the press had been singing the praises of traditional party discipline and regularity. "It is idle to think of accomplishing any great political object without partisan association," a stand-patter wrote to the Buchananite New York *Journal of Commerce* in late 1857. "We cannot conceive how a Democrat from principle, who has any of the true faith in him, can affiliate and cooperate with the party which may be organized to maintain an opposition to the Democracy. . . . Under no circumstances should those who are dissatisfied with the nominee of their party, go farther at an election than to withhold their hands from his support for it is nothing short of political suicide to lend a hand to the Opposition."[21] As antislavery Democrats developed their alliance with Republicans to stop the Lecompton Constitution, the party press issued stern warnings to the bolters to "recognize, at all times and in all places, the binding force of political obligation." The minority must concede to the wishes of a majority expressed through the customary round of conventions, nominations, and platforms.[22]

Buchananites depicted their opponents in and out of the party in terms usually attributed to youth and adolescence. "The agitators belong to a different class" from the "conservative, reflecting, Union-loving men of the country; men who are opposed alike to the fanaticism of the North, and the hot-headed secession doctrines which prevail in some portions of the South," the New York *Journal of Commerce* declared as the Lecompton fight heated up in the House.

They are the nervous, active, restless, and uneasy spirits, who constantly see something which in their opinion needs reforming. Hence they are always ready for a tilt with whoever is opposed to their views. The world is too slow for them, and they are in a great hurry to "all men conform to their own peculiar views." The Anti-Slavery party is largely composed of these "fast men." Not content with the exemption of their own community from the evils of slavery, and unwilling to leave to other communities the responsibility of disposing of that and other domestic questions in their own way and time, they are very impatient to "hurry things up" as fast as possible, and dictate to distant States and Territories, the mode and time in which *their* duties shall be performed.[23]

As "Civis" rhapsodized on the front page of the paper:

Even if it pass, with fools, in fashion;

'Twould desolate, degrade, and mash one,
And play the mischief with the nation.
So, when you curse the Democrats,
Remember—barn how cured of rats!
And even wait for slavery,
Deliberating, still to see;
Nor think it wisdom, if a curse,
T'exchange it only for what's worse,
Since not for party, pride, or passion,
Ought patriots to fire the nation!
As fury only burns and mashes,
Intoxicated in its flashes;
And tends to ruinous heaps of ashes.
As thought and principle are strong,
Passion is weakness, ever wrong.
No State exists without its evils;
Yet statesmen, such above all cavils,
Deliberate in history wise,
And learn in all to economize.
While men of passion, like young brats,
That value barns much less than rats,

Feeling to gratify, or party,
Go at it furious and hearty,
As doctors, when their patients tease,
Kill them—to vanquish the disease!
And show the potent remedy
Mere dreadful, when their victims die,
Than was the previous malady.
Thus fools, with treason in communion,
Compute the value of the UNION;
Complot and swagger in their cups,
Like oracles between their sups,
As if a Goth could ever build,
Instead of burn, what ages yield.
To govern is an easy thing
With Absalom—'make me a King;
The way to do it right I'll show
And all because—I love 'em so.'[24]

By 1860, Buchanan had stiffened his resolve to suppress the
Douglas faction in the party, calling them "disorganizers" who
threatened the party's existence. Most of his efforts to influence
the nomination and the election boiled down to a determined effort
to control the delegations and the electoral votes of Pennsylvania,
the one Northern state where the administration still had some
influence and respectability. The Keystone State had gone for Buchanan in 1856, but only with the aid of purchased voters and a
campaign of fear over the fate of the Union. By 1860, Buchanan's
hold on his followers had slipped considerably as Douglas's star
rose in the aftermath of the fight over Lecompton. Decisions made
early in the administration had demoralized significant portions of
the president's supporters and cost him the influence of John Forney's Philadelphia *Pennsylvanian*. Now, as his friends wrestled
with Douglas Democrats for control of the state's convention delegates, Buchanan's only weapon was the patronage. Unfortunately,
the most powerful federal officers in the state were warring with
each other, so that by early spring 1860 the weary president's mail-
box was filled with mutual recriminations and charges of betrayal.
Open war broke out at the state convention at Reading in late
February. "The standard of your Administration was lowered there,
in my judgement, by gross mismanagement and want of skill on
the part of those who took the lead with affairs in the Convention,"
a friend reported to him. "I never witnessed such a chaos of Political Principles, Men & Measures." Although the state delegation would support the administration in Charleston, it contained

enough dissidents to signal the eclipse of Buchanan's influence in Pennsylvania.[25]

The feud with Douglas festered at Charleston, and Buchanan did little to heal it.[26] The struggle was for the control of the party and both men dug in their heels while professing to desire national reconciliation. "The question simply is, shall Douglas kill the Democratic Party, and maintain a successful war upon yourself and friends, or shall we kill him," Robert Tyler wrote to Buchanan as the two mapped strategy for the convention. "I, for one, am for skinning and quartering this Demagogue. We must have a strong platform—the strongest, I think—We must drive him from the Party, or cut him in two with a platform. Besides our only chance for an election is in a Platform. A rally of the Democratic Party will not do—we haven't votes enough—the Opposition must be demoralized and broken."[27] Buchanan's lieutenants at the Charleston convention included William Bigler of Pennsylvania, John Slidell of Louisiana, Jesse Bright of Indiana, Caleb Cushing of Massachusetts, and Howell Cobb of Georgia, all confirmed Douglas-haters who had every incentive to disregard the president's hope that some accommodation be arranged. Although Buchanan had indicated that he would be satisfied with a Southern man running on a Northern platform, the strategy adopted by his subordinates at Charleston retreated before the demands of Southern delegates that the party commit its platform to a federal slave code for the territories; a simple reaffirmation of the 1856 platform would not suit them. When Douglas's men succeeded in thwarting that scheme, eight deep South delegations bolted the convention, to the surprise and consternation of the administration men. After Douglas failed to win the nomination, Buchanan and Douglas had the opportunity to isolate the seceders and heal the split in the party by supporting a compromise candidate, such as R. M. T. Hunter of Virginia, or James K. Guthrie of Kentucky, without surrendering their views on the territories. Both refused.[28]

Buchanan's insistence on a platform that protected Southern interests and permitted the enactment of a federal slave code for the territories guaranteed that the split with Douglas would be permanent. The test of party loyalty would be the "old Democratic doctrine of state sovereignty," he argued. Criticizing squatter sovereignty as a new invention of troublemakers and disorganizers, Buchanan rejected a broad, flexible, and loose platform that avoided specific qualifications on popular sovereignty and would mollify enough Northerners to save Pennsylvania and New York from the Republicans. Unwilling to bend on the platform, Bu-

chanan was unable to manage an effective campaign to fuse the
party factions and conservative oppositionists in John Bell's Constitutional Union Party into an anti-Republican coalition.

The party reconvened in Baltimore in June, where Northern
votes succeeded in splitting the delegations of the Charleston seceders, precipitating a walkout by the administration forces and
making Douglas's nomination by the remaining delegates a cer-
tainty. Cushing reconvened the bolters down the street and the
new convention nominated Breckinridge on a Southern rights platform.[29] The disruption of the party prompted a flurry of complicated and byzantine movements first to substitute a compromise
candidate for Bell, Douglas, and Breckinridge and,[30] failing that,
to arrange a fusion of anti-Republican forces in Pennsylvania, New
York, and New Jersey. Buchanan gave these movements his blessing, but they foundered on Douglas's refusal to join the effort and
on Buchanan's own patronage policies. The president indulged his
supporters' demand that he purge the federal patronage of Douglas
Democrats and force local politicians to bend to the administration's will. In mid-August, he answered the demand of New
York "hard" leaders, including Daniel Dickinson, that he remove
C. Comstock, editor of the Albany *Atlas & Argus* and the state's
leading Douglas organ, from his postmastership. Dissent against
this impolitic decision even from his own supporters drew a stiff
reply. "This organ, not only does not sustain the principles of my
administration, but is in direct antagonism to them," Buchanan
lectured Gerard Hallock, editor of the New York *Journal of Commerce.* "It maintains political doctrines in violation of the Constitution of the United States as propounded by the Supreme Court.
Unless these doctrines can be overthrown there never will be a
reunion between the democratic party North and the Democratic
party South, or in other words, a democratic party co-extensive
with the Union. Without this, the Constitution and the Union cannot be perpetuated."[31] Similar reasoning justified removals in Pennsylvania and Illinois.

Buchanan complicated matters with his tepid support for Breckinridge. In a speech on 9 July, Buchanan unenthusiastically endorsed his vice-president. Noting that Breckinridge's candidacy
was not "a regular nomination" and that every Democrat was free
to vote his conscience, he would still support him on similarity of
principle. Buchanan then signaled Breckinridge's dispensability by
supporting efforts to unite the party under a different candidate.[32]
Breckinridge had supported Douglas in the Little Giant's first contest with Abraham Lincoln in 1858 and, although he ran on a plat-

form endorsed by the administration, his utterances during the campaign took a more moderate tone than that of Buchanan's allies in the press and the executive departments. By September, Buchanan was endorsing any effort to create combined anti-Lincoln tickets. In Pennsylvania, a convention at Cresson cobbled together a shaky union of the Bell and Breckinridge men, and Buchanan urged that all party candidates be forced to pledge to it. Efforts at fusion in New York resulted in a similar ticket, which foundered on Douglas's refusal to countenance any bargain with the administration men. The fatal feud between Douglas and Buchanan bore its rotten fruit in November, as Breckinridge, Douglas, and Bell fell before the Republican onslaught. Few presidents have equaled Buchanan's record for misjudging public opinion and rigidly insulating the White House from the trend of national events.

At every turn, Buchanan was overwhelmed by the energetic and innovative efforts of his opponents. The Republicans in particular saw their opportunity and conducted a campaign noteworthy for the eminence of its candidates and the youthful vigor of its tone. The corruption issue was political dynamite. In March 1860, "Honest" John Covode, a Pennsylvania Republican, launched a House fishing expedition into the administration's efforts to pass the Lecompton Constitution. The inquiry spread into the affairs of the major departments and uncovered a pattern of scandal and vote purchasing unequaled in the past. Former supporters of the administration, angry at being refused office, talked freely and laid open the administration's parlous condition in its home base of Pennsylvania. The use of a House investigating committee was itself a major departure, as was the unlimited scope and magnitude of the inquiry. Although the Congress had previously investigated abuses and used the results as campaign fodder, this year the Republicans planned and executed the movement as a campaign strategy. The committee report splashed across the papers just as the Baltimore conventions ratified the division of the Democratic Party. Antiadministration Democrats rallied to the cause and denounced Buchanan. "Singing psalms will not save him now, sir," Congressman Isaac N. Morris of Illinois claimed. "He has already sinned away his day of grace, and all hope for him has become extinct." The administration had wrecked the party and true Democrats should leave it. "We cannot go into the canvass of 1860 with any hope of success, with its rotten and fetid carcass tied to the party."[33]

Buchanan could do nothing about this. He sent in two sternly worded protests against the House's action, which were greeted with hoots of derision and buried in committee. He denounced the investigation as unconstitutional and unprecedented while claiming that its revelations of lax ethics in high office vindicated him by failing to produce a formal bill of impeachment. The president's helplessness was evident on all sides.

In attempting to explain the irony of a career politician making so many miscalculations about his friends and his enemies, historians have come up with a number of answers, each of which contributes to an emerging picture of Jacksonian politics in decline and of a new Civil War party system in its birth pangs. First, scholars point to Buchanan's own pro-Southern philosophy, which many regard as the pivot around which his policies would turn. The policies of his administration reflected the president's belief that the South had been repeatedly wronged in the sectional quarrel, and have given credence to the now general impression that his pro-Southern orientation cut him off from Northern supporters and prevented him from reconciling with Stephen Douglas. This portrait of a president determined to defend the South shows us a Democratic administration entirely captive to powerful Southern interests determined to advance their proslavery agenda. Buchanan himself provided some of the most compelling evidence for this view. In his apologia for the administration published after the Civil War, Buchanan labored to prove that the essential cause of the war was abolitionist fanaticism, which had poisoned Northerners against the South and had driven Southerners into the cardinal error of seceding from the Union.

Second, some historians have noted that the president's cast of mind left him inflexible and uncompromising when the spirit of the law and the needs of practical politics rendered legalistic hair-splitting a self-defeating policy. Buchanan's defense of the Lecompton constitutional convention winked at the patina of legality shrouding this notoriously corrupt assembly and led him into open warfare with his hand-picked governor of the territory. He rigidly demanded that the Democrats impose as a party standard what he called the "old Democratic doctrine" of state sovereignty as expounded by the Supreme Court. Buchanan's ideological reflexes preferred the constitutional sophistry of Calhounism at the expense of a reaffirmation of the party's flexible and servicable Cincinnati platform of 1856. For example, his veto of a homestead bill that had attracted sponsors in both sections in effect told nonslaveholding farmers that adherence to state rights was more important than obtaining land in the West, and cost him the assistance of up-and-coming leaders like Andrew Johnson of Tennessee.

Some scholars have pointed to the bachelor president's insecure, parsonage mentality, which frosted relations within the cabinet and led Buchanan to pry into the private affairs and correspondence of family and nonrelatives alike. Bereft of intimate female companions to broaden his social circle and soften his harried schedule of appointments and decisions, Buchanan retreated to a coterie of like-minded friends for guidance and support. He thus fell prey to a "Directory" of stronger, pro-Southern, spirits in and outside the administration and turned a blind eye to their abuses of power. For example, soon after he entered office, Buchanan fell out with Vice-President Breckinridge. When Breckinridge asked to visit and consult with him, Buchanan demurred, referring him to his niece Harriet Lane for an appointment. Breckinridge felt insulted and refused, only to discover too late that Buchanan always shuttled important visitors to Miss Lane, whose visitors Buchanan would leave any other meeting to greet. Thereafter, Breckinridge noted, he was shut out of the corridors of power in the White House.[34]

And finally, the unprecedented extent of political corruption in his administration has been connected to underlying developments in the economy, which made control of the federal purse ever more important to business interests and sharpers out to make a killing. The old Jacksonian party system had thrived in a decentralized federal structure that diffused party politics and lobbying by special interests across the states. The party strife over federal economic policy had waned in the late 1840s as a wave of prosperity and a series of national compromises over the tariff and internal improvements rendered the Whig program of federal economic development irrelevant for the time being. The states carried on the work of assisting business interests in developing a banking and transportation system and helped to inure Americans to the idea that the government had an important role to play in promoting economic growth. Late in the 1850s, economic issues returned to national politics as businessmen and politicians arranged for the dispensation of public lands, the construction of railroads, and the settlement of the territories. Higher stakes attracted an army of grafters and spoilsmen and overwhelmed the federal government's feeble accounting practices and almost nonexistent controls over conflicts of interest. Buchanan's administration became the most corrupt in the history of the country.

Each of these explanations for Buchanan's behavior reveals much about the condition of the party system as the 1860 campaign got underway. The second party system had fallen into such disarray that a national administration had become the tool of one section. The sectionalization of politics pushed conservatives like

Buchanan into more rigid, ideological, and reactionary positions on public affairs and imparted a tone of desperation and fear to their actions. Eight years of Democratic rule and increasingly shrill denunciations of the opposition as treasonous had encased the White House in a siege mentality that brooked no dissent within the party and reinforced Buchanan's loneliness, isolation, and aloofness. Rampant spoilsmanship had revealed the dry rot within the party and the federal government and contributed to a crisis of legitimacy that sapped the government's public support.

To his dying day, Buchanan remained supremely confident that his reading of the public mind and his conception of the strategies needed to grapple with the crisis were correct. The problems in his administration and his ultimate defeat suggest to us a president completely out of touch with his public and unable to cultivate any popular understanding of his policies or purposes. It is arguable, however, that Buchanan's dilemmas were attributable to yet another cause at work in the political system and increasingly evident in the campaign of 1860: the increasing futility of political practices associated with a dying party system and challenged by a rising generation of new leaders who were innovative in political techniques at the dawn of a new age. Buchanan, in short, presided over the onset of the Civil War party system, whose emergence heralded a new set of political customs, a new arrangement of the civic culture, and a new host of issues that confounded him at every turn. In response, Buchanan wielded rusty weapons from an old and familiar arsenal and in the end went down in the history books as one of the worst presidents the country ever had. The realignment of the 1850s demonstrated that new parties meant new political styles and issues, and that the customs supporting the Jacksonian system were being transformed in the heat of party warfare over slavery and popular disgust with politics as usual.

The Republicans exploited this sentiment and outgeneraled their opponents—especially Buchanan—in channeling it toward victorious ends. Of special interest to the young party's managers were two vital groups in the electorate: old-line Whig and American supporters of Fillmore from 1856, and young, new voters just entering politics. In the former case, the Republicans plied nativist themes in strong Fillmore areas of the country, especially Philadelphia, the lower North, and Connecticut. In the latter case, the Republicans built on their 1856 strategy of using a young, charismatic Frémont candidacy to lure young voters away from the rough-and-tumble Know-Nothings. This time they mobilized youth through the "Wide-Awake" military clubs that they spread through-

STATE OF AFFAIRS AT WASHINGTON.

Member after Member of the Cabinet resigns, or is allowed to withdraw; the Public Chest is empty, and the President does nothing but wring his hands and bemoan himself.—*Washington Letter.*

A cartoon unsympathetic to Buchanan's situation in the winter of 1860–61 as members of his cabinet depart and the secession crisis grows, while "the President does nothing but wring his hands and bemoan himself." Courtesy of Dickinson College.

out the North. The Wide-Awakes recruited new and young voters, adopted military styles of dress, parade, and symbol that anticipated the similar types of campaigning in the third party system. The party brimmed over with young leaders charged with the confidence and vigor born of crusading adolescence.[35] Striking effectively at the old fogies running the Bell and Buchanan campaigns, the Republicans announced that they had infused their party with a depth of conviction found only in new parties. And most important, the Republicans abandoned—if reluctantly and with considerable debate—any conciliatory Southern strategy to "nationalize" their party along the lines of the old Jacksonian system.[36]

The Republicans' use of new techniques such as the Covode investigation and the Wide-Awake clubs and their willingness to confront the slavery question directly and firmly suggests that they saw real opportunity in exploiting the growing sense in the country that the cycle of politics was turning away from the old fogies and that they were to be the ones to set its future course. After the war, Buchanan noted that a new generation was indeed coming into prominence, albeit for the most sinister of purposes. Recognizing that the leadership of the country was changing, Buchanan could only lament it and fight back with familiar weapons. He noted after the war that in 1860 "an entire new generation had now come upon the stage in the South, in the midst of the anti-slavery agitation. The former generation, which had enjoyed the blessings of peace and security under the Constitution and the Union, had passed away. That now existing had grown up and been educated amid assaults upon their rights, and attacks from the North upon the domestic institution inherited from their fathers."[37] Yet that new generation spoke a language and pursued a political agenda that Buchanan barely understood, if at all. Included among new Southern leaders were men such as John Slidell, with whom Buchanan had consorted with for years, and who now backed Breckinridge. Breckinridge himself, like Franklin Pierce and Stephen Douglas, appealed to the vibrant spirit of the 1850s and stood in contrast to Buchanan's shopworn image of Jacksonian rectitude. Few of these men developed a close working relationship with Buchanan, who failed to understand the magnitude of their popular appeal.[38] Douglas's popular sovereignty struck a responsive chord in the rising, muscular Northwest, a region of the country Buchanan was unfamiliar with. It did not surprise Buchanan that this loose doctrine would propel Douglas out of the party mainstream as Buchanan had defined it, and into the ranks of the disorganizers and demagogues of the new generation. Douglas also broke with precedent during the campaign, launching a furious, courageous, and ultimately futile electioneering effort that took him into the deep South, up through the crucial border, and into New England. Although some other presidential candidates had attempted similar feats, Douglas was clearly breaking the mold, prompted by the tremendous stakes in the election and fueled by his own undomitable energy.

Buchanan's experience with the 1860 campaign suggests that historians should examine periods of realignment for signs of generational pressures in the electorate. It is rare for such pressures to stem directly from a discernible demographic bulge in the age distribution of the population. It is more likely that when a social and political crisis approaches the magnitude of the calamity facing the country in 1860, a widespread revulsion against an entire class of leaders and the age they represent will make "old fogyism" an issue of real significance to the voters. In such a situation, the different socializing experience of the current leadership would greatly complicate its ability to understand the demands of new and young citizens.[39] The Republicans implemented a clear and successful strategy to capture this portion of the electorate and, in combination with the confidence and clarity of a broad and assertive platform ranged against a weak and divided gaggle of conservatives, laid the foundations of the Civil War generation in the North.

Notes

1. Roy F. Nichols, *The Disruption of American Democracy* (New York: Macmillan, 1948), 341. Four candidates were in the field: John C. Breckinridge for the Southern Democrats; Stephen A. Douglas for the Northern Democrats; John Bell for the Constitutional Union Party, a coalition of conservative Whigs and nativists; and Abraham Lincoln of the Republican Party. Despite the voluminous periodical literature on the election, there is no modern study of the campaign; see Emerson D. Fite, *The Presidential Campaign of 1860,* (New York: Macmillan, 1911); Ollinger Crenshaw, *The Slave States in the Presidential Election of 1860,* in Johns Hopkins University Studies in Historical and Political Science ser. 63, no. 3 (Baltimore: Johns Hopkins Press, 1945). The candidates' perspective on the campaign can be followed in their biographies: William C. Davis, *John C. Breckinridge: Soldier, Statesman, Symbol* (Baton Rouge: Louisiana State University Press, 1974); Joseph Parks, *John Bell of Tennessee* (Baton Rouge: Louisiana State University Press, 1950); Robert W. Johannsen, *Stephen A. Douglas* (New York: Oxford University Press, 1973); Reinhard H. Luthin, *The First Lincoln Campaign* (Cambridge, Mass.: Harvard University Press, 1974). Allan Nevins, *The Emergence of Lincoln,* 2 vols. (New York: Scribners, 1947), 2:171–317, provides an insightful and sprightly overview.

2. Joel Silbey, *The American Political Nation, 1838–1893* (Stanford, Calif.: Stanford University Press, 1993); William E. Gienapp, *The Origins of the Republican Party, 1852–1856* (New York: Oxford University Press, 1987), 3–11; and Joel Silbey, *The Partisan Imperative: The Dynamics of American Politics before the Civil War* (New York: Oxford University Press, 1984), 33–59 provide the most succinct and forceful outlines of the system and its stabilizing effects before the 1850s.

3. Michael F. Holt, *The Political Crisis of the 1850s* (New York: Wiley, 1978), 216.

4. Marvin Rintala, "Political Generations," *International Encyclopedia of the Social Sciences,* ed. David Sills (New York: 1968), 6:93. On the concept of political generations, see Samuel P. Huntington, "Generations, Cycles, and Their Role in American Development," in Richard J. Samuels, ed. *Political Generations and Political Development* (Lexington, Mass.: Lexington Books, 1976), 9–28. For a discussion of historical applications, see Alan B. Spitzer, "The Historical Problem of Generations," *American Historical Review* 78 (December 1973): 1353–85; Morton Keller, "Reflections on Politics and Generations in America," in Stephen R. Graubard, ed., *Generations* (New York: W. W. Norton, 1979), 123–31; William Strauss and Neil Howe, *Generations: A History of America's Future* (New York: 1991). For applications to the Civil War era, see for example Daniel J. Elazar,

Building toward Civil War: Generational Rhythms in American Politics (Washington, D.C.: 1992); George Forgie, *Patricide in the House Divided: A Psychological Portrait of Lincoln and His Age* (New York: W. W. Norton, 1979); and Reid Mitchell, *The Vacant Chair: The Northern Soldier Leaves Home* (New York: Oxford University Press, 1992).

5. On political socialization, see Christine B. Williams, "A Socialization Explanation of Political Change," in John C. Pierce and John L Sullivan, eds., *The Electorate Reconsidered* (Beverly Hills, Calif.: Sage, 1980), 111–34; Paul R. Abrahamson, *Generational Change in American Politics* (Lexington, Mass.: Lexington Books, 1975); Paul Allen Beck, "A Socialization Theory of Partisan Realignment," in *The Politics of Future Citizens: New Dimensions in the Political Socialization of Children,* ed. Richard G. Niemi (San Francisco: W. H. Freeman, 1974), 199–219.

6. 21 August, 18 September 1858, in Roy P. Basler, ed., *Collected Works of Abraham Lincoln* (New Brunswick, N.J.: Rutgers University Press, 1953), 3:2, 168–71. At the seventh and final debate in Alton (15 October 1858, in ibid., 3:321), Douglas could not resist the temptation to tell the whole melodramatic story about Clay returning from retirement to save the Union, and to associate himself with the ultimate victory: "Lincoln is the man, in connection with Seward, Chase, Giddings, and other Abolitionists who got up that strife that I helped Clay to put down." For a good example of Union Party appeals to the spirit of the old system, see "Address of the National Union Men," January 1860, Millard Fillmore Papers, State University of New York at Oswego.

7. At the time the Act was passed, Buchanan was safely stationed in England; but he opposed it then and later because it permitted territorial legislatures to deny slaveholders their property rights. See his speech in support of Breckinridge and Lane, 9 July 1860, in John Bassett Moore, ed., *The Works of James Buchanan: Comprising His Speeches, State Papers, and Private Correspondence,* 12 vols. (New York, 1908–11; reprint, 1960), 10:459–63, and Klein, *President James Buchanan,* 213–14. Old Whigs agreed with Republicans and Buchananites that Douglas had opened a can of worms. See Millard Fillmore to New York Union meeting, printed in Washington *Daily National Intelligencer,* 30 December 1859 and manuscript copy 18 December 1860 in Fillmore Papers, Oswego; R. H. McCurdy to Fillmore, New York City, 30 January 1860, Fillmore Papers, Oswego; Nashville *Republican Banner,* 5, 8, 13, 20, 22 January 1860.

8. See especially Paul Kleppner, *The Third Electoral System, 1853–1892: Parties, Voters and Political Cultures* (Chapel Hill: University of North Carolina Press, 1979), which confines its analysis of political culture to specific patterns of voting behavior. The question of linkages between realignment and policy change is analyzed in David W. Brady, "Elections, Congress, and Public Policy Changes: 1886–1960," in Bruce A. Campbell and Richard J. Trilling, eds., *Realignment in American Politics: Toward a Theory* (Austin: University of Texas Press, 1980), 176–201.

9. An excellent review of the corruption issue and its larger significance for the 1850s is Mark W. Summers, *The Plundering Generation: Corruption and the Crisis of the Union, 1849–1861* (New York: Oxford University Press, 1987).

10. Campbell and Trilling, *Realignment in American Politics,* 4–10.

11. Tyler Anbinder, *Nativism and Slavery: The Northern Know Nothings and the Politics of the 1850s* (New York: Oxford University Press, 1993), 40–42, argues that youthfulness was not a unique characteristic of the Northern Know-Nothings. But see Hendrik Booraem, *The Formation of the Republican Party in*

New York: Politics and Conscience in the Antebellum North (New York: New York University Press, 1983), 244 n44; George Haynes, "A Chapter from the Local History of Knownothingism," *New England Magazine* 21 (1896): 82–96; Michael F. Holt, "The Politics of Impatience: The Origins of Know Nothingism," *Journal of American History* 60 (September 1973): 309–31.

12. Dale Baum, *The Civil War Party System: The Case of Massachusetts, 1848–1876* (Chapel Hill: University of North Carolina Press, 8–20. See also Roy Shortridge, "The Voter Realignment in the Midwest during the 1850s," *American Politics Quarterly* 4 (April 1976): 193–222.

13. Larry Gara, *The Presidency of Franklin Pierce* (Lawrence: University Press of Kansas, 1992).

14. Buchanan to Hendrick B. Wright (copy), Wheatland, 26 June 1856, Buchanan Papers, Historical Society of Pennsylvania (HSP). See also Elbert B. Smith, *The Presidency of James Buchanan* (Lawrence: University Press of Kansas, 1975), 17.

15. "Party Systems and the Political Process," reprinted in Walter Dean Burnham, ed., *The Current Crisis in American Politics,* (New York: Oxford University Press, 1982), 92–117.

16. Buchanan to John L. Henry et al., Washington, D.C., 17 July 1860, Buchanan Papers.

17. Kenneth Stampp, *America in 1857: A Nation on the Brink* (New York: Oxford University Press, 1990), 62.

18. Philip S. Klein, *President James Buchanan: A Biography* (University Park: Pennsylvania State University Press, 1962), 147–50, 213–15.

19. Lincoln pressed the theme in his speech at Springfield, but see also speeches at Carlinville, Clinton, and Bloomington Ill., 31 August, 2, 4 September 1858, in Basler, *Collected Works* 3:77–78, 81–84, 85–90.

20. New York *Daily Tribune,* 14, 11 May 1860.

21. New York *Journal of Commerce,* 15 December 1857.

22. Ibid., 13 February 1858.

23. Ibid., 16 February 1858.

24. "Let It Slide," ibid., 3 March 1858.

25. Vincent L. Bradford to Buchanan (private), Philadelphia, 2 March 1860, Buchanan Papers, HSP. See also James C. Van Dyke to Buchanan (private and confidential), Philadelphia, 7 March 1860, and Joseph B. Baker to Buchanan, Washington, 9 March 1860, in ibid.

26. Smith, *Presidency of James Buchanan,* 102–3, 113, argues that Buchanan determined at the outset never to compromise with Douglas and to use every means available to prevent his nomination.

27. Robert Tyler to Buchanan, Philadelphia, 20 March 1860, Buchanan Papers, HSP.

28. George N. Sanders, who had been attempting to manage Douglas's nomination, telegraphed Buchanan from Charleston on 27 April pleading with him to reciprocate Douglas's support of Buchanan in 1856 by coming out for the Little Giant; the collect telegram cost the annoyed president $27, in ibid., and Nevins, *Emergence of Lincoln,* 2:218. Klein, *President James Buchanan,* 342–44, argues that Buchanan sought such a compromise, but the last-minute desperation of his henchmen in attempting to prevent a Southern bolt suggests that he and his closest advisers were serenely confident that the schism would be minor and that they could eventually hogtie Douglas to an administration-backed platform.

29. Nevins, *Emergence of Lincoln,* 2:268–72.

30. Davis, *John C. Breckinridge,* 226–27, details these efforts by Davis, Robert Toombs, and administration men to get Douglas out of the race.

31. Buchanan to Gerard Hallock (copy, private and confidential), Washington, D.C., 11 August 1860, Buchanan Papers, HSP; see Buchanan to Comstock (private copy) Washington, D.C., 5 July 1860, and Hallock to Buchanan, New York City, 6 August 1860, both in ibid.

32. See Davis, *John C. Breckinridge,* 226–27; Johannsen, *Douglas,* pp. 792–93.

33. Nevins, *Emergence of Lincoln,* 2:196–200, and Summers, *Plundering Generation,* 257–60, review the Covode Investigation and its impact; Morton quoted in Summers, p. 257. See also David Meerse, "Buchanan, Corruption, and the Election of 1860," *Civil War History* 12 (June 1966): 116–31.

34. The "Directory" thesis is most assertively pursued by Nevins ("Buchanan was by nature a man easily subservient to others. There was no question in which direction his subservience would fall"; *Ordeal of the Union,* 2 vols. [Charles Scribner's Sons: New York, 1947] 2: 514), especially in *Emergence of Lincoln* 1:62–72. The episode with Breckinridge is described in Davis, *John C. Breckinridge,* 170–71.

35. William E. Gienapp, "Who Voted for Lincoln?" in John L. Thomas, ed., *Abraham Lincoln and the American Political Tradition,* (Amherst: University of Massachusetts Press, 1986), 60–62.

36. See, for instance, Hartford *Evening Press,* 25 October 1860, in Howard Cecil Perkins, ed., *Northern Editorials on Secession,* 2 vols. (New York: 1942) 1:60–61; New York *Daily Tribune,* 9 May 1850; Gienapp, "Who Voted for Lincoln?", 53–54; Richard H. Abbott, *The Republican Party and the South, 1855–1877: The First Southern Strategy* (Chapel Hill: University of North Carolina Press, 1986), 11–19.

37. Buchanan, *Mr. Buchanan's Administration on the Eve of the Rebellion* (1866), in Moore, *Works,* 12:70.

38. There is even some evidence that Breckinridge leaders in the South were younger and less experienced than the Bell men. See William Barney, *The Secessionist Impulse: Alabama and Mississippi in 1860* (Princeton: Princeton University Press, 1974), 95–96.

39. See Paul Abrahamson, "Generational Change and the Decline of Party Identification," in Richard G. Niemi and Herbert F. Weisberg, eds., *Controversies in American Voting Behavior* (San Francisco: W. H. Freeman, 1976), 324.

The Presidency of James Buchanan: A Reassessment

[What follows is an edited transcription of the panel discussion at the James Buchanan Conference held at Franklin and Marshall College, 21 September 1991. Panelists were Don Fehrenbacher of Stanford University; Kenneth M. Stampp of the University of California at Berkeley; Robert Johannsen of the University of Illinois, Urbana-Champaign; and Elbert Smith of the University of Maryland, College Park.]

Michael Birkner: In the winter of 1857, as James Buchanan was preparing to assume the office that he had sought for so long, much of the American public felt that it had been rescued from a dangerous crisis. Because had the Republican Party captured the White House in 1856, many Southern Democrats said they simply would not accept the results. Who could foretell the consequences had John Charles Frémont been elected president in James Buchanan's stead? And we all know that it was, indeed, a very close call. The breakup of the Union seemed possible, if not necessarily imminent, as a consequence of a Republican victory in 1856. But Frémont wasn't elected in 1856. Buchanan was elected primarily because of his strong showing in the South where Frémont won virtually no votes at all. He was a Black Republican to Southerners and simply unacceptable. Buchanan was acceptable to Southerners. He was a canny politician. He had real skills and he was, most importantly, a Union man to the core—a man who had no views that were anathema to the South. The question facing Buchanan and the country, as he prepared to assume the presidency in March 1857, was whether he could hold his party together and the nation together in the face of sectional distrust and deep sectional antagonism. This, of course, is the problematic of Buchanan's presidency. How things turned out for Buchanan comprises the topic for discussion this morning. We are very fortunate to have with us four scholars who have written extensively on the 1850s. Each has offered valuable commentary on Buchanan in the course of writing broader works on the period.

I would like to begin with Professor Smith, if I can, and begin properly at the beginning. I'd like to set the scene for March 1857 as Buchanan prepares to assume the presidency. What was uppermost on his mind as he planned his inaugural?

Elbert Smith: Buchanan had this in mind: how do I make certain the Republicans don't win in 1860? On the other hand, I don't think he thought through this very clearly. Incidentally, it is important to note that he wrote his own speeches and he wrote his own inaugural, unlike most presidents today. He had also been very seriously ill with dysentery, a form of Legionnaires' Disease, and whether or not that affected his judgment, we don't know. The North needed reassuring if it was going to stop attacking the South and thereby playing into the hands of the Southern radicals and Buchanan did not do this. . . .

He never understood that the Free-Soil movement, the idea that slavery should not expand, was a mass opinion, that great numbers of Northerners believed this. This was not just the idea of a small number of Republican fanatics. His immediate problem was how to handle the question that had been the major part of his platform, popular sovereignty. And the big question was when should the decision be made. Should it be made at the point when a territorial government was created or should it be made at the point when a territory became a state? The Democrats very wisely didn't tackle that part of it at all. So that Southerners could believe that popular sovereignty meant deciding on slavery at statehood, and the Northerners could believe the opposite. You might ask what's the difference. A very significant difference it seems to me. If after the South had access to a territory for a reasonable length of time, and then that territory voted to be a free state, you could say, well it's because of climate, geography, economics, all kinds of different reasons. On the other hand, if you cut off slavery at the beginning, it could only be for moral reasons, and the South, I think, very much objected to this. In 1848, for example, when they were debating over Oregon, and Thomas Hart Benton and Sam Houston said who's going, when are you leaving, who's taking slaves to Oregon, [John C.] Calhoun said that doesn't matter. The admission of Oregon without slavery is an insult to my heritage. It's an insult to my descendants, and that's more than enough reason for secession. On that basis, we should secede. So Buchanan has to deal with this and he wrote letters to two Supreme Court justices; he knew they had the Dred Scott case, and I'm going to leave that to Professor Fehrenbacher, who is a real expert on it. But Buchanan definitely used influence on one Pennsylvania judge to get him to fall in line with this. Knowing the South would be very happy with it, apparently completely blind to the reaction it would cause in the North, he predicts it and makes it clear that he knows that it's coming and says in his inaugural address, "Some people have asked the question when do we decide this." "Well," he said, "the whole question of territorial slavery is going to be answered by the Supreme Court in a few days." Therefore, when the case does come out he is completely identified with it. Those, it seems to me, are his main points. He doesn't think slavery will go to the West; he doesn't really want slavery to go to the West. But he's perfectly willing to give the South the right to take slavery to the West or anywhere else, not thinking it will mean anything and, again, quite oblivious to the reaction this is going to have in the North.

Birkner: I think it might be appropriate now to talk a little about the man who takes the presidency in 1857. We've had numerous comments made in the papers today and in side comments here for the last two days that on paper Buchanan was well qualified to be president of the United States and he was in many ways someone who gave people a sense of confidence and comfort because he would not have to be trained for the job. And yet, he does not live up to expectations. Professor Stampp might be in a position to help us understand the disjunction between the paper credentials and the reality.

Kenneth Stampp: You might ask whether it was just that Buchanan was elected at the wrong time. I think probably he never would have done very well. [*Laughter*] I don't know that there was ever a right time. He might have done as well as Warren Harding. [*Laughter*] I'd like to give two explanations of why I think so. One relates to the matter in which he formed his cabinet and another relates to, I think, an excellent example of how he bungled even the use of patronage. It's true that Buchanan was superbly trained. We've already heard about his background in Congress and the Senate, diplomatic service in the State Department, and his background and experience contrasted with Lincoln's lack of experience. One spent one term in the Congress and two terms in the state legislature. I don't think we ought to use this as an example of how it always will be—that it is better to have an inexperienced

President-elect James Buchanan greets members of the "committee of arrangement" that will guide him to the inaugural procession, 4 March 1857. From Leslie's Illustrated Magazine. Courtesy of Dickinson College.

man like Lincoln than a well-trained, superbly trained, president like James Buchanan. Because I don't think it's going to work that way invariably. I think we have had many examples of the opposite. But in choosing his cabinet Buchanan showed no interest at all in harmonizing the various divisions and factions in the party. The Democratic Party, like the Republican Party, was full of factions and divisions. In the South, you had Conservative-Union Democrats, you had out-and-out secessionists, and States' Rights Democrats ready to jump off the reservation at the first thing that they would regard as a provocation. In the North, you had Doughfaces, Northern men with Southern principles, you had young Democrats who looked to Stephen A. Douglas, the so-called Young America wing of the party. And somehow, Buchanan should have, I think, brought representatives of all of these groups into his cabinet. Instead, he set up a cabinet of men who agreed with him. He wanted no conflict in his cabinet. He wanted sort of to be chairman of the board and have a cabinet that would work in harmony with him. As a result, I think, it is absolutely wrong to say that Buchanan was dominated by a directory, by a group of powerful cabinet members, for example, Jeremiah Black of Pennsylvania and Howell

Cobb of Georgia. He simply agreed with them. They agreed with him. There was no dispute. The cabinet was a most harmonious group. There is lots of testimony from Cobb and others: we meet together, we are fond of each other, we have no difference of opinion. Consider the way he picked a secretary of state. There were two possibilities: Howell Cobb of Georgia, who is eminently qualified, and Robert J. Walker of Mississippi, a Northerner who had moved to Mississippi, also eminently qualified. The trouble was that if either one of them had been brought into his cabinet there would be problems. Both of them had lots of enemies, so in the end he took the advice of his friend, J. Glancy Jones of Pennsylvania, who suggested "why not bring in Lewis Cass." Now Lewis Cass is incompetent, he's much too old, but he won't offend anybody. Nobody will regard him as a political rival. So Buchanan decided in the end to forget about Cobb and Walker, and invite Lewis Cass to come into the cabinet on condition that he would let Buchanan pick his assistant secretary of state, a close friend of Buchanan's, and really on condition that Buchanan and the assistant secretary of state would run the State Department and Lewis Cass would sign things. Cass was so happy, his term in the Senate was just expiring, he was so happy to stay on in Washington that he agreed to these terms and he was for four years a cipher in the Buchanan administration, till the very end. At the very end Cass suddenly decided that Buchanan wasn't a staunch enough of a Unionist and he resigned from the cabinet in indignation. It was the only thing he did of any significance in the four years as Secretary of State. His resignation was the great moment of his four years. [*Laughter*]

Now let me give you one example of his bungling with patronage. Unquestionably, the man who made it possible for Buchanan to be elected in 1856 was John W. Forney, a Pennsylvanian newspaperman, who was chairman of the Democratic Committee in Pennsylvania who was responsible for carrying that state. He had many ways of doing it. He got lots of Irish voters in Philadelphia and eastern Pennsylvania on the voting lists in time to cast their votes for Buchanan, who incidentally carried Pennsylvania by a scant 1,000 votes. Buchanan was so grateful to Forney for the work he did in Pennsylvania and for other things (he contributed his own money to the campaign in Pennsylvania) that he told Forney that he was going to offer him the editorship of the Washington *Union,* which was a Democratic newspaper in Washington and that is exactly what Forney wanted. He was a superb editor but, also, it meant that he could, after four years, retire in comfort because

Portrait of Jeremiah Black, Buchanan's close friend in Pennsylvania politics and his trusted attorney general. Courtesy of Dickinson College.

printing contracts would come to him from the Democratic Congress that would put him on easy street. The trouble was that Buchanan had never checked to see how the party would react to Forney becoming the editor of the Washington *Union* and he discovered, shortly after the election, that a vast number of Southerners were almost livid at the thought of Forney editing the Washington *Union*. They didn't trust him, and there were reasons why they shouldn't trust him. In any case, Buchanan discovered that it would be impossible and so he called Forney in and said, "I'm sorry. I can't give you the editorship. I've got to find something else for you." Very quickly, after that disappointment, Forney came to Buchanan and said "I'll tell you what. I would really like to go to the United States Senate and there is going to be a vacancy. The Democrats are the majority in the legislature. I'd like you to support me for the Senate." Well, Buchanan said, "all right" and that would take care of that. There was one little problem and that is that he had already promised Jeremiah Black that he was going to support him for the Senate. So the first thing that he had to do was to write to Black and say, "Would you please permit me to withdraw my offer to support you for the Senate?" Black, somewhat reluctantly, fortunately he was a good friend of Forney's, agreed to do it. So Buchanan let it be known that Forney was his candidate for the Senate. Well, the Democrats had a majority in the legislature. It was very thin majority. Lots of Democrats resented Buchanan's intervening and, in the end, several Democrats switched, several refused to vote, and several switched to the Republican candidate, that prince of a man, Simon Cameron [*Laughter*], and Buchanan suffered a humiliating defeat and there was still the Forney problem. What next? Well, Forney would have loved to have gotten into the cabinet. Buchanan thought Forney wasn't fit for that. Forney was rather erratic, he got into his cups quite frequently, and he was not tactful in his conversations, and that was out of the question. Buchanan finally said, "How would you like to be American Consul in Liverpool?" Forney said, "After what I've done for you, Mr. President, that's a pretty humiliating thing. I'm not going to take that." For a long time nothing happened. Poor Mrs. Forney, who had several children and was expecting another one, went to Buchanan and said, "What is to become of my family? Surely, you can give him the postmastership [in Philadelphia]. He won't disgrace you if you give him the Postmastership." Nothing happened. Forney became increasingly desperate. He wrote to Jeremiah Black, his friend. He wrote to Buchanan. Finally, he announced in June 1857 that he was going to start his own newspaper in Philadelphia, the Philadelphia *Press*. Well that really worried Buchanan, and he had reason to worry, suspecting that Forney was not about to edit a proadministration newspaper. Forney assured him that he was going to be loyal to the administration. Well, he started the Philadelphia *Press* and it quickly became the most popular Democratic newspaper in Pennsylvania. It practically drove the Philadelphia *Pennsylvanian,* which was run by an incompetent editor, to the wall and by the late fall of 1857 he had

broken with Buchanan over the Lecompton issue. He was supporting Douglas; he was now giving his loyalty to Douglas as he had
given it to Buchanan for so many years. And that was a beautiful
example of his mishandling of patronage. Incidentally, in addition
to that, Forney had succeeded in talking Buchanan out of bringing
the one man from Pennsylvania that he wanted in his cabinet and
that was J. Glancy Jones, who was a Congressman and a very close
friend of Buchanan's. Forney said "over my dead body. You cannot
put that man into the administration." And so Buchanan had to
write a letter to Jones saying, "I wish you'd permit me to withdraw
my offer of a position within the cabinet." Jones said, "I know
who's behind this. I know it's Forney and his clan. For heaven's
sake, don't appoint Jeremiah Black to your cabinet because everybody knows he is nothing but a tool of Forney's." He reluctantly
did give his consent to withdrawing his candidacy for the cabinet
and promised to be a loyal supporter of Buchanan, and he was.
Buchanan wrote again and said "now that you've withdrawn, I
have to ask you one more favor, would you please agree that Black
can go into the cabinet." And Jones had to concede to that. This
is about as bad a job of handling a number of important appointments as you can imagine. I think these examples are enough to
illustrate my point that he simply wasn't the man cut out to be the
chief executive of the United States then or any other time, and
I'll stop there.

Birkner: One of the things that we learn here is that Buchanan set
off on the wrong foot on the issue of patronage. At least in retrospect it appears that he may have gotten off on the wrong foot in
terms of his relationship with another branch of government, the
Supreme Court. And I thought since it occurs right at the beginning
of the Buchanan presidency we might want to get some sense of
what he is up to even before his inauguration, in terms of a crucial
decision about to be handed down on the slavery issue by the
Supreme Court. I think Professor Fehrenbacher is the right person
to ask this. What is going on and what does it tell you about
Buchanan?

Don Fehrenbacher: Well, let me say just a word first about why
Buchanan took the attitude that he did toward the Dred Scott case
and the decision that was forthcoming. Buchanan was an active
presidential candidate for about ten years, from about 1846 to 1856,
and in 1850, during the crisis of that year, some enemies turned
up a newspaper report from 1819 showing that he had been a mem-

Portrait of Supreme Court Chief Justice Roger Brooke Taney, author of the famous obiter dicta in *Dred Scott* v. *Sandford* (1857). Courtesy of Dickinson College.

Supreme Court Justice Robert C. Grier, like Taney and Buchanan a graduate of Dickinson College, and a key actor in maneuvering behind the scenes over the Dred Scott decision. Courtesy of Dickinson College.

ber of a Resolutions Committee for a meeting right here in Lancaster that had opposed the Missouri Compromise, which he later urged and recommended, and had favored the proposed antislavery restriction on Missouri. He immediately began to get queries, particularly a letter from Jefferson Davis, and so he wrote a letter to Jefferson Davis in which he attributed this to his youth and to the influence of the chairman of the meeting, who was an old friend, and then he went on, "through my whole public career I have been uniform in maintaining the just constitutional rights of the South.

I have made more speeches on this subject, both on the floor of the Senate and at home, than probably any other man now living." This letter was not put before the public until during the Civil War when *Harper's Weekly* called it a "cringing, fawning, supplicating, shivering, slobbering piece of servile obsequiousness." [*Laughter*] Which is an interesting bit of nineteenth-century tautological redundancy. I don't think lackey of the South is quite the right term. I agree with that. Proslavery is not quite the right term. Certain, pro-Southern or, perhaps, anti-antislavery would be as good a description of Buchanan's attitude at least from the late 1820s and early 1830s. From his experience in Congress and, particularly in the Senate during the great controversy over petitions, Buchanan became absolutely convinced that the slavery issue, if agitated, was going to destroy the Union. I think he believed that sincerely. I think that was the strongest motivation that he had. Mind you, he had other reasons to be pro-Southern. It was politically suitable for him to be pro-Southern. There were other reasons why he was anti-antislavery. He was temperamentally not tuned in to the abolitionist self-righteous approach. He was a man of the middle ground. Basically, the thing that drove him most was his fear of a breakup of the Union owing to the slavery agitation. He became increasingly convinced that that had to somehow be repressed or suppressed if the Union was to survive, and he had that feeling, certainly, at the time of his inauguration. Now, the Dred Scott case had been in the works for a decade and there was no doubt that the Court was going to decide against poor Dred Scott himself and send him back to slavery. There was no doubt about that. The main question was whether the Court was going to give a broad decision or a narrow decision, and it could have avoided all of the major issues by simply upholding the view of a lower court that Dred Scott, whatever had happened to him in Illinois and in Minnesota, when he returned to Missouri, had returned to Missouri law and was, therefore, still a slave, and the Court had actually decided that was the decision that was to be issued. Justice [Samuel] Nelson of New York was to issue this narrow decision, and he even wrote it. In fact you can read it because he submitted it eventually as his concurring opinion. But then, for various reasons, the Court changed its mind and decided to address the larger questions. One, the question of Negro citizenship, was really not politically important. Although, historically, it's important to us today, it was not politically important at that time. And the question of whether Congress had the power to prohibit slavery in the territories or, in other words, the constitutionality of the Missouri Compromise line.

A decision was made to render the broader decision. Buchanan, it is thought by some people, played a critical role in that decision. It was quite clear that the five Southern Justices on the Court were prepared to rule against the constitutionality of the Missouri Compromise but, if they got only five votes, all Southern, declaring that, the effect of the decision was liable to be very doubtful, to say the least. What was badly needed, from Buchanan's point of view, was at least one justice from the North who would go along with the invalidation of the Missouri Compromise line. Well, two justices were out of the question because they were opposed to the entire attitude of the majority. They were going to be dissenters. Nelson had already made up his mind that he preferred the narrow decision. That left only one, a Pennsylvanian named [Robert C.] Grier, and it was upon Grier that Buchanan, at the urging of another justice, another member of the Court, brought some pressure, and we know then that, as a consequence, the Court divided six to two, two really not voting, on the question of whether the Missouri Compromise line was really unconstitutional. And that made it appear, at least a bit more, as a national decision rather than a strictly sectional one. Roy Nichols thinks that the Dred Scott would have been entirely different without Buchanan's intervention behind the scenes. What is ignored in most of these presentations, and in the idea that it was the fault of the two dissenting justices, that the broader decision was issued, is the failure to take into account the determination of the chief justice who issued a broader decision. The willpower really in effect here, was not so much Buchanan's, not the dissenting justices', but it was [Roger Brooke] Taney's. I am convinced of that and, therefore, while Buchanan certainly made it easier by the pressure he brought on Grier, the Dred Scott decision as issued was, in its broader frame, what the chief justice desired. Of course, Buchanan wanted a decision because it would presumably remove from politics the issue that was troubling not only the United States as a whole, it was not only causing the quarrel between Republicans and Democrats, that is the question of whether slavery could or should be forbidden in the territories; the whole question was dividing the Democratic Party itself. As has already been suggested, the Democratic Party had endorsed the principle of popular sovereignty. What does popular sovereignty mean? Well, to most of the people who use the term it meant that the people in the territory should decide whether they were to have slavery. But Southerners claimed that it meant making the decision only at the time of statehood, which really was no popular sovereignty at all because everyone had always admitted that a free state had the right to decide whether it should be free or slave. The Democratic Party had hung together now for several years by having a policy of popular sovereignty which was defined in two ways: one in the North, and one in the South. And it was to the advantage of the Democratic Party to continue that ambiguity. Yet Buchanan and a number of other Democrats unwisely encouraged the Court to remove that ambiguity by, in effect, adopting the Southern interpretation of popular sovereignty—that is, by declaring that the Missouri Compromise was unconstitutional. That was to take the Southern side completely. One of the mysteries is that Buchanan did not, if you look at his inaugural, say that this was the question before the Court. He did not say that the Missouri Compromise issue was before the Court, or the question of slavery in the territories. He said that the issue troubling the Democrats was before the Court, that is whether popular sovereignty could take effect at the time of the organization of the territory or at the time of the organization of the state. Therefore, he said, happily this question is now before the Court. Which was not true at all. The Court had no reason, in considering the Dred Scott case, to take up the question that divided the Southerners from [Stephen] Douglas. Furthermore, the Court didn't decide that. There is nothing in the decision except in the opinion of the chief justice as a statement that probably did not have the standing of law. So, the mystery to me is how Buchanan got the notion that the Court was going to decide that question of the timing of popular sovereignty. He couldn't have gotten it from the two justices with whom he was in communication. The only answer that I can suggest is that he was also, perhaps orally, personally in communication with the chief justice. Because it was only in the chief justice's opinion that a decision was rendered that, in effect, outlawed Douglas-style popular sovereignty as well as Republican-style prohibition of slavery in the territories.

Birkner: I suppose one of the other mysteries of the Dred Scott case may be that Buchanan should have expected that it would quiet deep sectional bitterness and the clamor over popular sovereignty.

Fehrenbacher: Yes, let me say that, as late as 1860 in his last annual message to Congress, he finally really commented on the substance of the Dred Scott case by congratulating the nation on the Dred Scott decision and how it had settled matters.

Birkner: So he sort of missed the boat. [*Laughter*] One thing we certainly know about the Dred Scott case is that it set the stage for tremendous drama which is played out in 1857, which Professor Stampp has written about in detail. But the story, for our purposes, is the personal drama. It's Buchanan and it's Douglas. Buchanan fixes on the Kansas issue. He is determined to take a path that Douglas ultimately cannot accept, and Douglas goes public in opposition to the president of his party's emphatic position on this issue. And it seems to me Professor Johannsen can help us understand the dynamics of Buchanan's decision and Douglas's decision. I hope you want also to say a word, if you would, Professor Johannsen, about something that festers underneath all of this, and that is that there was bad blood between Buchanan and Douglas.

Robert Johannsen: I don't want to say too much about that. The title of this panel discussion is "A Reassessment of Buchanan." I think we need a lot more work on Buchanan. Everybody is an expert on Buchanan based on sharp focusing on certain aspects of his presidency. Buchanan is treated primarily by historians as a sort of supporting character, supporting player, to a study of somebody else—Abraham Lincoln or the study of a single year in the Buchanan administration, or something like that. I am just amazed that there hasn't been more work on Buchanan. We have two biographies of Buchanan, in 1883 George Ticknor Curtis's *Life and Letters of James Buchanan* and then we have Philip Klein's 1962 *President James Buchanan: A Biography,* and thirdly we have E. B. Smith's study of the presidency. But isn't there a lot more to be said about James Buchanan than can be said in these three widely spaced studies? I have always felt that we need to know more about Buchanan, more about his career, more about his position on the issues over the years, the stands he took, and that sort of thing. Don Fehrenbacher has mentioned the importance of the abolitionist controversy of the 1830s.

So, I think, one thing we need to do is spend more time looking at Buchanan's total career instead of picking out an episode, things that he couldn't do, his incompetence in this respect or in that respect. Andrew Jackson mishandled patronage from time to time. There are some glaring examples; it's not unique. We've got to look at him in greater perspective; we've got to know more about him. Many years ago, I reviewed a couple of books on James Buchanan. At that time, I expressed some disappointment because I found little written about him that would explain Buchanan's approach to the presidential office, his concept of the presidency so

As president, Buchanan presided over many ceremonies at the White House, among them this reception for the Japanese Embassy. From *Leslie's Illustrated Magazine.* Courtesy of Dickinson College.

to speak. I asked a number of questions that I thought might place Buchanan, give us a better notion of what Buchanan meant, what Buchanan stood for, and a better understanding of how and why he acted as he did. Because certainly we know that this administration was beset with a great many crises. How did he bring his experience to bear on the problems he faced? The constitutional issues? What was the character of that? How did he define his presidential role in the face of deep national crisis? What was his concept, his view, of the power of the presidency, the function, the obligation, the responsibilities of the presidential office? I think that there is a lot that could be done in that respect.

Yesterday morning, we were given a classic description of the Jacksonian presidency. The Jackson concept of a strong, aggressive president, director of all his people, and so forth. Professor [William] Gienapp suggested that Lincoln followed this Jacksonian concept, but Buchanan fell dreadfully short. Well, not all political leaders in the United States, presidential aspirants or otherwise, agreed with Andrew Jackson's concept of the presidency.

With respect to [Stephen] Douglas, I feel that Douglas has been treated much the same way we find Buchanan described here to-day. So I feel a kind of empathy with the Old Public Functionary, because I have been struggling against similar charges. Douglas was allegedly a tool of the South, no matter what he did, he was down on his narrow bones before the altar of the slave power and the minion of the proslavery forces, that sort of thing. The same sorts of things were said about Buchanan, captive of the South. We never speak of anybody during this period as being the captive of the North, a captive of the abolitionists who argues against slavery. We still struggle against, feel the impact of the legacy of the Civil War.

Now the Douglas-Buchanan split was not regarded by all con-temporaries as an earthshaking development. Abraham Lincoln in 1858 said that the rift between Douglas and Buchanan over the Lecompton Constitution was of no real importance. He advised Republicans to ignore it, pay no attention to it, it doesn't matter. On the contrary, Lincoln saw Douglas and Buchanan as working together in spite of this rift.

Fehrenbacher: Excuse me. Lincoln did that for strategic reasons. He was working against the efforts of certain Republicans in the East to paint Douglas as—

Johannsen: I know. But why don't we give Buchanan or Douglas credit sometimes for working for strategic reasons.

Smith: Lincoln wants to get elected senator, and everybody knows that everybody in Illinois hates Buchanan so he identifies Bu-chanan with Douglas to defeat Douglas in the election.

Fehrenbacher: He's trying to push Douglas as close as he possibly can to the proslavery side.

Johannsen: You didn't let me complete my thought.

Fehrenbacher: I'm sorry, go ahead. I won't interrupt you again until you deserve it. [*Laughter*]

Johannsen: I would be disappointed if you didn't. I want interaction.

Stampp: You mention that Douglas and Buchanan were constantly called tools of the slave powers, and that no one was ever called a tool of the North. Which Southerners did you have in mind to play these roles? I was just wondering whether there was one.

Johannsen: But you see, I'm asking the question.

Stampp: But in the case of the so-called doughfaces, these were Northerners who were tools of the South. I was wondering which Southerners were tools of the North.

Smith: Some people call Zachary Taylor a tool of the North even though he owned 140 slaves.

Johannsen: One thing I have been impressed with is that we have difficulty recognizing the fact that some fifteen slaveholding states were actually part of the Union, they were part of the United States. We talk about how they were somehow not really Americans, not really a part of the Union. I suppose this is the legacy of the Civil War. The North won the Civil War. The North interprets the history of the United States in the antebellum period, and we are still arguing it.

Fehrenbacher: But there was a Doughface factor in American politics down to the Civil War which meant that you cannot name any person who achieved high executive office who didn't have, in some way or the other, to make his peace with the South. And Southerners, to hold high executive office, did *not* have to make their peace with the antislavery forces. A John C. Calhoun could be unanimously approved by the Senate for the position of secretary of state, but no person could become secretary of state who was in any way associated with a strong antislavery viewpoint, until the time of Lincoln. This had been building up for years, so that when we talk about antislavery we should think of anti-Southernism, too, in the North and resentment of the extent to which the South had dominated the country.

Johannsen: The position that Buchanan took was to be fair and just to both sides, because if it wasn't, the balance in the Union is askew, and Douglas felt, as you said Buchanan felt earlier in the 1830s, that the antislavery agitation would destroy the Union. Douglas felt you can't argue, in the political context, you can't argue moral arguments because there is no compromise, there is no way minds can meet. Southerners have their standards of morality, and Northerners have their standards of morality and never the twain shall meet. And he said, a number of times, the only way this question would be settled was through fighting or bloodshed, a bloody civil war. Of course, that's what happened.

Smith: Here you have two people who apparently agree with each other on most of these policies, and yet Buchanan does everything he possibly can to keep Douglas from getting elected president in 1860 and senator in 1858. My question simply is, Did personal relations play that big a part in keeping these two people at each other's throat?

Johannsen: Yes, I think it fed on itself. Douglas did feel aggrieved that he wasn't consulted by Buchanan. . . .

Smith: I think it's significant that Douglas claimed that he spent $42,000 of his own money helping Buchanan get elected, and Buchanan wrote him a letter of thanks addressed to The Honorable Samuel A. Douglas. That would upset anybody.

Johannsen: Do you think that was a deliberate slight?

Smith: Are you going to say that he didn't know Douglas's first name?

Fehrenbacher: Maybe he was getting old. [*Laughter*] Bob, let me ask you one further question about Douglas in the break with Buchanan. Would you be willing to agree, to some extent, that Douglas by 1858 had come to recognize that as far as his constituency in Illinois was concerned he was carrying all the Southern weight that he could and, in fact, had to make some gesture toward antislavery in order to stay in power?

Johannsen: Well, you use the word gesture and carrying weight, suggesting the problem was sincerity.

Fehrenbacher: No, no. I wouldn't want to exclude that but I'm saying that simply as a matter of political strategy, the same strategy that Lincoln would use and did, in what Lincoln had to say about Negro equality. Wasn't Douglas consulting political strategy to some extent for his own benefit in the stand that he took against Lecompton?

Johannsen: Sure. You're absolutely right. He was simply reflecting the wisdom of his constituents and he was simply building on statements he had made in 1854 and 1850 and even the late 1840s. There was nothing new about his stand. In fact in 1858, he confronted Lincoln, questioned Lincoln's irrepressible conflict notion. It's exactly what he's afraid of. Let me just add, when he questioned Lincoln's use of the "house divided" metaphor, Lincoln responded, "Mr. Douglas, your quarrel is not with me, but with a higher authority," because this was a paraphrase of Jesus Christ, "A house divided against itself cannot stand." He said, "If you believe that a house divided can stand, then you're at war with our Savior, not with me."

Birkner: If I could exercise a moderator's privilege here, I think old Buck deserves to be factored back into the action. It seems to me whether we are dealing with a sympathetic view of Buchanan's presidency such as you get in the biography by Professor Klein or a less than sympathetic reading such as you get in *America in 1857,* a recent book by Professor Stampp, Buchanan has to make some very hard decisions about the Kansas issue. We can't leave Kansas out of the story quite so readily perhaps as Professor Johannsen would have us do. I would like to ask Professor Stampp about something that intrigues me, because I hadn't read it until I looked at his book, and that is the kinds of options that Buchanan had in 1857. It seems that his options were, perhaps, broader than is typically thought. Would you comment on that?

Stampp: Well, I think he had two options. One, doing what he did, which was disastrous; and the other, doing what he said he was going to do. And that was to insist that the Lecompton Constitution be submitted to an honest vote, the whole constitution. He made the commitment in his inaugural address, where he talked about submitting the document. He made the commitment to Robert J. Walker when Walker agreed to be governor of Kansas. Walker sent a note to Buchanan saying, "It is my understanding that you and your cabinet are in agreement with my proposal that this constitution must be submitted for ratification." Walker mentioned that in his inaugural address in Kansas and told the delegates to the convention that he would urge Congress not to admit Kansas if the constitution were not submitted for ratification. He got a lot of static out of the South, and Buchanan's organ, the Washington *Union,* stood by Walker. Buchanan wrote a letter to Walker on 12 July 1857, saying, "I will stand or fall on my commitment of the submission of the constitution for ratification." There is no evidence whatsoever that Buchanan indicated that he was breaking away from that until the Lecompton convention executed that, so called, juggle, of letting the people vote for the future admission of slaves or not. But, by providing that, the slaves there would continue in slavery, and Buchanan suddenly discovered then that that's what he had meant all along. He had never intended that the whole constitution be submitted to ratification. The only important issue, as he expressed through [Jeremiah] Black in an editorial in the Washington *Union,* was the question of the further admission of slaves into Kansas. As far as the slaves already in Kansas, he said the Dred Scott decision protected them. Which is utter nonsense. The Dred Scott decision did no such thing. Any state had the right to abolish slavery, whatever slavery there was in that state. The Dred Scott decision did not abolish that right. He claimed that was the only issue, and it wasn't the only issue. The Lecompton Constitution rigged representation in Kansas. It provided that all the fraudulent votes that had been cast in Magee County and Oxford precinct were to be counted as legal, and representation was to be based on the illegal votes that had been cast. There were questions involving the expenditure of money for internal improvements; there were questions for banking; there were questions for the location of the capital of Kansas. All of them were crucial issues, and it's probably true that the people in Kansas, the majority in Kansas, wouldn't have voted for that constitution if it had been written by the most honest body of men you could imagine. They weren't going to have anything to do with the Lecompton Constitution, and one of the arguments used against submitting it was that if they had submitted it, it would have been voted down by the people, so what's the point of submitting it, they won't even consider it. You've got to go behind the motives of the voters. If they vote against it for the wrong reasons, they have no right to be given the chance to vote for it in the first place. It was an unbelievable switch in strategy on Buchanan's part. But let me say this in defense of Buchanan. Buchanan really thought he could pull it off and, remember, he came awfully close. He got it through the Senate easily. He came within eight votes of getting that approved by the House of Representatives. Five votes the other way would have switched it. If they could have bought five more men, they could have passed it. [*Laughter*] And you know, I don't know whether Buchanan ever thought about this, but Douglas had really set a precedent for him. Douglas had raised a hell of a fuss back in 1854 with his Kansas-Nebraska Act, and two years later the Democrats won the presidential election again. This is 1857, Buchanan was raising a hell of a fuss, but supposing he brought Kansas in under the Lecompton Constitution, as he almost did. What would have been the situation in 1860? I don't know. But he might have thought, they'll cool off by 1860 and we'll have a harmonious convention and a chance to win the presidency again. It was a bad guess. It was a terrible miscalculation. But it almost did work.

Fehrenbacher: He thought, didn't he, that by 1860, Kansas as an independent state would have abolished slavery?

Stampp: Right.

Birkner: So far it seems as if the Buchanan presidency goes into a black hole after the Lecompton Constitution fight plays down. I'm just curious whether any of our panelists here, as part of this reassessment, want to say anything about the fact that we tend as historians to focus on the Lecompton Constitution, or some foreign policy episodes as Professor May spoke about this morning, and then we proceed to the secession crisis. Is this, as Professor Johannsen suggests, an understudied presidency?

Smith: It seems to me that Phil Klein has told us all that we ever need to know about Buchanan as a person. He was a highly intelligent, extremely ambitious man who wanted to be president. Over a long period he had formed a great many personal friendships with Southerners, I suspect because they were the ones who left their wives at home when they came to Washington, and so he spent his time in Washington with Southerners at boarding houses and so on. He obviously had very deep personal affections there and, so when he gets into the White House and become president, he acts on these emotions and these ideas and these feelings that he has. I don't know what else we would try to learn about him. Professor Johannsen says that we need to learn more about him. Where would we start?

Stampp: Professor Summers gave us some idea of what was going on between 1857 and 1860, and that's an important part of the Buchanan administration.

Birkner: I see that Professor Klein is seeking the floor and I think he's entitled to it.
[Philip S. Klein stands up from the floor and speaks in favor of

Buchanan's plan for Kansas since it was likely to result in the freeing of slaves in Kansas.]

Smith: Could a majority, was a majority big enough to amend the constitution? And the Lecompton Constitution said you can't change it until 1864.

Fehrenbacher: From the Northern viewpoint, why should the Free-Soil majority in Kansas have to accept slave-state status, and then abolish slavery later on. At least that was their attitude and that's why they rejected it. I'd like to ask Professor Johannsen, why did Douglas reject the English compromise, which would have seemed to have met most of his objections?

Stampp: Let me give one reason. Senator [David C.] Broderick said that, if he endorsed any compromise, he was going to publicly denounce Douglas. Douglas did waver but the anti-Lecompton Democrats got to him and threatened him if he broke away, and so he changed his mind and denounced it.

Johannsen: At the same time, he regarded that compromise as being kind of a compromise of his initial position and his stringent insistence that this was a travesty on popular sovereignty. The constitution should have been presented in its entirety to the electorate.

Fehrenbacher: But everyone knew it was a Southern surrender agreement, a face-saving Southern surrender.

Johannsen: The English bill? Yes. That's right, because Southerners faced the prospect if they did win the Lecompton Constitution, if they did bring Kansas into the Union as a slave state, it would be a Republican slave state and that so confused the situation. But Douglas felt that the constitution should be submitted without a lot of this compromise language.

Stampp: He wanted a flat vote for or against the Lecompton Constitution and the English bill phrased it in such a way it was a subterfuge. It sounded as if they were voting on the land grant, and that's what the Republicans objected to, that's what most of the anti-Lecompton Democrats objected to, and that's ultimately, when Douglas denounced it, that's the point he made. Well, he made two points actually, and that is for not ratifying it, there was a penalty, and that is they wouldn't be admitted to statehood until they had the 93,000 or whatever population was required, whereas, if they ratified it, they'd be admitted to statehood immediately, and Douglas said that is unfair. It penalized them for rejecting the constitution and rewarded them for ratifying it. So it's another joke.

Birkner: We are going to come in a moment or two to the end of the formal part of an informal session, so that people in the audience will have the opportunity to ask their questions. Before we do though I wanted to give Professor Fehrenbacher a chance to comment on the debate on the African slave trade, the opening of which some Southerners were for and some were not. Professor Fehrenbacher has a comment I think he would like to share with us.

Fehrenbacher: Very briefly, I won't go into any detail but I will say, simply, that there were two slave-trade crises that Buchanan faced. One was the effort by certain Southerners to revive the African slave trade, both by direct action, in the case of actually going and getting slaves in the case of the ship *Wanderer,* and also urging a repeal of the federal laws against it. Buchanan took a definite stand against that. The other thing is that a crisis with England over the British search of American ships involved in the slave trade to Cuba, which was the only slave trade that Americans had been involved in for forty years. And the Buchanan administration in rejecting British intervention, took the stand that the United States could do its own law enforcing and, therefore, was under some obligation to do a better job of law enforcing. As a result— this is something that few people know—the Buchanan administration has the best record of any administration on suppression of the African slave trade. More slave ships were captured in the Buchanan administration, and particularly in the years 1859, 1860, and 1861, than in any previous administration by far. And one of those ships captured was the *Erie,* which was captained by a certain Nathaniel Gordon, who some of you may remember was the only person ever executed for slave trading under American law, and Lincoln refused to commute his sentence or pardon him. He was actually hanged. But he was arrested during the Buchanan administration.

Stampp: There is another point to be made. He was taken to New York and tried there, and not in Florida or Georgia.

Fort Pickens, in Pensacola Harbor, Florida, remained in federal hands during the secession crisis as Buchanan worked out a compromise with Floridians whereby the garrison could be supplied but not reinforced. Courtesy of Dickinson College.

Smith: He had a lot of people arrested but nobody convicted up till Gordon.

Fehrenbacher: No. In a number of other criminal trials, Southerners had refused to convict. But the arrest was during the Buchanan administration.

Birkner: I'd like to get the panelists briefly, to give us a one-minute reassessment of Buchanan. If they prefer not to express a personal opinion, I'd like them to tell us where they think Buchanan studies ought to be going. If I could ask them each to be brief so that the audience could then have a shot. I thought we'd start with Professor Johannsen.

Johannsen: Well, one thing I would like to point out, one thing I would like to suggest here in addition to what I said already about knowing more about Buchanan, studying him further, is a new look at Buchanan during the secession crisis, and especially the 8 January message to Congress, which I find almost not mentioned at all in the books on Buchanan and in other studies of the secession crisis. And yet as I read that message, 8 January 1861, I was reminded of Abraham Lincoln on 4 March 1961, and I find Lincoln echoing the points that Buchanan made in that special message. And I hesitate to present this because people are going to jump all over me because of what I'm saying about Lincoln. But it seems to me that there is a linkage, and I wish I had time before coming here to look into this, to see to what extent Lincoln's newspaper in Springfield reported these things, made these points, and so forth. A great many Northern people supported this message, supported Buchanan in these statements, including Dr. Stampp, in *And the War Came*. So I think here is a point that ought to be reached, that Buchanan's stiffening position with respect to the Union and his statements in the 8 January message in which he says "the right and duty of the federal government to use military force defensively against those who resist federal officers in the execution of their legal functions and against those who assail the property of the federal government is clear and undeniable." And that's italicized. He emphasizes that statement, and we find that echoed in Lincoln's inaugural. Well, Lincoln gets all the credit; we should give some credit to James Buchanan.

Stampp: Let me amplify that a bit, because that's what I wanted to talk about. Having given a rather negative assessment at the beginning, I would like to say that I absolutely agree with Professor Johannsen that his response to the secession crisis was altogether honorable and not only in his message of 8 January but in his regular message, which was so much maligned in the public press. What he did in that message was to say exactly what Lincoln said. There is a difference between enforcing the law and protecting American property and coercing a state, and Buchanan denied the right of the federal government to coerce a state and so did Lincoln. But he also said that the government had the right to protect its property. He said further that the powers of the president, as then defined by federal law, were not adequate, and he threw it up to Congress to provide additional powers and the Congress never did, even after the South left the Union, and resigned from Congress and the Republicans had a majority. In January and February, 1861, the Republicans did absolutely nothing to strengthen the power of the president. Lincoln, of course, had to go beyond the power of the president; that Buchanan was not willing to do. In his message of 8 January, he made the same point: he refused to recognize the right of a state to secede; he defended the right of the federal government to repel aggression against the federal govern-

SOUTH CAROLINA'S "ULTIMATUM".

Cartoon in early 1861 portrays Buchanan as eager to thrust aside his responsibilities to Fort Sumter. Buchanan is seen urging South Carolina Governor Pickens not to fire on Sumter "till I get out of office." Published by Currier and Ives. Courtesy of Dickinson College.

ment; he insisted that he had no intentions, and it was illegal, to coerce a state. It was a meaningless distinction, but Lincoln made it and so did Buchanan, and Buchanan left office without compromising Lincoln; the Confederacy had not been recognized. He had not launched a war, and he had every right to feel that this crisis belonged to Lincoln. It was awful that one had to wait four months for a new president to come in, but I think Buchanan did what was the right thing for him to do during that period. Another place where he differs from Lincoln, of course, is that he kept advocating compromise and Lincoln did everything that he could do to prevent compromise. But as far as protecting the integrity of the Union, I think Buchanan's record is first-rate during the secession crisis.

Johannsen: Even Lincoln endorsed compromise. During his inaugural address, he said if you come up with an amendment in Congress to solve this problem, I'll support it.

Stampp: Well, that's not a compromise because no Southerner said that was adequate.

Fehrenbacher: Two men could say approximately the same thing, but they've said it out of totally different backgrounds, and that's what made the difference. Lincoln said it out of an antislavery background and back of Buchanan was thirty years and more of pro-Southern, anti-antislavery service and actions, and the credibility of the two when they said these things—similar things—was, therefore, very different, at least, throughout the North.

Stampp: Can I make one point? And that is that Jefferson Davis said, "If Abraham Lincoln follows the policy of James Buchanan, we're going to have a civil war." So Jefferson Davis saw no difference.

Fehrenbacher: But Northerners remembered Buchanan for what he had been and that is why, I think, that much more needs to be done with investigating more thoroughly Buchanan's earlier history set against the background of what was going on during his more than twenty years in Congress in order to understand why he believed, and I think he sincerely believed, that the one major problem of his time, the one that was above all others, was that of preventing the breakup of the Union as a result of slavery agitation. And I think that he acted on those terms until maybe right at the very end, when circumstances were going to force him to depart them.

Smith: My primary criticism of Buchanan rests on the fact that the only way really you were going to prevent secession was to prevent the election of a Republican president, and so everything you did that created the wrong image or an anti-Democratic image, or an anti-Southern image, and made it stronger in the North increased the possibility that a Republican candidate in 1860 would, as Lincoln did, get enough Northern votes to win the presidency even though he had only 40 percent of the total vote. Certainly, the Lecompton Constitution played a great role in causing a lot of Democrats to become Republicans, a lot of former Know-Nothings to become Republicans. If the Lecompton Constitution had passed that would have been even greater. That's one man's opinion. I thoroughly agree with Professor Stampp about Buchanan's role in the crisis. He stood firm. He would not accept any Southerners as delegates. He said you come here as private citizens. He made it clear that he would maintain control of the forts. His reputation has suffered a good deal because of the out-and-out falsehoods of General Winfield Scott. Buchanan wanted to reinforce Fort Sumter

Artist's rendering of Fort Sumter, before the South Carolina bombardment of April 1861 sparked the Civil War. Courtesy of Dickinson College.

with the *U.S.S. Brooklyn* and Scott talked him out of it, so they sent the smaller, weak, unarmed ship that was driven away. Scott later implied that he was the one who wanted to send the *Brooklyn*, and Buchanan had talked him out of it. This is not true. Buchanan did stand firm. If he had given up Fort Sumter, Lincoln would not have had his cause for the war. Fort Sumter was still on the plate for Lincoln because Buchanan did stand firm in this crisis.

Birkner: Let's open the floor to questions now.

Member of the Audience: Would somebody comment, please, on Buchanan's views on Manifest Destiny?

Stampp: He was for it.

Robert May: I know I've already had my say, but in response to Michael Birkner mentioning the black hole of Buchanan's presidency, something might be added about his foreign policy. Recently we've had several presidents in this country who have been described as foreign policy presidents—that is, that they had no domestic agenda. It seems to me that James Buchanan, who vetoed various kinds of internal development bills, was a president who essentially had a foreign policy agenda. Buchanan intended to be a foreign policy president, and had the idea of resolving the Utah problem and the slavery in the territories problem smack at the beginning of his presidency, which would leave him free to follow a Manifest Destiny kind of agenda that he had set a long time earlier. Although he did not approve of illegal expansion, that is, filibustering, he definitely approved of buying Cuba, of a protectorate over northern Mexico, and things like that, as well as of commercial expansion—which many scholars have pointed out was a rising thing in the country. If he could arrange markets in Asia, the whole country would prosper. So I would throw that out as a possible interpretive handle for Buchanan's presidency. Slavery could go on forever with Cuba as its source. The South would always have a supply of slaves. As Professor Fehrenbacher and others have said, this is an anti-antislavery president. He did not love the peculiar institution. Philip Klein's biography makes it clear that he criticized slavery in the abstract but he certainly did not have an antislavery soul. I think he would have tolerated a perpetuation of slavery indefinitely.

Smith: He sent 2,500 men and nineteen ships up the Parana River against Paraguay and I've never figured out what he hoped to gain from this. He was avenging the murder of one American.

Birkner: In his fascinating diary for this period, George Templeton Strong was obsessed with Buchanan's lack of backbone. People did talk about it. Would any of the panelists like to comment upon this?

Johannsen: I would suggest that this is a period of time when the United States looked upon the presidency as a weaker branch of the government than the legislative branch. Since the Polk administration, perhaps, it's the Congress that exercised the leadership in the nation. This is off the top of my head but I think that's probably the case. You have a series of more or less passive presidents. This is what makes the contrast with Lincoln, that was drawn the other day, so glaring because Lincoln harks back to the old Jacksonian concept. But this is a period of weak executives or at least of a perception that this is the way it ought to be—weak executives, strong legislative branch. . . .

Member of the Audience: What evidence do we have that Buchanan communicated directly with the Supreme Court in the Dred Scott decision?

Fehrenbacher: We have letters. . . . Justice [John] Catron is the one that he corresponded with first, and then Catron urged him to bring some pressure on Grier. He wrote to Grier and Grier replied. So we have that correspondence.

Smith: I'd like to say something quickly on this, on whether it made any difference. I think if Buchanan and Douglas had liked each other, presented a united front, brought about a fair and honest election in Kansas, which would have gone Free-Soil, I don't think the Democratic Party would have lost the South and, I think, they would have kept a lot of Democrats from going Republican in 1860. I think it could have made a big difference.

Johannsen: At the same time, we get awfully close here at times to a kind of devil thing with respect to the Civil War. I think William Gienapp said somewhere yesterday that Buchanan made the secession crisis, or the North-South crisis, insolvable.

Gienapp: No, I didn't say that.

Johannsen: I wrote it down. Anyway, it's because of Buchanan that the Democratic Party splits, and it's because of that the Republicans win in 1860. We have people, apparently this is a kind of neorevisionist point of view, the Blundering Generation, and Buchanan was the chief blunderer who brings about the Civil War.

Birkner: We have time for two more questions and then we're going to have to pursue questions more informally.

Member of the Audience: I would like to ask these gentlemen—we may never get a chance to do this again, since they know Buchanan so well—to give us each a brief analysis of Buchanan's character.

Stampp: I'll use a few adjectives to try to—cautious, conservative. He really disliked agitators. He happened to focus on abolitionists, but, I think, he probably would have had the same feelings toward women's rights agitators, temperance agitators, and all the other agitators. He hated abolitionists; he hated Republicans. It was unrealistic, but he really did feel, as many Democrats did, and as they frequently virtually said, that the Republican Party was an illegitimate political organization because it was a standing threat to the survival of the Union and because it was a sectional party. He believed these things and, therefore, in his eyes, it was a perfectly legitimate agenda to stop sectional agitation. He felt, "What good does it do? It doesn't do any good for slaves or anyone." Moreover, Buchanan accepted Southerners' assurances that the slaves are well cared for it because it's in the interest of their masters and that they are being civilized and that we could only make things worse by agitating for the abolition of slavery. That's not exactly proslavery, but it comes awfully close to it.

Smith: I have a theory. He's a bachelor. He has an affectionate nature. He desperately needs affection. He doesn't want to be lonely. He doesn't like being lonely, and so when he goes to Washington, he takes up with the people who are also without their wives and kids there, and they give him affection and they win his affection. And, I think, there is this deep personal affection for a number of Southerners, because they were the ones that he was put in with when he went to Washington. I think that has a big impact on the way he felt. I think our personal friendship and our personal relationships have a lot to do with our behavior.

Stampp: Well, there are some qualifications there. Some of them did bring their wives, and he loved their wives.

Smith: Well, that's true too. The ones that came with their wives were always trying to match him up with somebody.

Fehrenbacher: I think the adjective erratic should be added to cautious. He was basically cautious, prudent—but he could be rash and stubborn. And the rashness is indicated, I think, in the move into Utah before he had enough information to be really justified.

Johannsen: He was a very stiff, uncompromising individual once he made up his mind. A constitutionalist, devoted to the constitution. An individual who treasured law, order, and stability. . . .

Fehrenbacher: I believe, like all politicians of that time, he was a constitutionalist only when it was to his advantage to be that. I think you could overstress his clinging to the constitution. He, like most Democrats, refused to accept the ruling of John Marshall that a national bank was constitutional. And the Democratic Party kept in its platform, right down through 1856, a statement that Congress had no power to incorporate a bank. And he was asked, "If you urge people to obey the Supreme Court with respect to the Dred Scott case, why did you take this stand against the Court's decision with regard to a bank?"

Johannsen: When I say constitutionalist, it's according to his interpretation always.

Birkner: I see a number of hands here, which would suggest that you haven't looked at your watches and noticed that we've been going for two hours. However, before I close this, I see Phil Klein and, I think, we owe him a debt of gratitude for his pioneering work on Buchanan. [*Applause*]

Selective Bibliography

Abbott, Richard H. *The Republican Party and the South, 1855–1877: The First Southern Strategy.* Chapel Hill: University of North Carolina Press, 1986.

Abrahamson, Paul R. "Generational Change and the Decline of Party Identification." In Richard G. Niemi and Herbert F. Weisberg, eds., *Controversies in American Voting Behavior.* San Francisco: W. H. Freeman, 1976.

———. *Generational Change in American Politics.* Lexington, Mass.: Lexington Books, 1975.

Anbinder, Tyler. *Nativism and Slavery: The Northern Know Nothings and the Politics of the 1850s.* New York: Oxford University Press, 1993.

Angle, Paul, ed. *Herndon's Life of Lincoln.* Cleveland, Ohio: World Publishing. 1942.

Auchampaugh, Philip Gerald. *James Buchanan and His Cabinet on the Eve of Secession.* Lancaster, Pa.: privately printed, 1926.

———. "Political Techniques, 1856—Or Why the Herald Went for Fremont." *Western Political Quarterly* 1 (1949): 243–51.

Baker, Jean H. *Affairs of Party: The Political Culture of the Northern Democrats in the Mid-Nineteenth Century.* Ithaca, NY: Cornell University Press, 1983.

———. *The Politics of Continuity: Maryland Political Parties from 1858 to 1870.* Baltimore: Johns Hopkins University Press, 1973.

Barney, William. *The Secessionist Impulse: Alabama and Mississippi in 1860.* Princeton: Princeton University Press, 1974.

Baum, Dale. *The Civil War Party System: The Case of Massachusetts, 1848–1876.* Chapel Hill: University of North Carolina Press, 1984.

Beck, Paul Allen. "A Socialization Theory of Partisan Realignment." In Richard G. Niemi, ed., *The Politics of Future Citizens: New Dimensions in the Political Socialization of Children.* San Francisco: W. H. Freeman, 1974.

Belohlavek, John M. *George Mifflin Dallas: Jacksonian Patrician.* University Park: Pennsylvania State University Press, 1977.

———. *Let the Eagle Soar: The Foreign Policy of Andrew Jackson.* Lincoln: University of Nebraska Press, 1985.

Bergeron, Paul H. *The Presidency of James K. Polk.* Lawrence: University Press of Kansas, 1987.

Bermann, Karl. *Under the Big Stick: Nicaragua and the United States since 1848.* Boston: South End Press, 1986.

Binder, Frederick Moore. "James Buchanan: Jacksonian Expansionist." *Historian* 55 (Autumn 1992): 69–84.

———. *James Buchanan and the American Empire.* Selinsgrove, Pa.: Susquehanna University Press, 1994.

Birkner, Michael J. "A Conversation with Philip S. Klein." *Pennsylvania History* 56 (October 1989): 243–75.

———. "Was There a Second Great Generation?" *Virginia Cavalcade* 40 (Autumn 1990): 52–64.

Blue, Frederick J. *Salmon P. Chase: A Life in Politics.* Kent Ohio: Kent State University Press, 1987.

Bogue, Allan G. *The Congressman's Civil War.* New York: Cambridge University Press, 1989.

Booraem, Hendrik. *The Formation of the Republican Party in New York: Politics and Conscience in the Antebellum North.* New York: New York University Press, 1983.

Brady, David W. "Elections, Congress, and Public Policy Changes: 1886–1960." In Bruce A. Campbell and Richard J. Trilling, eds., *Realignment in American Politics: Toward a Theory.* Austin: University of Texas Press, 1980.

Brown, Charles H. *Agents of Manifest Destiny: The Lives and Times of the Filibusters.* Chapel Hill: University of North Carolina Press, 1980.

Bruns, Roger, and Bryan Kennedy. "El Presidente Gringo: William Walker and the Conquest of Nicaragua." In Robert James Maddox, ed., *Annual Editions: American History.* Guilford, Colo.: Duskin, 1991.

Buchanan, James. *Mr. Buchanan's Administration on the Eve of Rebellion.* New York: D. Appleton and Company, 1866.

Burnham, Walter Dean. "Party Systems and the Political Process." In *The Current Crisis in American Politics.* New York: Oxford University Press, 1982.

Carman, Harry J., and Reinhard H. Luthin. *Lincoln and the Patronage.* New York: Columbia University Press, 1943.

Chambers, William Nisbet. *Old Bullion Benton: Senator from the New West.* New York: Russell and Russell, 1956.

Coleman, John F. *The Disruption of the Pennsylvania Democracy, 1848–1860.* Harrisburg: Pennsylvania Historical and Museum Commission, 1975.

Collins, Bruce. "The Democrats' Loss of Pennsylvania in 1858." *Pennsylania Magazine of History and Biography* 109 (October 1985): 499–536.

Cortada, James W. *Two Nations over Time: Spain and the United States, 1776–1977.* Westport, Conn.: Greenwood Press, 1978.

Cox, Henry Bartholomew. *War, Foreign Affairs, and Constitution Power: 1829–1901.* Cambridge, Mass.: Ballinger, 1984.

Crenshaw, Ollinger. *The Slave States in the Presidential Election of 1860.* Johns Hopkins Studies in the Historical and Political Science, ser. 63, no. 3. Baltimore: Johns Hopkins Press, 1945.

Davis, Robert Ralph, Jr. "James Buchanan and the Suppression of the Slave Trade, 1859–1861." *Pennsylvania History* 33 (October 1966): 446–59.

Davis, William C. *John C. Breckinridge: Soldier, Statesman, Symbol.* Baton Rouge: Louisiana State University Press, 1974.

Dennett, Tyler. *Americans in Eastern Asia: A Critical Study of the Policy of the United States with Reference to China, Japan and Korea in the 19th Century.* New York: Barnes and Noble, 1941.

———, ed. *Lincoln and the Civil War in the Diaries and Letters of John Hay.* New York: Dodd, Mead, 1939.

Donald, David Herbert. *Liberty and Union*. Boston: Little, Brown, 1978.

———. *Lincoln Reconsidered: Essays on the Civil War Era*. New York: Knopf, 1972.

———. ed. *Inside Lincoln's Cabinet: The Civil War Diaries of Salmon P. Chase*. New York: Longmans, Green, 1954.

Dunbar, Willis Frederick. *Lewis Cass*. Grand Rapids, Mich.: Eerdmans, 1970.

Elazar, Daniel J. *Building toward Civil War: Generational Rhythms in American Politics*. Lanham Md.: Madison Books, 1992.

Farley, Foster M. "William B. Reed: Presidential Buchanan's Minister to China, 1857–1858." *Pennsylvania History* 37 (July 1970): 269–80.

Fehrenbacher, Don E. *Chicago Giant: A Biography of "Long John" Wentworth*. Madison, Wi.: American History Research Center, 1957.

———. *The Dred Scott Case: Its Significance in American Law and Politics*. New York: Oxford University Press, 1978.

———. "The Republican Decision at Chicago." In *Politics and the Crisis of 1860*. Urbana: University of Illinois Press, 1961.

———. *Slavery, Law and Politics: The Dred Scott Case in Historical Perspective*. New York: Oxford University Press, 1981.

Feipel, Louis N. "The Navy and Filibustering in the Fifties." *United States Naval Institute Proceedings* 44 (April–July 1918): 1529.

Fermer, Douglas. *James Gordon Bennett and the New York Herald: A Study of Editorial Opinion in the Civil War Era, 1854–1867*. New York: St. Martin's Press, 1986.

Fite, Emerson D. *The Presidential Campaign of 1860*. New York: Macmillan, 1911.

Foner, Eric. *Free Soil, Labor, Free Men: The Ideology of the Republican Party before the Civil War*. New York: Oxford University Press, 1970.

Forgie, George. *Patricide in the House Divided: A Psychological Portrait of Lincoln and His Age*. New York: W. W. Norton, 1979.

Forney, John W. *Anecdotes of Public Men*. New York: Harper and Brothers, 1873.

French, Benjamin B. *Witness to the Young Republic: A Yankee's Journal, 1828–1870*. Hanover, N.H.: University Press of New England, 1989.

Gara, Larry. *The Presidency of Franklin Pierce*. Lawrence: University Press of Kansas, 1992.

Garraty, John A. *Silas Wright*. New York: Columbia University Press, 1949.

Gienapp, William E. "Nebraska, Nativism and Rum: The Failure of Fusion in Pennsylvania, 1854." *Pennsylvania Magazine of History and Biography* 109 (October 1985): 425–71.

———. *The Origins of the Republican Party, 1852–1856*. New York: Oxford University Press, 1987.

Glatthaar, Joseph T. *Partners in Command: The Relationships between Leaders in the Civil War*. New York: Free Press, 1994.

Graebner, Norman A., ed. *Politics and the Crisis of 1860*. Urbana: University of Illinois Press, 1961. S.v. "The Republican Decision at Chicago," by Don E. Fehrenbacher.

Hagan, Kenneth J. *This People's Navy: The Making of American Sea Power*. New York: Free Press, 1991.

Halstead, Mural. *Trimmers, Trucklers, and Temporizers.* Madison: State Historical Society of Wisconsin, 1961.

Hendrickson, James E. *Joe Lane of Oregon: Machine Politics and the Sectional Crisis.* New Haven: Yale University Press, 1967.

Hesseline, William B., ed. *Three against Lincoln: Mural Halstead Reports the Caucuses of 1860.* Baton Rouge: Louisiana State University Press, 1960.

Holt, Michael F. *The Political Crisis of the 1850s.* New York: Wiley, 1978.

————. *Political Parties and American Political Development: From the Age of Jackson to the Age of Lincoln.* Baton Rouge: Louisiana State University Press, 1992.

————. "The Election of 1856." In Arthur M. Schlesinger, Jr., ed, *Running for President: The Candidates and Their Images.* New York: Simon and Schuster, 1994.

————. "The Politics of Impatience: The Origins of Know Nothingism." *Journal of American History* 60 (September 1973): 309–31.

Huntington, Samuel P. "Generations, Cycles, and Their Role in American Development." In Richard J. Samuels, ed., *Political Generations and Political Development.* Lexington, Mass.: Lexington Books, 1976.

Huston, James L. "The Demise of the Pennsylvania American Party, 1854–1858." *Pennsylvania Magazine of History and Biography* 109 (October 1985): 473–97.

————. *The Panic of 1857 and the Coming of the Civil War.* Baton Rouge: Louisiana State University Press, 1987.

Hyman, Harold M. *A More Perfect Union: The Impact of the Civil War and Reconstruction on the Constitution.* New York: Knopf, 1973.

Hyman, Harold M., and William M. Wiecek. *Equal Justice under Law: Constitutional Development, 1835–1875.* New York: Harper and Row, 1982.

Johannsen, Robert W. *Stephen A. Douglas.* New York: Oxford University Press, 1973.

Klein, Philip S. *President James Buchanan: A Biography.* University Park: Pennsylvania State University Press, 1962.

Kleppner, Paul. *The Third Electoral System, 1853–1892: Parties, Voters and Political Cultures.* Chapel Hill: University of North Carolina Press, 1979.

Knoles, George Harmon. *The Crisis of the Union, 1860–1861.* Baton Rouge, LA: Louisiana State University Press, 1965.

Knupfer, Peter B. *The Union as It Is: Constitutional Unionism and Sectional Compromise, 1787–1861.* Chapel Hill: University of North Carolina Press, 1991.

Lightner, David L. "The Interstate Trade in Antislavery Politics." *Civil War History* 36 (June 1990): 119–36.

Long, David F. *Gold Braid and Foreign Relations: Diplomatic Activities of U.S. Naval Officers, 1798–1883.* Annapolis, Md.: Naval Institute Press, 1988.

Luthin, Reinhard H. *The First Lincoln Campaign.* Cambridge, Mass.: Harvard University Press, 1944.

Maizlish, Stephen E. and John J. Kashma. *Essays on American Antebellum Politics, 1840–1860.* College Station, Tx: Texas A&M University Press, 1982.

May, Robert E. *The Southern Dream of a Caribbean Empire, 1854–1861.* Baton Rouge: Louisiana State University Press, 1973.

McLaughlin, Andrew C. *Lewis Cass.* Boston: Houghton, Mifflin, 1891.

McPherson, James M. *Battle Cry of Freedom: The Civil War Era*. New York: Oxford University Press, 1988.

Meerse, David E. "Buchanan, Corruption, and the Election of 1860." *Civil War History* 12 (June 1966): 116–31.

———. "Buchanan's Patronage Policy: An Attempt to Achieve Political Strength." *Pennsylvania History* 40 (January 1973): 37–57.

Merk, Frederick. *The Monroe Doctrine and American Expansion, 1843–1849*. New York: Alfred A. Knopf, 1966.

Murray, Robert K., and Tim H. Blessing. *Greatness in the White House: Rating the Presidents, Washington through Carter*. University Park: Pennsylvania State University Press, 1988.

———. "The Presidential Performance Study: A Progress Report." *Journal of American History* 70 (December 1983): 535–55.

Nevins, Allan. *The Emergence of Lincoln*. 2 vols. New York: Charles Scribner's Sons, 1950.

———. *Ordeal of the Union: A House Dividing, 1852–1857*. New York: Charles Scribner's Sons, 1947.

———. *The Statesmanship of the Civil War*. New York: Collier Books, 1962.

Nevins, Allan, and Milton Halsey Thomas, eds. *The Diary of George Templeton Strong, 1835–1875*. New York: Macmillan, 1952.

Nichols, Roy F. *The Disruption of American Democracy*. New York: Macmillan, 1948.

———. "James Buchanan: Lessons in Leadership in Trying Times." In *Boyd Lee Spahr Lectures in Americana*, p. 165–174. Carlisle, Pa.: Library of Dickinson College, 1950.

Nichols, Roy F., and Philip S. Klein. "The Election of 1856." In Arthur M. Schlesinger, Jr., and Fred L. Israel, eds., *History of American Presidential Elections, 1789–1968*. Vol. 2. New York: Chelsea House, 1971.

Niven, John. *John C. Calhoun and the Price of Union: A Biography*. Baton Rouge: Louisiana State University Press, 1988.

———. *Martin Van Buren: The Romantic Age of American Politics* New York: Oxford University Press, 1987.

Olliff, Jonathon C. *Reforma Mexico and the United States: A Search for Alternatives to Annexation, 1854–1861*. University: University of Alabama Press, 1981.

Parks, Joseph. *John Bell of Tennessee*. Baton Rouge: Louisiana State University Press, 1950.

Potter, David M. *The Impending Crisis, 1848–1861*. New York: Harper and Row, 1976.

———. *Lincoln and His Party in the Secession Crisis*. New Haven: Yale University Press, 1942.

Quaife, Milo Milton, ed. *The Diary of James K. Polk during His Presidency, 1845 to 1849*. 4 vols. Chicago: A. C. Maclurg & Company, 1910.

Randall, James G. *Constitutional Problems under Lincoln*. Rev. ed. Urbana: University of Illinois Press, 1951.

———. *Lincoln, the President*. New York: Dodd, Mead, 1945–55.

Rauch, Basil. *American Interest in Cuba, 1848–1855*. New York: Columbia University Press, 1948.

Rawley, James A. *Race and Politics: "Bleeding Kansas" and the Coming of the Civil War.* Philadelphia: Lippincott, 1969.

Samuels, Richard J., ed. *Political Generations and Political Development.* Lexington, Mass.: Lexington Books, 1976. S.v. "Generations, Cycles, and Their Role in American Development," by Samuel P. Huntington.

Schroeder, John H. *Shaping a Maritime Empire: The Commercial and Diplomatic Role of the American Navy, 1829–1861.* Westport, Conn. Greenwood Press, 1985.

Scroggs, William O. *Filibusters and Financiers: The Story of William Walker and His Associates.* New York: Macmillan, 1916.

Sears, Louis Martin. *A History of American Foreign Relations.* Rev. ed. New York: Thomas Y. Crowell, 1935.

Sellers, Charles G. *James K. Polk: Continentalist, 1843–1846.* Princeton: Princeton University Press, 1966.

Shenton, James P. *Robert John Walker: A Politician From Jackson to Lincoln.* New York: Columbia University Press, 1961.

Shortridge, Roy. "The Voter Realignment in the Midwest during the 1850s." *American Politics Quarterly* 4 (April 1976): 193–222.

Silbey, Joel. *The American Political Nation, 1838–1893.* Stanford, Calif.: Stanford University Press, 1993.

———. *The Partisan Imperative: The Dynamics of American Politics before the Civil War.* New York: Oxford University Press, 1984.

Simpson, John Eddins. *Howell Cobb: The Politics of Ambition.* Chicago: Adams Press, 1973.

Smith, Elbert B. *The Press, Politics, and Patronage: The American Government's Use of Newspapers, 1789–1875.* Athens: University of Georgia Press, 1977.

Smith, Elbert B. *The Death of Slavery, 1837–1865.* Chicago: University of Chicago Press, 1967.

———. *The Presidency of James Buchanan.* Lawrence: University Press of Kansas, 1975.

Southerland, James E. "John Forsyth and the Frustrated 1857 Mexican Loan and Land Grab." *West Georgia College Studies in the Social Sciences* 11 (June 1972): 18–25.

Spitzer, Alan B. "The Historical Problem of Generations." *American Historical Review* 78 (December 1973): 1353–85.

Stampp, Kenneth M. *America in 1857: A Nation on the Brink.* New York: Oxford University Press, 1990.

———. *And the War Came: The North and the Secession Crisis, 1860–1861.* Baton Rouge: Louisiana State University Press, 1950.

———. "The Republican National Convention of 1860." In *The Imperiled Union: Essays on the Background of the Civil War.* New York: Oxford University Press, 1978.

Summers, Mark W. *The Plundering Generation: Corruption and the Crisis of the Union, 1849–1861.* New York: Oxford University Press, 1987.

Thompson, William Y. *Robert Toombs of Georgia.* Baton Rouge: Louisiana State University Press, 1966.

Updike, John. *Buchanan Dying: A Play.* New York: Knopf, 1974.

————. *Memories of the Ford Administration: A Novel*. New York: Knopf, 1992.

Van Deusen, Glyndon G. *William Henry Seward*. New York: Oxford University Press, 1967.

Varg, Paul A. *United States Foreign Relations, 1820–1860*. East Lansing: Michigan State University Press, 1979.

Walsh, Justin E. *To Print the News and Raise Hell! A Biography of Wilbur F. Storey*. Chapel Hill: University of North Carolina Press, 1963.

Williams, Christine B. "A Socialization Explanation of Political Change." In John C. Pierce and John L. Sullivan, eds., *The Electorate Reconsidered*. Beverly Hills, Calif.: Sage, 1980.

Walther, Eric. *The Fire-eaters*. Baton Rouge, LA: Louisiana State University Press, 1992.

Williams, T. Harry. *Lincoln and His Generals*. New York: Knopf, 1952.

Wilson, Howard L. "President Buchanan's Proposed Intervention in Mexico." *American Historical Review* 5 (July 1900): 687–701.

Woodford, Frank B. *Lewis Cass: The Last Jeffersonian*. New Brunswick, N.J.: Rutgers University Press, 1950.

Zornow, William Frank. *Lincoln and the Party Divided*. Norman: University of Oklahoma Press, 1954.

Zwikl, Kurt D. "The Political Ascent of James Buchanan." *Pennsylvania Heritage* 17 (Spring 1991): 16–21.

Contributors

MICHAEL J. BIRKNER is Professor and Chair of the Department of History at Gettysburg College. He received his Ph.D. from the University of Virginia. His books include *Samuel L. Southard: Jeffersonian Whig* (1984), *The Papers of Daniel Webster: Correspondence, 1850–1852* (with Charles M. Wiltse) and, most recently, *A Country Place No More: The Transformation of Bergenfield, New Jersey, 1894–1994* (1994).

DON E. FEHRENBACHER, Emeritus Professor of History and American Studies at Stanford University, is the author of many books on nineteenth-century American political history. Among the numerous honors earned during his scholarly career, he has been the Harmsworth Professor of American History at Oxford University, and his book, *The Dred Scott Case* (1978) won the Pulitzer Prize in History.

WILLIAM E. GIENAPP is Professor of History at Harvard University. He holds the Ph.D. from the University of California, Berkeley. Gienapp is the author of *The Origins of the Republican Party, 1852–1856* (1987), which received the Avery O. Craven Award from the Organization of American Historians, as well as a number of articles and journals and edited collections. He is also a coauthor of *Nation of Nations,* a textbook in United States history. He is currently at work on a brief biography of Abraham Lincoln.

MICHAEL F. HOLT, Langbourne M. Williams Professor of American History at the University of Virginia, is the author of three books on antebellum political history, including *The Political Crisis of the 1850s* (1978). His Ph.D. is from the Johns Hopkins University. In 1993–94 he was the Pitt Professor of American History and Institutions at the University of Cambridge. He is nearing completion of a full-scale history of the Whig Party.

ROBERT JOHANNSEN, James G. Randall Distinguished Professor of History at the University of Illinois, has published a dozen books, including a biography of Stephen A. Douglas which won the Francis Parkman Prize in 1973. His most recent book is *Lincoln, the South and Slavery: The Political Dimension* (1991).

PETER KNUPFER is Associate Professor of History at Kansas State University. He received his Ph.D. from the University of Wisconsin in 1988. Knupfer is the author of *The Union as It Is: Constitutional Unionism and Sectional Compromise, 1787–1861* (1991) and "Crisis in Conservatism: Northern Unionism and the Harpers Ferry Raid," in Paul Finkelman, ed. *His Soul Goes Marching On: Responses to John Brown's Raid* (1994). He is currently working on a study of the election of 1860.

ROBERT E. MAY is Professor of History at Purdue University. His doctorate is from the University of Wisconsin. May is the author of *The Southern Dream of a Caribbean Empire, 1854–1861* (1973) and *John A. Quitman: Old South Crusader* (1985). His most recent work is an edited book about Civil War diplomacy entitled *The Union, the Confederacy, and the Atlantic Rim* (1995).

ELBERT SMITH is emeritus Professor of History at the University of Maryland. Among his many publications on nineteenth-century American politics and biography is *The Presidency of James Buchanan* (1975), which won the Phi Alpha Theta Book Prize. Smith has served several times as a Fulbright exchange professor, and remains active in the Fulbright Scholars organization.

KENNETH M. STAMPP is emeritus Professor of History at the University of California at Berkeley. He has been writing books about the Civil War era since 1949, when his monograph on Indiana politics during the Civil War was published. Stampp's many books include the prize-winning *The Peculiar Institution* (1956) and, most recently, *America in 1857: A Nation on the Brink* (1990). Stampp has been president of the Organization of American Historians and, like Don Fehrenbacher, Harmsworth Professor at Oxford University.

MARK W. SUMMERS is Professor of History at the University of Kentucky. He received his Ph.D. from the University of California, Berkeley. Summers is the author of many books and articles on the Civil War era and the Gilded Age, including *The Plundering Generation: Corruption and the Crisis of the Union, 1849–1861* (1987) and *The Era of Good Stealings* (1993).

Index